ESSENTIALS
OF ENGLISH GRAMMAR

ESSENTIALS

OF

ENGLISH GRAMMAR

BY

OTTO JESPERSEN

PH.D. LITT.D. LL.D.

CORRESPONDING FELLOW OF THE
BRITISH ACADEMY

UNIVERSITY OF ALABAMA PRESS

University, Alabama

FOURTH PRINTING, 1969

Copyright © 1964 by
UNIVERSITY OF ALABAMA PRESS
Standard Book Number: 8173-0450-9
Library of Congress Catalog Card Number: 64-21942
Printed in the United States of America

PREFACE

THE appearance of this book is due to urgent appeals from some English friends (among them Professors W. E. Collinson, G. C. Moore Smith, and R. A. Williams), who asked me to bring out a one-volume grammar embodying the principles explained in *The Philosophy of Grammar* and partly carried out in the four volumes of my *Modern English Grammar*. After some years of hesitation I have now made the attempt, but of course the responsibility for its shortcomings rests exclusively upon me. Parts of the manuscript have been submitted to various friends, to whose kind criticisms I owe a great debt of gratitude. I must mention Dr E. R. Edwards, who read nearly the whole of the manuscript; Professors C. A. Bodelsen and G. E. K. Braunholtz, Miss Isabel Fry, Dr G. E. Fuhrken, and Miss J. Young, Ph.D., who all of them read a greater or lesser number of chapters and communicated to me their remarks. Niels Haislund, M.A., assisted me in copying the manuscript, and gave me valuable assistance in reading the proofs. My heartfelt thanks to all these kind scholars!

To the student I may perhaps offer two pieces of advice : to read in general the examples before the rules, and, if he is not particularly interested in phonetics, to skip Chapters II-VI until he has finished the rest of the book.

I may be allowed here to repeat what I wrote in 1909 in the first volume of my bigger Grammar :

" It has been my endeavour in this work to represent English Grammar not as a set of stiff dogmatic precepts, according to which some things are correct and others absolutely wrong, but as something living and developing under continual fluctuations and undulations, something that is founded on the past and prepares the way for the future, something that is not always consistent or perfect, but progressing and perfectible—in one word, human."

A detailed exposition of the reasons that have led me to

deviate from much of what is usually found in English grammars, and some criticism of the views of other scholars, will be found in a paper on " The System of Grammar," which will be printed in a volume, " Linguistica : Selected Papers in English, French, and German," and will also be sold separately.[1]

OTTO JESPERSEN

Gentofte, Copenhagen
January 1933

[1] London : George Allen & Unwin Ltd.

CONTENTS

CHAPTER I

What is grammar ?—Local and social dialects.—Spoken and written language.—Formulas and free expressions.—Expression, suppression, and impression.—Prescriptive, descriptive, explanatory, historical, appreciative grammar.—Purpose and plan of this grammar.

CHAPTER II

Phonetic script.—Lips.—Tip of the tongue.—Blade.—Front and back of the tongue.—Vowels.—Soft palate.—Vocal chords. —Table of consonants.—Syllables.—Diphthongs.—Length.— Stress and tone.

CHAPTER III

Sound laws.—Alternations.—Stress.—The great vowel-shift.— New [aꞏ, ɔꞏ].

CHAPTER IV

Weakening of *r.*—Short vowels before *r.*—*ar, or,* etc.—Alternations with and without *r.*—Influence of stress on vowels.— Loss of *e.*—Vowels in weak syllables.—Loss of vowels in groups. —Alternations in compounds.—Strong and weak forms of the same word.

CHAPTER V

Consonants. — Tolerated consonant groups. — Consonants dropped.—Voiced and voiceless consonants.—H.—Assibilation.—Stump-words.

CHAPTER VI

Causes of unphonetic spelling.—French influence : *ch, g, c, ou, u, o.*—Doubling of letters.—Differentiation of *i, j, u, v.*— Learned spellings.

CHAPTER XIII

PAGE

Extraposition.—Quasi-predicatives.—Real predicatives.—Link-verb.—No verb.—Predicatives of becoming.—What can be a predicative ?—Article or no article with substantives as predicatives.—Predicative left out.

CHAPTER XIV

Cases in pronouns.—Nominative and objective.—After *than* and *as*.—*But, save, except*.—Case after *let*.—Relative attraction.—Predicative.—Objective in independent position.—*Himself*.—*Who*.—Second person.—Cases in substantives.—Common case and genitive.—Group-genitive.—Difficulties with pronouns.—The meaning of genitive.—Restrictions in the use of the genitive.—Lifeless things.—Measures.—Genitives as primaries.—Genitive after *of*.

CHAPTER XV

Three persons.—Substitutes for pronouns.—Indirect speech.—Vocative.—Imperative.—Verbs.—Difficulties.—Generic person.

CHAPTER XVI

Division of pronouns.—Pronouns of contextual indication (Personal pronouns).—Ambiguities.—Unspecified *they*.—The *self*-pronouns.—*It*.—Preparatory *it*.—Unspecified *it*.—Emphatic *it*.—Pronouns of pointing : *this, that, yon*.—Representative *that*.—Indefinite *that*.—*Hereafter*, etc.—*Thus*.—*So*.—The definite article.—Demonstrative *the*.—The article of complete determination.—Words without article.—Proper names.—Times and dates.—The typical.—Distributive.—Languages.—Diseases.—No article.—Repetition.—The article of incomplete determination.—Adjectives with proper names.—The pronoun of identity (*same*).—The pronoun of similarity (*such*).

CHAPTER XVII

Indefinite unity (*one*).—Indefinite article.—Place of indefinite article.—Pronoun of difference (*other*).—Pronoun of discretion (*certain*).—Pronoun of unspecified quantity (*some*).—Pronouns of indifference (*any, either*).

CHAPTER XVIII

CHAPTER XIX

CHAPTER XX

CHAPTER XXI

CHAPTER XXII

CHAPTER XXIII

CHAPTER XXIV

CHAPTER XXV

CHAPTER XXVI

CHAPTER XXVII

CHAPTER XXVIII

CHAPTER XXIX

CHAPTER XXX

CHAPTER XXXI

CHAPTER XXXII

CHAPTER XXXIII

CHAPTER XXXIV

CHAPTER XXXV

CHAPTER XXXVI

ESSENTIALS
OF ENGLISH GRAMMAR

CHAPTER I

INTRODUCTORY

What is grammar?—Local and social dialects.—Spoken and written language.—Formulas and free expressions.—Expression, suppression, and impression.—Prescriptive, descriptive, explanatory, historical, appreciative grammar.—Purpose and plan of this grammar.

1.1₁. Grammar deals with the structure of languages, English grammar with the structure of English, French grammar with the structure of French, etc. Language consists of words, but the way in which these words are modified and joined together to express thoughts and feelings differs from one language to another.

English and French have many words in common but treat them in a totally different way. Take the word *excuse*, which is spelt in the same way in the two languages. But the pronunciation is different, the vowel in the last syllable of the French word being unknown in English. In English we make a difference in pronunciation between *to excuse* and *an excuse*, but no such difference is made in French. Still greater differences appear when we make up complete sentences. Compare, for instance, the following :

Excuse me.	Excusez-moi.
Don't excuse me.	Ne m'excusez pas.
Do you excuse her?	L'excusez-vous? *or* Est-ce que vous l'excusez?
We excuse her.	Nous l'excusons.
Let us excuse her.	Excusons-la.
We must excuse her.	Il faut l'excuser.
We shall excuse her.	Nous l'excuserons.
Shall we excuse her?	Est-ce que nous l'excuserons? etc., etc.

1.1₂. The grammar of each language constitutes a system of its own, each element of which stands in a certain relation to, and is more or less dependent on, all the others. No linguistic system, however, is either completely rigid or perfectly harmonious, and we shall see in some of the subsequent chapters that there are loopholes and deficiencies in the English grammatical system.

Language is nothing but a set of human habits, the purpose of which is to give expression to thoughts and feelings, and especially to impart them to others. As with other habits it is not to be expected that they should be perfectly consistent. No one can speak exactly as everybody else or speak exactly in the same way under all circumstances and at all moments, hence a good deal of vacillation here and there. The divergencies would certainly be greater if it were not for the fact that the chief purpose of language is to make oneself understood by other members of the same community; this presupposes and brings about a more or less complete agreement on all essential points. The closer and more intimate the social life of a community is, the greater will be the concordance in speech between its members. In old times, when communication between various parts of the country was not easy and when the population was, on the whole, very stationary, a great many local **dialects** arose which differed very considerably from one another ; the divergencies naturally became greater among the uneducated than among the educated and richer classes, as the latter moved more about and had more intercourse with people from other parts of the country. In recent times the enormously increased facilities of communication have to a great extent counteracted the tendency towards the splitting up of the language into dialects—class dialects and local dialects. In this grammar we must in many places call attention to various types of divergencies : geographical (English in the strictest sense with various sub-divisions, Scottish, Irish, American), and social (educated, colloquial, literary, poetical, on the one hand, and vulgar on the other). But it should be remembered that these strata cannot be strictly separated from, but are constantly influencing one another. Our chief concern will be with the normal speech of the educated class, what may be called Standard English, but we must remember that the speech even of "standard speakers" varies a good deal according to circumstances and surroundings as well as to the mood of the moment. Nor must we imagine that people in their everyday speech arrange their thoughts in the same orderly way as when they write, let alone when they are engaged on literary work. Grammatical expressions have been formed in the course of centuries by innumerable generations of illiterate speakers, and even in the most elevated literary style we are obliged to conform to what has become, in this way, the general practice. Hence many established idioms which on closer inspection may appear to the trained thinker illogical or irrational. The influence of emotions, as distinct from orderly rational thinking, is conspicuous in many parts of grammar—see, for instance, the chapters on gender, on expanded tenses, and on *will* and *shall*.

1.1₃. In our so-called civilized life print plays such an important part that educated people are apt to forget that **language is primarily speech,** *i.e.* chiefly conversation (dialogue), while the written (and printed) word is only a kind of substitute— in many ways a most valuable, but in other respects a poor one —for the spoken and heard word. Many things that have vital importance in speech—stress, pitch, colour of the voice, thus especially those elements which give expression to emotions rather than to logical thinking—disappear in the comparatively rigid medium of writing, or are imperfectly rendered by such means as underlining (italicizing) and punctuation. What is called the life of language consists in oral intercourse with its continual give-and-take between speaker and hearer. It should also be always remembered that this linguistic intercourse takes place not in isolated words as we see them in dictionaries, but by means of connected communications, chiefly in the form of sentences, though not always such complete and well-arranged sentences as form the delight of logicians and rhetoricians. Such sentences are chiefly found in writing, but the enormous increase which has taken place during the last few centuries in education and reading has exercised a profound influence on grammar, even on that of everyday speech.

1.2₁. There is an important distinction between **formulas** (or formular units) and **free expressions.** Some things in language are of the formula character—that is to say, no one can change anything in them. A phrase like " How do you do? " is entirely different from such a phrase as " I gave the boy a lump of sugar." In the former everything is fixed : you cannot even change the stress or make a pause between the words, and it is not natural to say, as in former times, " How does your father do? " or " How did you do? " The phrase is for all practical purposes one unchanged and unchangeable formula, the meaning of which is really independent of that of the separate words into which it may be analysed. But " I gave the boy sixpence " is of a totally different order. Here it is possible to stress any of the words and to make a pause, for instance, after " boy," or to substitute " he " or " she " for " I," " lent " for " gave," " Tom " for " the boy," etc. One may insert " never " or make other alterations. While in handling formulas memory is everything, free expressions involve another kind of mental activity ; they have to be created in each case anew by the speaker, who inserts the words that fit the particular situation, and shapes and arranges them according to certain patterns. The words that make up the sentences are variable, but the type is fixed.

Now this distinction pervades all parts of grammar. Let us here take two examples only. To form the plural—that is, the expression of more than one—we have old formulas in the case of *men, feet, oxen* and a few other words, which are used so often in the plural that they are committed to memory at a very early age by each English-speaking child. But they are so irregular that they could not serve as patterns for new words. On the other hand, we have an *s*-ending in innumerable old words (*kings, princes, bishops, days, hours,* etc.), and this type is now so universal that it can be freely applied to all words except the few old irregular words. As soon as a new word comes into existence, no one hesitates about forming a plural in this way : *automobiles, kodaks, aeroplanes, hooligans, ions, stunts,* etc. In the sentence " He recovered his lost umbrella and had it re- covered," the first *recovered* is a formular unit, the second (with a long vowel in the first syllable) is freely formed from *cover* in its ordinary meaning (**4.6**$_2$).

1.2$_2$. In all speech activity there are, further, three things to be distinguished, **expression, suppression,** and **impression.** Expression is what the speaker gives, suppression is what he does not give, though he might have given it, and impression is what the hearer receives. It is important to notice that an impression is often produced not only by what is said expressly, but also by what is suppressed. Suggestion is impression through suppression. Only bores want to express everything, but even bores find it impossible to express everything. Not only is the writer's art rightly said to consist largely in knowing what to leave in the inkstand, but in the most everyday remarks we suppress a great many things which it would be pedantic to say expressly. " Two third returns, Brighton," stands for something like : " Would you please sell me two third-class tickets from London to Brighton and back again, and I will pay you the usual fare for such tickets." Compound nouns state two terms, but say nothing of the way in which the relation between them is to be understood : *home life*, life at home ; *home letters*, letters from home ; *home journey*, journey (to) home ; compare, further, *life boat, life insurance, life member* ; *sunrise, sunworship, sunflower, sunburnt, Sunday, sun-bright*, etc.

As in the structure of compounds, so also in the structure of sentences much is left to the sympathetic imagination of the hearer, and what from the point of view of the trained thinker, or the pedantic schoolmaster, is only part of an utterance, is frequently the only thing said, and the only thing required to make the meaning clear to the hearer.

1.3. The chief object in teaching grammar today—especially that of a foreign language—would appear to be to give rules which must be obeyed if one wants to speak and write the language correctly—rules which as often as not seem quite arbitrary. Of greater value, however, than this **prescriptive** grammar is a purely **descriptive** grammar which, instead of serving as a guide to what should be said or written, aims at finding out what is actually said and written by the speakers of the language investigated, and thus may lead to a scientific understanding of the rules followed instinctively by speakers and writers.   Such a grammar should also be **explanatory,** giving, as far as this is possible, the reasons why the usage is such and such.   These reasons may, according to circumstances, be phonetic or psychological, or in some cases both combined.   Not infrequently the explanation will be found in an earlier stage of the same language : what in one period was a regular phenomenon may later become isolated and appear as an irregularity, an exception to what has now become the prevailing rule.   Our grammar must therefore be **historical** to a certain extent.   Finally, grammar may be **appreciative,** examining whether the rules obtained from the language in question are in every way clear (unambiguous, logical), expressive and easy, or whether in any one of these respects other forms or rules would have been preferable.

This book aims at giving a descriptive and, to some extent, explanatory and appreciative account of the grammatical system of Modern English, historical explanations being only given where this can be done without presupposing any detailed knowledge of Old English (OE., *i.e.* the language before A.D. 1000) or Middle English (ME., *i.e.* the language between 1000 and 1500) or any cognate language.   Prescriptions as to correctness will be kept in the background, as the primary object of the book is not to teach English to foreigners, but to prepare for an intelligent understanding of the structure of a language which it is supposed that the reader knows already.

1.4. Grammatical rules have to be illustrated by **examples.** It has been endeavoured to give everywhere examples that are at once natural, characteristic, and as varied as possible.   Many have been taken from everyday educated speech, while others have been chosen from the writings of well-known authors.   It should be noted that in quotations from old books the spellings of the original editions have been retained; Shakespearian quotations are given in the spellings of the First Folio (1623), and Biblical quotations in the spelling of the Authorized Version (1611, abbreviated AV.), the only deviations being that the use of capitals and of the letters *i, j, u, v* has been made to conform to modern usage.

Apart from the phonological part which deals with sounds, grammar is usually divided into two parts : **accidence**—also called morphology—*i.e.* the doctrine of all the forms (inflexions) of the language, and **syntax,** *i.e.* the doctrine of sentence structure and the use of the forms. This type of division has been disregarded in this book, which substitutes for it a division in the main according to the chief grammatical categories. In most of the chapters the forms have first been considered and then their use, but more stress has everywhere been laid on the latter than on the former. In this way it is thought that a clearer conception is gained of the whole system, as what really belongs together is thus brought closely together.

1.5. As the system in this book differs from that followed in most grammars, a few new **technical terms** have been found necessary, but they will offer no serious difficulty ; in fact, they are far less numerous than the terminological novelties introduced in recent books on psychology and other sciences. On the other hand, we have been able to dispense with a great many of the learned terms that are often found abundantly in grammatical treatises and which really say nothing that cannot be expressed clearly in simple everyday language.

CHAPTER II

SOUNDS

Phonetic script.—Lips.—Tip of the tongue.—Blade.—Front and back of the tongue.—Vowels.—Soft palate.—Vocal chords.—Table of consonants.—Syllables.—Diphthongs.—Length.—Stress and tone.

2.1₁. All language is primarily spoken and thus consists of sounds (**1.1₃**). It is therefore necessary at the very outset to get a clear idea of the sounds that make up the spoken language, and to understand how they are produced by means of the organs of speech, viz., the lips, the tongue, the soft palate, the vocal chords, and the lungs.

In order to avoid confusion between sounds and the letters of ordinary spelling it is necessary to use **phonetic script,** which in this book is made as simple as possible without any difficult complications. Sound symbols are here printed in square brackets [ ]. In phonetic script as here used [·] after a symbol indicates length of a sound, *e.g.* [wi·] means *we* or *wee*. Stress is marked by means of ['] *before* the beginning of the accented syllable, *e.g.* [bi'li·v] =*believe*.

Only the barest outline of the phonetics of English can be given in this book, and only the principal sounds are described, *i.e.* those that can be used significantly to distinguish words. In our rapid survey of the organs of speech we begin with the lips, because they are most easily accessible to immediate inspection, and then move gradually inwards.

To get a clear conception of the essence of **sounds** it is necessary to pronounce them separately, thus [p] or [m] without a vowel, not [pi·] or [em] as in the ordinary names of the **letters.**

2.1₂. The two **lips** may be completely closed as for [p, b, m] : these sounds thus are lip **stops.** Or they may be more or less opened. The smallest aperture is found in [w], which is a lip **fricative ;** fricatives are sounds formed with such a small aperture that an audible friction is produced.

2.1₃. If next we take such a series of vowels as [u·] in *too*, [ou] in *so*, and [ɔ·] in *saw*, we find a gradual increase in the size of the aperture, but the shape of the aperture is essentially the same as for [w] : all these sounds have lip-rounding and are therefore termed **round.**

A different series is found in [i·] in *see*, [ei] in *day*, [æ] in *hat*, [a·] in *far* : here the lips are not rounded, but more or less **spread.**

2.1₄. The sounds [f] and [v] are fricatives just as much as [w], but differ from that sound by being produced by the lower lip alone, which is approached to the upper teeth.

2.2₁. By means of the **tip of the tongue** are formed first the three stops [t, d, n], then three fricatives [þ, ð], as in *thin, then* against the front teeth, and [r] against the gums, often with a distinctly " flapping " movement. Further, we have [l], in which the tip of the tongue touches the gums so as to leave an aperture on one side or one on either side of the tongue through which the air can escape (**lateral** aperture).

2.2₂. With the **blade** of the tongue (immediately behind the tip) are formed the two hissing fricatives [s, z] as in *seal, zeal*, characterized by a chink in the tongue through which a very thin stream of air passes. If the air-channel is made a trifle broader, and the tip of the tongue is turned a little farther back, we get the sounds [ʃ, ʒ] as in *she, mission, vision* [ʃi·, miʃən, viʒən] ; they are often combined with [t, d] as in *chin, gin* [tʃin, dʒin].

2.3. We next have the fricative [j] as in *yield*, formed with the **front of the tongue** against the hard palate.

The **back of the tongue** forms the stops [k, g, ŋ] ; [ŋ] is the final sound in *sing* [siŋ] and often occurs before [g, k] as in *finger, sink* [fiŋgə, siŋk].

A fricative formed with the back of the tongue is [w], which is thus formed at two places, see on the lips **2.1₂.**

2.4. The tongue is also instrumental in forming the **vowels.**

These are either **front, central** or **back,** according to the part of
the tongue that is highest. The distance between the tongue
and the roof of the mouth also varies a good deal, so that we
may draw up the following scheme of English, showing their
approximate position in the mouth :

front	central	back
[iˑ]		[uˑ]
[i]		[u]
[e]	[əˑ]	[o]
[ɛ]	[ə]	[ʌ]
[æ]		[ɔˑ]
	[aˑ]	[ɔ]

Examples of these vowels :

[iˑ] *see, seed, seat* [siˑ, siˑd, siˑt].

[i] *hid, hit, silly* [hid, hit, sili].

[e] *led, let* [led, let].

[ɛ] *bear, air* [bɛˑə, ɛˑə].

[æ] *had, hat* [hæd, hæt].

[əˑ] *fir, fur, heard, hurt* [fəˑ, həˑd, həˑt].

[ə] *ago, connect, suppose* [ə'gou, kə'nekt, sə'pouz]

[ʌ] *bud, but* [bʌd, bʌt].

[aˑ] *hard, heart, half, papa* [haˑd, haˑt, haˑf, pə'paˑ].

[uˑ] *brood, brute, who* [bruˑd, bruˑt, huˑ].

[u] *wood, foot* [wud, fut].

[o] *low* [lou], see **2.8**.

[ɔˑ] *broad, brought, saw* [brɔˑd, brɔˑt, sɔˑ].

[ɔ] *nod, not* [nɔd, nɔt].

The last five vowels are round, the others not.

Note that [iˑ] and [i], [əˑ] and [ə], [uˑ] and [u], [ɔˑ] and [ɔ] are
not exactly pairs of identical vowels, those here marked short
are more slack and open than those marked long. In an exact
phonetic script we should therefore use different symbols for
these vowels.

2.5. The **soft palate** is movable, and is either raised so as to shut off the mouth from the cavity of the nose—then we have purely **oral** sounds—or else it may be lowered so as to allow the air to pass through the nose—in that case we have **nasal** sounds. The only nasal sounds in English are [m, n, ŋ], which correspond to [b, d, g] respectively and differ from them only through the soft palate being lowered. All other sounds are oral.

2.6. If the **vocal chords** (in the larynx, popularly called " Adam's apple ") are brought together and made to vibrate, the result is a **voiced** sound; if they are separated from each other and kept still, the sound is **voiceless.** All vowels, and normally also the nasals [m, n, ŋ], [l], [r], and [j] are voiced. With the other consonants we have voiced and voiceless sounds corresponding to one another, thus :

voiced	voiceless
[b] : *bat, cab*	[p] : *pat, cap*
[v] : *vine, leave*	[f] : *fine, leaf*
[d] : *doe, had*	[t] : *toe, hat*
[ð] : *then, teethe*	[þ] : *thin, teeth*
[z] : *zeal, dies*	[s] : *seal, dice*
[ʒ] : *vision*	[ʃ] : *she, mission*
([dʒ] : *jest, ridge*	[tʃ] : *chest, rich*)
[g] : *gain, bag*	[k] : *cane, back*

Where the spelling has *wh*, as in *whet, which*, some speakers have the voiceless sound corresponding to the voiced [w] in *wet, witch*, while others make no distinction, but pronounce the voiced sound everywhere (**5.1₃**).

[h] is a fricative produced by the vocal chords.

The innermost organ of speech is the lungs, which produce the air-current necessary to generate speech-sounds.

2.7. We can now tabulate English consonants:

ORGAN	PLACE	STOP			FRICATIVE		LATERAL
		Voiced	Voiced	Unvoiced	Voiced	Unvoiced	Voiced
Lip	Lip	m	b	p	w	(hw)	
	Front teeth				v	f	
Tip of tongue	Front teeth				ð	þ	
	Gum	n	d	t	r		l
Blade of tongue	Gum			{	z ʒ	s ʃ	
Front of tongue	Hard palate				j		
Back of tongue	Soft palate	ŋ	g	k	w	(hw)	
Vocal chords						h	

Nasal ⏟ Oral

2.8₁. Syllables. Most syllables contain one vowel, which is then the " top " of the syllable.

In some cases we have two vowels in the same syllable; together they form a **diphthong.** There are three kinds of diphthongs in English:

(1) full (long-distance) diphthongs, in which the constituents are widely apart:

> [ai] as in *hide, height*
> [oi] as in *noise, choice*
> [au] as in *loud, lout*

(2) slow (short-distance) diphthongs, in which the movement is lesser and slower:

> [ei] as in *laid, late*
> [ou] as in *code, coat*

(3) **murmur**-diphthongs ending in the indistinct central
vowel [ə] :

[iə] as in *peer*
[ɛ·ə] as in *pair*
[uə] as in *poor*
[a·ə] as in *far*
[ɔ·ə] as in *war*

In the two last-mentioned diphthongs [ə] tends to disappear
completely, thus in *hard, hart* [ha·d, ha·t], *ward, wart* [wɔ·d,
wɔ·t].

2.8₂. Finally, we have syllables without a vowel; the consonant which then is the top of the syllable is termed **syllabic.**
Thus [l] is syllabic in *battle* [bætl], [n] in *rotten* [rɔtn] (**4.**7).

2.9₁. By the **length** or quantity of a sound we understand the
time occupied in its production. The absolute length is sus-
ceptible of infinite gradations; it is determined by a variety of
causes, quality of the sound itself, its surroundings, position in
syllable, stress and finally the momentary frame of mind of the
speaker. Under the influence of emotion the [ɔ·] of " How
glorious ! " may become very long indeed; even the ordinarily
short initial consonant of " No ! " may be considerably lengthened. It should be distinctly understood that the length
denoted in phonetic script is only relative, not absolute, thus
the long [i·] in *beat* as contrasted with the short [i] in *bit*. The
vowel [æ] of *bat*, and especially of *bad*, though marked short, is
really longer, measured absolutely, than the " long " [i·] of *beat*
and *bead*.

The voice or voicelessness of a final consonant has considerable
influence on the length of the preceding sounds; compare thus
the vowels of *bead* and *beat*, of *heard* and *hurt*, the diphthongs
of *raise* and *race*, of *code* and *coat*, of *eyes* and *ice*, the [l] of *felled*
and *felt*, the [n] of *send* and *sent* : in all these pairs the sound is
longer in the former than in the latter word.

2.9₂. **Stress,** which distinguishes, for instance, the first syllable
of *photograph*, the second of *photography*, and the third of

photographical, from the rest of the word, or which marks out the second, fifth and seventh words of the sentence : *the man in the car was ill,* from the weaker words, depends not only on the force with which the air is expelled from the lungs, but also on the total energy with which the sounds are articulated, thus on energetic action on the part of all organs of speech. In the larynx this is shown particularly in the energetic way in which the vocal chords act in producing higher or lower tones, or in jumping or gliding up and down, in stressed voiced sounds. Thus are produced variations of intonation, which are of the utmost importance for the meaning of the sentences. The student should notice, for instance, the way in which the meaning of the sentence :

Won't you come and dine with me today ?

is modified according as each of the words *won't, you, dine, me,* and *today* receives the stress and the characteristic interrogatory tone. (From a poem by Mr W. de la Mare.)

EVOLUTION OF THE SOUND-SYSTEM

Sound laws.—Alternations.—Stress.—The great vowel-shift.—
New [aˑ, ɔˑ].

3.1₁. In course of time, languages change in respect to sounds
as well as in everything else. Very often these changes affect
at the same time whole series of words with great regularity :
then we speak of **sound laws,** though these are not to be compared with natural laws because they are not like these universal
with regard to time and space, but are merely formulas of what
happened at one particular period in one particular language or
dialect. Just as a geologist from the aspect of a piece of scenery
can draw conclusions as to what has happened at that place
perhaps hundreds or thousands of years ago, the trained philolo-
gist sees in our present English language traces of phonetic
changes, some of them dating very far back, while others are
more recent.

The symbol > means " has become phonetically," and inversely < " has developed from."

3.1₂. We have survivals of a prehistoric sound law called
apophony or gradation (German *ablaut*) in many verbal forms,
e.g. *drink, drank, drunk* or *write, wrote, written,* and also in some
substantives, e.g. *burden* (cp. *bear, bore*) and *writ* (cp. *write*).
Another prehistoric sound law is mutation (German *umlaut*),
where a vowel is coloured by that of a following syllable, which
was subsequently lost. This explains the plurals of some substantives, e.g. *men, geese* from *man, goose,* and the formation of
derivatives like *fill* from *full, filth* from *foul, heat* from *hot.* An
isolated survival of a prehistoric consonant change is seen in
were as the plural of *was.*

3.1₃. In the following pages a survey is given of the most
important changes that have affected the English sound-system ;
all minor changes have been disregarded, but it should be clearly

understood that the sound history of English is so very complicated that a complete and detailed exposition would require several hundred pages.   Only such sound laws are mentioned as have taken place in the full daylight of history, *i.e.* since the English began to write down their own language.   No attempt has been made to present the phenomena in a strictly chronological order.

It will be seen in various pages of this survey that the sounds of words cannot be studied without regard to their meanings : there is in fact a constant interplay between the outer and inner aspect of language which should not be overlooked.

3.2. As a rule, sound changes do not affect the same sound wherever it is found, but only under certain **phonetic conditions** —in one particular position (initial, medial, or final), in stressed syllables or in unstressed syllables, etc.   A long vowel may be changed while the corresponding short vowel is kept unchanged, or *vice versa*.   In this way sound changes may give rise to **phonetic alternations,** through which closely connected words, which formerly had the same, or practically the same sound, become more or less differentiated in sound.   For instance, when initial [k] before [n] was dropped, *e.g.* in *know, knock, knit,* it was kept when protected by a preceding vowel, hence we get the alternation between *knowledge* and *acknowledge*.   An [n] became mute after [m], but only at the end of a word, hence the alternation between *damn* and *damnation, solemn* and *solemnity, autumn* and *autumnal*.   In some cases, especially when the same word has been affected by several subsequent sound changes, the result is that two words which originally belonged closely together are torn completely asunder ; thus no one now has an immediate feeling that the first syllable of *woman* contains the same word as *wife* (OE. *wīfman* ; the shortened *i* is still heard in the plural *women,* though disguised in the spelling).

In the following chapters alternations are indicated by the sign ‖, thus *knowledge ‖ acknowledge ; solemn ‖ solemnity,* etc.

Stress

3.3₁. In OE. words the root-syllable, *i.e.* the syllable that was felt as the most important and significant one, received stronger stress than other syllables. This is still the case with native words, e.g. *better, happiness, careless*, etc. The root-syllable is generally the first as in the examples just given, but it may be preceded by a weak prefix, as in *believe, arise, indeed, forgive*.

3.3₂. In all old compounds the first element is stressed as being the distinctive part of the word : *statesman, postman, holiday, twelvemonth, goldfish, blackbird, Gloucester, Gloucestershire, daisy* (originally *dayes-ye*, " day's-eye "), etc. The feeling of one sense-unit is very strong in all these. But in many recent compounds each part is felt as a unit in itself and as equally important as the other, and this leads to equal or nearly equal stress on the two parts, *e.g.* in *lead pencil, gold coin, country town, back garden, head quarters, cock pheasant, home-made*. This is even the case with some compounds that are generally spelt as one word, e.g. *plumpudding, headmaster*. In connected speech the stress may vary for rhythmical reasons, *e.g.* in '*this after'noon*, but '*afternoon 'tea, 'home-made 'jam*, but *it's 'all home-'made*, '*square miles*, but *two 'thousand square 'miles, 'coat 'tails*, but '*coat-tail 'pocket*. Contrast also may determine stress in these compounds, as when '*rice pudding* is said in contrast to '*plumpudding*.

The two parts of such compounds are so independent that we may say that they form really two words, the first of which is an adjunct of the second; note that this is shown by the possibility of the use of *one* as in *two gold watches and a silver one*, and of an adverb as in *on merely business grounds* or *on strictly party lines* (**8.5**).

3.3₃. While numerals in *-ty* always stress the first syllable, those in *-teen* have rhythmically changing stress; *she is just fif'teen*, but *she is 'fifteen years*.

3.3₄. In some words a distinction is made between a substantive with stress on the first and a verb with stress on the second element :

> 'forecast || fore'cast
> 'overthrow || over'throw
> 'underline || under'line

3.4₁. Into this consistent and comparatively simple system there came an inrush of hundreds of French—and later of Latin and Greek—words with a totally different stress system. End-stress was retained in such words as resembled native words with weak prefixes, e.g. *arrive, affair, accuse, connect, complete, desire, escape, endure, expect, prepare, propose, succeed.* But in most other words the stress was shifted ; thus in those words of two syllables whose endings resembled native unstressed suffixes, e.g. *cousin, dozen, mason, punish, barber, error, country, medal.*

3.4₂. In longer words rhythm often determines which syllable attracts the stress : in such a word as *radical, cal* was originally the strongest, but *rad* had a secondary stress because separated from *cal* by the weak *i* and later acquired the chief stress ; similarly the third from the ending is stressed in *individual, occupy, verity, necessity, tyranny, elegant, innocent, sentiment, separate, interrogative, catholic, popular* and many others. Words in *-ory, -ary* from Old French *-'orie, -'arie* (modern *-oire, -aire*) follow the same principle of having the stress on the vowel removed by one syllable from the original stress, hence we have *pre'paratory, 'military, 'necessary* ; Americans still preserve the memory of the original stress by giving *-o-* and *-a-* a secondary stress, while these syllables are weak or even slurred over in British pronunciation. In the endings *-ion, -ian, -ious* the *i* originally counted as a full syllable, though not now pronounced in that way, hence we have *opinion, condition, diffusion, musician, tedious* and others with stress on what is now the last syllable but one.

Rhythmical stressing of the third-last syllable accounts for the alternation in many word-families like the following :

'colony ‖ co'lonial
'origin ‖ o'riginal ‖ origi'nality
'contemplate ‖ con'templative ‖ contem'plation
'victory ‖ vic'torious
'solid ‖ so'lidity ‖ soli'darity
'photograph ‖ pho'tography

3.4₃. In many words analogy has been strong enough to counteract this rhythmical principle, thus *arrive, refuse* drag along *a'rrival, re'fusal; a'cquaint, a'cquaintance; a'llow, a'llowance; em'ploy, em'ployment; a'ttract, a'ttractive,* etc. The British stress in *advertisement* [əd'vəˑtizmənt] is rhythmical, but Americans generally say [ædvə'taizmənt]. *Capitalist* and *pianist* vacillate between rhythmical and analogical accentuation. *Aristocrat* is [ə'ristəkræt] rhythmically or ['æristəkræt] from *aristocracy* [ˌæri'stɔkrəsi]. Some adjectives in *-able* have rhythmical stress : *'admirable, 'lamentable, 'preferable;* these are traditional forms handed over from generation to generation. But very often a speaker would be simply thinking of the verb and then add the ending *-able*: this would lead to a different accentuation, thus *a'greeable, de'plorable, re'markable,* etc. Thus we often find two conflicting pronunciations : *'acceptable*—the old rhythmic form, is found in Shakespeare and is still used sometimes in the reading of the Prayer Book, but generally the word is pronounced *ac'ceptable.* Shakespeare's and Spenser's *'detestable* has been supplanted by *de'testable.*

In long words rhythm generally determines the place of secondary stresses, e.g. *ˌincon'venience, inˌcompreˌhensi'bility.*

3.4₄. In many words stress serves to distinguish substantives (or adjectives) and verbs, e.g. *absent, accent, conduct, frequent, object, present, rebel, record, subject,* cf. the corresponding differentiation in native words (**3.3₄**). In longer words a corresponding distinction is made through a secondary stress on the last syllable in the verb : *experiment* [sb. eks'perimənt, vb. eks'periˌment], similarly *compliment* and others. Words in *-ate* have [-it] or [-ət] as adjectives, [-eit] with secondary stress as verbs, e.g. *moderate, separate.*

The Great Vowel-Shift

3.5₁. The greatest revolution that has taken place in the phonetic system of English is the vowel-shift, which began in the fourteenth century and resulted in the general raising of Middle English long vowels, with the exception of the two highest [iˑ, uˑ], which could not be further raised, but were diphthongized into [ai, au]. The transitions may be provisionally represented in this way :

[iˑ > ai]	[uˑ > au]
[eˑ > iˑ]	[oˑ > uˑ]
[ɛˑ > eˑ]	[ɔˑ > oˑ]

$$[aˑ > ɛˑ]$$

The movement was, on the whole, parallel in the two series of vowels, front and back. After the two high vowels [iˑ] and [uˑ] had become diphthongs, each of the other long vowels climbed, as it were, up the ladder to the next higher position, keeping all the time the original distance, and in this way preventing disturbing clashings of words that were originally kept apart by vowels distant from each other by one degree only.

A few examples of each vowel may here be given, arranged according to the Middle English vowels, but written here in the modern spelling :

[iˑ] : *bite, wise, by*	[uˑ] : *foul, fowl, house, cow*
[eˑ] : *beet, freeze, see*	[oˑ] : *fool, goose, shoe*
[ɛˑ] : *beat, please, sea*	[ɔˑ] : *foal, rose, no*

[aˑ] : *hate, graze*

3.5₂. A closer inspection of the facts gives rise to the following remarks :

(1) These thoroughgoing changes are disguised in the traditional spelling, which reflects medieval conditions with much greater fidelity than modern ones. The spelling *ou* in *foul, house,* etc., is only seemingly a phonetic rendering of the modern diphthong, for *ou* (with its variant *ow*) was originally taken over from French to denote the vowel [u].

(2) In the above diagram ME. [aˑ] has been placed midway

between the front and the back-round series.   When it was
raised it entered the front series, while an older [a·] had become
[ɔ·] : OE. *stān* > ME. *ston*, modern *stone*.

(3) The notations [ɛ·] and [o·] as the results of ME. [a·] and
[ɔ·] do not correspond with present pronunciation, for the vowels
have become diphthongs, though of a different order from [ai,
au], as their movement is slow, so that they might be written
[ɛ·i, o·u] in exact notation.   Here they are for practical reasons
written [ei, ou] : [heit, greiz, foul, rouz, nou].   They have thus
fallen together with the diphthongs developed from ME. *ai* or
ei and *ou*, with the result that we have the diphthong :

[ei] in *ale, lade, vane* as well as in *ail, laid, vain, vein*, and
[ou] in *sole, road, rode, sloe* as well as in *soul, rowed, slow*.

The pronunciation is more clearly diphthongic in the South of
England than in the North or some parts of the United States.

(4) Middle English had two *e-* as well as two *o*-sounds, in the
above diagram denoted as [e·, ɛ·] and [o·, ɔ·] respectively.   In
earlier centuries these sounds were neatly distinguished, and
even in their upward movement kept their distance.   This is
still the case in the back-round series, where the vowels in *fool*
and *foal* are still distinct.   But in the front series the vowel
resulting from the open ME. [ɛ·] was—a century or two after the
general shift was completed—further raised one step to [i·] and
thus fell together with the result of the old close [e·].   Consequently we have [i·] in *heal, read, sea, meat*, as well as in *heel,
reed, see, meet*.

3.5₃. At a time when the old [e·] had been raised to [i·], while
the old [ɛ·] was still a comparatively open [ɛ]-sound, it became
usual in some words to write the former sound *ie* and the latter
ea, thus *field, thief, believe* ; for *ea* see the list just given.   At the
same time, the spelling *oa* became similarly usual in many words
after *oo* had come to be looked upon as the ordinary symbol for
[u·], e.g. *loan, boat, coach*.

3.5₄. Besides the [u·] which is due to the raising of [o·] we have
another [u·] in the combination [ju·], which is developed from an

earlier [iu] from various sources, e.g. *dew, due, use, hue, suit.* On the loss of [j] in *true*, etc., see **5.1₂**.

3.6. While loan-words adopted before the time of the great vowel-shift had, as a matter of course, to participate in it along with native words (see, e.g. *cry, arrive, type, agree, creed, peace, beast, take, fate, Satan, couch, spouse, roast, move*), recent loans have the same sound (or approximately the same sound) as the language from which they were adopted; thus we have [i·] in *esteem*, Fr. *estimer, breeze*, Sp. *briza*, or with retention of the French spelling, *marine, routine, police*, and others; in *machine* and *chemise* both *ch* [ʃ] and *i* [i·] testify to recent loans. Further, *route, rouge, bouquet, beau, éclat, mirage* (note [ʒ], not [dʒ] in some of these), *moustache* (note [ʃ]), *tomato*. Note the French end-stress in many of these recent loans.

Tower [tauə] and *tour* [tuə] are two French words *tour*, taken over at two different times.

3.7. While the long ME. vowels have thus undergone violent changes, the short vowels have been much better preserved and have, on the whole, the same values as in the Middle Ages. Still *a* has become [æ], e.g. *hat, sad, man, act*, etc., and in most cases the short [u] has become [ʌ], *i.e.* has been unrounded and lowered, e.g. *up, nut, some, touch.*

In some words, however, [u] has been kept, especially under the influence of lip-sounds and *l*, e.g. *full, pull, wolf, wool, put, bush*, etc.

The three words *food, blood*, and *good* had originally the same vowel [o·], which was raised to [u·], but while *food* has remained long, *blood* was shortened before [u] became [ʌ], and *good* after that change had taken place.

3.8. In consequence of the great vowel-shift numerous alternations, which at first depended on length of vowel only, have become more considerable:

[ai ‖ i] : *child ‖ children, five ‖ fifth, wise ‖ wisdom, hide ‖ hid, life ‖ live, dine ‖ dinner, type ‖ typical.*

[au ‖ ʌ] : *South ‖ Southern Suffolk, out ‖ utter, flower ‖ flourish.*

[i· || e] : *keep* || *kept*, *mean* || *meant*, *bleed* || *bled*, *read* || *read*, *deep* || *depth*, *sheep* || *shepherd*, *please* || *pleasant*.

[u· || ɔ] : *fool* || *folly*, *goose* || *gosling*.

[ou || ɔ] : *holy* || *holiday*, *throat* || *throttle*, *nose* || *nostril*, *know* || *knowledge*, *clothe* || *cloth*.

[ei || æ] : *shade* || *shadow*, *pale* || *pallor*, *vain* || *vanity*, *Spain* || *Spanish*, *late* || *latter*.

3.9$_1$. On referring to the diagram above (**3.**5$_1$) the reader will see that through the vowel-shift the lowest places, those for [a·, ɔ·], have been abandoned. This does not, however, mean that these vowels are non-existent in Modern English, for after the general shift new [a·]s and [ɔ·]s have developed in many words, often through the loss of a consonant, but also from other causes, which are not always easy to unravel. In many cases length of the vowel is uncertain, thus especially before [f, þ, s], where many speakers, especially in the North of England and in America, have [æ] or [æ·] corresponding to Southern English [a·], and [ɔ] corresponding to Southern [ɔ·]. These fluctuations are not specially indicated below.

[a·] is found :

(1) with loss of [l] before a lip-consonant : *alms, palm, half, halve.*
(2) before original *r* : *charm, large, heart, far* (**4.**3$_3$).
(3) before [f] : *staff, telegraph, laugh, laughter, craft.*
(4) before [þ] : *bath, path.*
(5) before [ð] : *paths, father, rather.*
(6) before [s] : *grass, glass, cast, master, ask, basket, clasp.*
(7) before [m] : *example,* (*ma'am*).
(8) before [nt] : *aunt, plant, advantage, shan't.*
(9) before [ns] : *dance, chance, France, answer.*
(10) before [nd] : *demand, command, Flanders, Alexander.*
(11) before [nʃ] : *branch, blanch.*
(12) finally : *ah, hurrah, papa, mamma.*

Further, in some recent loans from other languages, e.g. *lava, mirage, mahdi, khaki, Cincinnati.*

In some words there is vacillation between [aˑ] and [ɔˑ] before
n-combinations; the spelling has *au* : *gaunt, haunt, Staunton,
jaundice, laundress, launch.*

How impossible it is to find fixed phonetic laws for many
of these combinations is shown by the fact that the following
words, which seemingly are quite parallel with the cases of [aˑ],
have always, or nearly always, short [æ] : *valve, camp, ample,
cant, scant, pantry, finance, fancy, gland, abandon, pander.*

We have a certain number of alternations between [ei] as the
normal continuation of ME. [aˑ], and the recent [aˑ] : *bathe* ||
bath, staves || *staff, graze* || *grass, pace* || *pass, halfpenny* || *half.*

3.9₂. [ɔˑ] is found :

(1) with loss of the back fricative denoted *gh* : *taught, brought,
    daughter.*
(2) before *l*, whether now lost or kept : *all, bald, talk, walk.*
(3) from original [au] : *saw, cause.*
(4) instead of [aˑ] through the influence of [w] : *water, war,
    quart.*
(5) before written *r* : *horse, lord, door* (**4.3₃, 4.4₂**).

Vacillation between long [ɔˑ] and short [ɔ] is found :

(1) before [ls, lt] : *false, also, fault, salt.*
(2) before [f] : *off, cough, soft.*
(3) before [þ] : *cloth, broth.*
(4) before [s] : *cross, toss, frost, lost.*

It will be seen that wherever this [ɔˑ] has developed from *a*,
there is always a [u] or [w] element to cause the rounding, either before (*war*) or after (*au*) ; this element was found
in the ME. consonant written *gh* in *taught*, etc., and in the
" hollow " [l].

3.9₃. A corresponding rounding is also caused by [w] in the
short *a* : *what, watch, quarrel.*

EVOLUTION OF THE SOUND-SYSTEM—*continued*

Weakening of *r*.—Short vowels before *r*.—*ar*, *or*, etc.—Alternations with and without *r*.—Influence of stress on vowels.—Loss of *e*.—Vowels in weak syllables.—Loss of vowels in groups.—Alternations in compounds.—Strong and weak forms of the same word.

R and R-Vowels

4.1₁. Originally *r* was a full point-trill everywhere. In order to pronounce this trill the tip of the tongue is made thin and elastic, and then raised and made to move rapidly to and fro several times : and in order to make the tip thin the bulk of the tongue-muscle must be shifted backwards. This articulation requires a good deal of energy, the sound is loud and noisy, and was therefore fit for the open-air life of olden times, just as it is nowadays preferred for singing in big concert-rooms. But the last few centuries, with their " civilized " indoor life, have in many countries witnessed a growing reduction of this point-trill *r* ; sometimes the point-element remains though without any trill, sometimes only the back-element is retained, which may or may not be accompanied with secondary trillings of the uvula (" Northumbrian burr "). Very often the degree of reduction is different according to the position in the syllable, the tendency being towards a stronger articulation before, and a weaker after the vowel ; in the latter position *r* may even totally disappear, especially before a consonant. Very often the *r* modifies a preceding vowel. Such tendencies are found all over the world, though not carried through everywhere to the same extent or in the same way.

4.1₂. In English *r* is now a consonant only when it immediately precedes a vowel (in the same or in the following word). It is not trilled except in out-of-the-way parts of Scotland, and occasionally after [b] or [p]. The tip of the tongue is raised against the innermost part of the gums so as to form a kind of broad aperture, which is smallest after [t, d], so that *tried,* *drove* sometimes come to resemble *chide, Jove* in sound. After a short vowel, as in *merry, hurry, carry*, the rapid movement up to the [r]-position and back is a " flap," but initially and after a long vowel, as in *rye, roll, roaring, Mary*, the movement is slower. In American pronunciation the point is more retracted, and the movements are generally slower in all positions. This is particularly conspicuous in such words as *very American*, where the [r] is apt to colour the preceding vowel and make it resemble [ə], the three sounds [eri] being nearly run together in contrast to the clearly cut British pronunciation.

4.1₃. When [r] was still a full consonant it proved stronger than a following [w] or [h], which disappeared : *Warwick* [wɔrik], *Berwick* [berik], *Harwich* [hæridʒ], *Durham* [dʌrəm], *Norham* [nɔrəm], *forehead* [fɔred, -id]. Where, on the other hand, there is a vivid feeling for each component, so that the combination is constantly being new-formed, [w] and [h] are maintained : *fir-wood, therewith, doorway, door-handle, war-horse, shareholder*, etc. It will be seen that the vulgar [fɔrəd] *forward* represents an older tradition than the polite [fɔ·(ə)wəd]. *Perhaps* is often made [præps], but also [phæps] with strongly aspirated [p].

4.2₁. A short vowel before *r* followed by a vowel generally has the same sound as it would have before most other consonants, e.g. *spirit, ferry, carry, hurry, horrid*. But in other positions *r* exercises a more or less deep-going influence on a preceding vowel.

4.2₂. A transition from *e* to *a* under the influence of a following *r* is very old in many words, e.g. *star, far* (ME. *sterre, ferre*), *Harry* from *Herry = Henry*, the name of the letter *R, heart* and *hart*. In some words the spelling *er* is still retained : *clerk, sergeant*, though as family names they are often spelt *Clark, Sargeant*; the occasional pronunciation with [ə·] is due to the spelling.

4.3₁. When not protected by an immediately following vowel, *r* is weakened and loses its value as a consonant as the distance between the tongue and the roof of the mouth is increased. The tip of the tongue at first was raised, though not to the full consonantal position ; this is still found in the western counties of England and in great parts of America, but in Standard British pronunciation the tip lies flat in the bottom of the mouth. The vowel-like quality of *r* is shown clearly after the diphthongs [au, ai], where a new syllable is frequently developed, *e.g.* in *shower*, OE. *scūr* ; *flower* and *flour* are two different spellings of what is etymologically and phonetically the same word ; *fire* and *hire* are disyllabics as early as in Shakespeare, who rhymes the former with *liar*.

4.3₂. Before this weakened *r*, original short *i*, *u*, and *e* (in so far as this had not become *a*) have fallen together, and we have now the same vowel [ə·] resulting from the vowel and *r* in *bird*, *word*, *herd*=*heard* [bə·d, wə·d, hə·d] ; other examples are *mirth*, *myrtle*, *cur*, *journey*, *earl*, etc. *Kerb* is merely a different spelling of *curb*.

4.3₃. With the short low vowels *a* and *o* the result is, in the southern pronunciation, a complete absorption of [r] before a consonant : *hard* [ha·d], *order* [ɔ·də] ; other examples, *cart*, *large*, *fork*, *horn*. Hence such rhymes as *crosses* : *horses*, *morning* : *dawning* (Keats) or *wrought* : *report*, *waters* : *quarters* (Kipling), which, of course, are avoided by poets who think much of spelling and the teaching of schools, as well as by those (Americans and others) who retain a trace of the *r*, even if it consists only in a very small raising of the tip towards the end of the vowel.

Those who have no trace of *r* or [ə] in the words here mentioned often pronounce [ə] when the sound is final : *far* [fa·ə], *nor* [nɔ·ə].

4.4₁ In all these cases an original short vowel has been lengthened through the influence of the fusion with the weakened *r*. We now come to the originally long vowels, and first note that *r* neutralizes the tendency towards diphthongs of the [ei, ou]-type and tends to lower vowels.

Thus instead of [ei]+*r* we get [ɛ·ə], which begins lower than

[ei] and glides off into [ə], e.g. *hare*=*hair* [hɛ·ə], *air*=*heir* [ɛ·ə], *fare*=*fair*, *their*, etc. Thus also in *prayer*, " act of praying," which is a sense-unit ; but when an agent-substantive in *-er* is formed from *pray*, *prayer*, " one who prays," it is possible to keep the two elements distinct and pronounce [eiə] ; thus also in *ratepayer*.

The diphthong [ɛ·ə] is also found in some cases of original *e* : *pear*, *tear* (vb.), *there* and others.

[ə] is pronounced between [ɛ·] and a consonantal [r] : *Mary* [mɛ·əri], *fairest*, *tearing*, etc.

4.4₂. The *r*, or the resulting vowel [ə], also prevents the formation of the up-gliding diphthong [ou] in words like *oar*, *board*, *door*, *floor*, *porch*, *court*. The vowel in these cases was in former times kept distinct from that in *fork*, etc. (**4.3₃**) by having the mouth less open ; this distinction is still maintained by many Northerners and Americans, but in Standard Southern pronunciation the vowel has been lowered : [ɔ·ə, bɔ·d], etc., so that *hoarse* and *horse*, *mourning* and *morning* are made identical [hɔ·s, mɔ·niŋ], even *court*=*caught*.

The combination [ouə] may, however, be heard in words that are clearly felt as formed from [ou]-words : *lower*, *playgoer*.

4.4₃. In words like *beer*, *deer*=*dear*, etc., we generally have not the full-length [i·] of *bee*, etc., followed by a short [ə], but two half-long elements, written phonetically for convenience' sake [iə] ; if final, [ə] may even tend to be long and to become the top of the syllable, thus especially in *year*, which instead of [jiə] becomes [jə·].

With consonantal [r] we have, for instance, *dearest* [diərist], *hero*, *nearing*.

4.4₄. Parallel to [iə] we have [uə] with both elements half-long rather than [u·ə] in *boor* [buə], *cure* [kjuə], *lure* [l(j)uə] ; before consonantal [r], e.g. *purity* [pjuəriti], *curious*. But there is a strong tendency to lower the vowel, especially in frequently used words like *your* [juə, jɔ·(ə)], *sure* [ʃuə, ʃɔ·(ə)].

Note that the first element of the name *Shoreditch* is identical with *sewer*, which is now made [sjuə] in refined pronunciation.

4.5₁. Consonantal [r] appears not only before a vowel in the same word, but also before one in the following word, if pronounced without any pause. Thus we get alternations like these :

> far below [faˑ(ə) biˈlou] || far above [faˑr əˈbʌv].
> more meat [mɔˑ(ə) miˑt] || more of that [mɔˑr əv ðæt].
> their things [ðɛˑə þiŋz] || their uncle [ðɛˑər ʌŋkl].
> dear Paul [diə pɔˑl] || dear Ann [diər æn].
> poor Paul [puə pɔˑl] || poor Ann [puər æn].
> our friend [auə frend] || our enemy [auər enimi].
> better paid [betə peid] || better off [betər ɔˑf].

4.5₂. As these alternations are generally unconscious, and as the [ə] developed from *r* is identical in sound with [ə] from weak vowels, there is a natural tendency to insert an unhistorical [r] in combinations like *idea of* [aiˈdiər əv], *a drama-r-of Ibsen*, *the law-r-of the land*, *Amelia-r-Ann*, etc. But a reaction has recently set in and has even led to the [r] being often omitted in *better and better* and similar combinations.

4.5₃. There are some comparatively old isolated instances of *r* being totally dropped, e.g. *Marlborough*, *Worcester*, *palsy* from *paralysie*. Vulgar *bust* from *burst* and *cussed* for *cursed* have developed in more recent times.

Influence of Stress on Vowel-Sounds

4.6₁. In English the difference between stressed and unstressed syllables is much stronger than in some other languages, for instance French, and this has had far-reaching consequences on the whole sound-system of the language. We notice a strong contrast between French *fraternité*, with all four syllables nearly equal in weight and with its four clear-cut vowels, on the one hand, and on the other, E. *fraternity* with *ter* much stronger than the rest of the word and with obscured *a* [ə] and *i*. Cp. also Fr. *capitaine* and E. *captain*, in which *i* has completely disappeared between *p* and *t*, while there is very little, if any, vowel left in the last syllable.

A great many weak *e*'s, which were still sounded in the four-teenth century, have since disappeared. In Chaucer's line :

> Of king*e*s, princ*e*s, erl*e*s, duk*e*s bold*e*

all the here italicized *e*'s were pronounced by him, but they have all of them disappeared, with the sole exception of that in *princes*, which has become [i], as have also all other *e*'s in the ending -*es* after a hissing sound : *noses, bridges, fetches.* Similarly the preterit ending -*ed* has lost its vowel : *filled, sinned, sobbed,* etc. ; after a voiceless sound we get the voiceless consonant [t] : *stopped, talked, kissed,* etc. But after -*d* and -*t* the ending is sounded [id] : *ended, handed, fitted.* In these cases the vowel [i] thus serves to keep the stem of the word and the ending from running together. We have also [i] in the superlative ending -*est* : *greatest, weakest,* in the ordinals like *twentieth,* and in the two obsolete verbal endings -*est* and -*eth,* e.g. (thou) *singest,* (he) *singeth.* Note that in all these cases in which *e* has become [i], it occurs before a point (or blade) consonant, whose tongue-position is not far removed from that of [i].

As final *e* in the older language served a great many gram-matical purposes, in the same way as it still does in German and the Scandinavian languages, its loss has meant an enormous simplification in the whole grammatical structure of English.

4.6₂. Among other instances of [i] in weak syllables we may mention the ending [-idʒ] in *college, knowledge, courage, marriage,* etc., [-it] in *summit, hamlet, Dorset, minute* ; *prophet* is generally pronounced like *profit* ; further, middle syllables like *compliment* =*complement, consequent, element, elegant.*

In some cases there is some vacillation between [i] in more familiar and [e] in more formal speech, thus in the endings -*ness* and -*less* : *goodness, careless, carelessness,* etc. While verbs in -*ate* have a secondary stress on that ending and therefore pronounce [-eit], adjectives and substantives have [-et], or more frequently, [-it] or [-ət] : *fortunate, aggregate* ; thus the verb *separate* is [sepəreit], the adjective [sep(ə)rit] or [seprət] ; the adverb is generally [seprətli].

Vacillation between weak [i] and [ə] is found, for instance, in *palace, palate, woollen, mountain, character, oracle*; *possible* and others in *-ible*. Some people pronounce [ə] in the endings *-less* and *-ness*.

Cp. the two spellings of the same name *Wallis* and *Wallace*.

Short [i] is found in the weak prefixes *be-, de-, re-, pre-* : *believe, before, depend, reject, prefer*. But when *re-* is added to a word with the full force of " again," it is stressed and pronounced ['riˑ] ; thus a difference is made between *reform*, " change," and *re-form*, " form again," *recover*, " get back," and *re-cover*, " cover again " (**1.**2).

4.6₃. The prevailing tendency in unstressed syllables is to reduce the vowel to the obscure [ə], which is produced with a minimum of tongue-activity, or even to leave out the vowel altogether.

Thus we have [ə] in a great many final syllables, *e.g.* :

> *-a : sofa, umbrella.*
> *-an : Roman, human.*
> *-ant* and *-ent : elegant, elephant, patient, obedient.*
> *-ance* and *-ence : elegance, distance, existence.*
> *-able : eatable.*
> *-at, -ot, -ut : combat, parrot, gamut.*
> *-us, -ous : Jesus, curious.*
> *-ar, -er, -or, -our : vicar, mother, writer, actor, humour.*

Final [ou] is generally kept : *hero, tomato, fellow, borrow* ; but in *thorough* and place-names like *Peterborough* the usual pronunciation is [pʌrə, piˑtəb(ə)rə]. In vulgar speech *fellow, window* become [felə, wində], often rendered *feller, winder*.

4.6₄. Further, [ə] occurs in many initial syllables :

> *a- : asleep, ajar, alone, agree, account,* etc.
> *ob-, oc-,* etc. *: obey, oblige, occasion, official.*
> *con-, com-, cor- : connect, content, commit, correct.*
> *sub-, sup-,* etc. *: submit, suppose, suffice.*
> *so- : solicitor, sonorous.*

A full vowel is found especially before consonant-groups and is naturally most frequent in literary words : *campaign, ambition, sanguineous* [æ].

[ə] is the natural pronunciation in the first syllable of such words as *police, potato, propose, produce, society,* etc. ; but [ou] is often heard in less familiar words, like *protest, phonetic, chronology,* and always in learned words like *procumbent, prolepsis.*

4.7₁. Complete disappearance of a weak vowel is particularly frequent, where the tongue-point can remain in contact with the roof of the mouth, the result being that [n] or [l] becomes syllabic.

Examples : *written* [ritn], *student* [stju·dnt], *Britain=Briton* [britn], *Brighton* [braitn], *basin* [beisn], *prison* [prizn], *boatswain* [bousn], *fatal* [feitl], *metal=mettle* (etymologically the same word) [metl], *victuals* [vitlz], *medal* [medl], *dismissal* [dis'misl], *weasel* [wi·zl].   Thus also generally after [ʃ, ʒ], e.g. *mission* [miʃn], *vision* [viʒn] ; but after [k, g] a very short vowel is retained in the pronunciation of many people, *e.g.* in *bacon* [beik(ə)n], *waggon* [wæg(ə)n].

A syllabic [m] is also found, when a vowel is left out, though [ə] is more frequent here than with [n] : *fathom* [fæð(ə)m], *circumstance* [sə·k(ə)mstəns], *tiresome* [taiəs(ə)m].

4.7₂. The weakening of unstressed vowels occasions a great many alternations.   In compounds the tendency to obscure or omit the vowel is naturally strongest in the most familiar words, especially if the meaning of the original composition has been obscured.   Examples :

man [mæn ‖ -mən], in *postman, gentleman, Englishman,* etc. But in some rarer compounds, like *nurseryman,* [-mæn] may be heard.

land [lænd ‖ -lənd] in *England, island, midland,* etc.   But such literary words as *dreamland, stageland* have the full vowel.

pan [pæn ‖ -pən] only in *saucepan.*

mast [ma·st] and *sail* [seil] ‖ sailors say [tɔpməst, tɔpsl], etc.

ful [ful ‖ -fəl] in *careful, awful,* etc.   But the original meaning and vowel are preserved in substantives like *spoonful, basketful,* etc.

mouth [mauþ ‖ -məþ] : *Plymouth, Portsmouth,* and other place-names.

town [taun ‖ -t(ə)n] : *Eaton, Newton, Easton,* etc.

folk [fouk ‖ -fək] in *Norfolk, Suffolk.*

stone [stoun ‖ -stən] in *brimstone,* cf. **4.8.**

come [kʌm ‖ -kəm] : *welcome, income.*

body [bɔdi ‖ -bədi] only in the pronouns *nobody, somebody*; but in *everybody* and *anybody* the rhythmic secondary stress preserves the full vowel; cp. also *busybody.*

penny, pence [peni, pens ‖ -pəni, -p(ə)ns] : *halfpenny, halfpence* (on [ei] see **5.3₂**), *twopence,* etc.

day [dei ‖ -di] generally in the names of the days of the week, *Sunday,* etc., and in *holiday* and *yesterday.* But other compounds, such as *weekday, birthday,* keep [-dei].

gate [geit ‖ -git] in a frequent pronunciation of names like *Highgate, Margate.*

4.8. Complete obscuration of sound as well as of meaning is seen in some original compounds, for instance, *cupboard* [kʌbəd] and *forehead* [fɔred] or even [fɔrid]. Such words have, to all intents and purposes, become separate units independent of the way in which they were at first framed as compounds. Compare also *breakfast* [brekfəst] : the independence is here shown in the flexion as well : *he breakfasted* instead of the old *he broke fast.* There may be some gain in the refashioning of *grindstone* as [graindstoun] instead of [grinstən] as it was sounded in former centuries, for the word means really a stone for grinding ; but the gain is more problematical when some people insist on pronouncing *waistcoat* [weistkout] instead of the unit-pronunciation [weskət], for *waist + coat* gives no adequate description of the thing. Such cases must be judged each on its own merits and not by any hard-and-fast rule.

4.9₁. We have further alternations between two (or even three) forms of the same word, according as it is pronounced with or (more frequently) without sentence-stress.

First, a series of pronouns :

We, me, he, she, with long or short [i].

her [hə·(r) ‖ hə(r)].

my [mai ‖ mi], not so frequently now as formerly, note [mi lɔ·d] to judges.

your [juə(r), jɔ·(r) ‖ jə(r)].

us [ʌs ‖ əs] ; [s] in *let's*.

them [ðem ‖ ðəm].

that [ðæt] demonstrative ‖ [ðət] conjunction (**33**.1, **34**.2).

the [ði· ‖ ði] before vowels, [ðə] before consonants.

some [sʌm ‖ səm].

an, a [æn, ei ‖ ən, ə].

4.9₂. Next, the most frequent verbs (auxiliaries) :

be [bi· ‖ bi].

been [bi·n ‖ bin]—but the latter form is by some used as a stressed form too.

am [æm ‖ əm, m] : *I'm*.

is [iz ‖ z] : *he's*, etc ; [s] after a voiceless consonant : *it's, what's*.

are [a·(r) ‖ ə(r)] : *we're*.

was [wɔz ‖ wəz].

were [wə·(r) ‖ wə(r)].

have [hæv ‖ həv, əv, v] : *we've*.

has [hæz ‖ həz, əz, z] : *he's been* ; [s] sometimes after voiceless : *it's been*.

had [hæd ‖ həd, əd, d] : *we'd been*.

shall [ʃæl ‖ ʃəl, ʃl].

should [ʃud ‖ ʃəd, ʃd].

will [wil ‖ l] : *I'll*.

would [wud ‖ wəd, əd, d] : *I'd*.

can [kæn ‖ kən, kn].

could [kud ‖ kəd].

may [mei ‖ mi, mə], comparatively rare.

must [mʌst ‖ məst, məs].

do [du· ‖ du, də, d] : *What d'you say?*

does [dʌz ‖ dəz].

4.9₃. Finally, some particles :

and [ænd ‖ ənd, ən, nd, n].

but [bʌt ‖ bət].

than [ðæn ‖ ðən].

as æz || əz], sometimes [z].

or [ɔˑə, ɔˑr || ə(r)].

at [æt || ət].

of [ɔv || əv, ə] ; cf. *off*, **5.6**₂.

to [tuˑ] ; in two senses spelt *too* : *too good, he too* || [tu] before vowel, [tə] before consonant.

from [frɔm || frəm].

for [fɔˑ(r) || fə(r)].

by [bai || bi], now rare : *by the by.*

till [til || tl] : *not till five.*

It should be noted that prepositions have the full vowel before weakly-stressed pronouns : *he looks at us* [æt əs], but with stress on *us* [ət 'ʌs] ; *she doesn't care for him* [fɔr im], but with stress on *him* [fə 'him].

Not [nɔt] becomes [nt] when fused with auxiliary verbs ; the [n] is syllabic after a consonant, as in *haven't, hadn't, hasn't, isn't, shouldn't, wouldn't, mustn't* [mʌsnt], but not after a vowel, as in *aren't, weren't* ; note the vowels in *can't* [kaˑnt], *shan't* [ʃaˑnt], *won't* [wount], *don't* [dount].

4.9₄. Note especially *there*, which has practically become two distinct words, [ðɛˑə(r)] with local meaning, and [ðə(r)] with obliterated meaning (" preparatory *there*," **10.**8) ; both forms of *there* may be combined in the same sentence : *there were many people there.*

4.9₅. Substantives have no such double forms according to stress ; the only exception is *sir*, the full form of which is [səˑ], while [sə(r)] is used before names : *Sir Thomas, Sir Arthur*, and often after *yes* or *no*. But it is worth recording that *mister* (*Mr*) and *missis* [misiz] (*Mrs*) were developed as weak-stress forms of *master* and *mistress* ; the latter has even been reduced to *miss*, which to begin with was only a form of depreciation for *mistress.*

One adjective has weak-stress forms :

saint [seint || sint, sənt, snt] : *St Andrew*, or without [t] before consonants : *St Paul.*

CHAPTER V

EVOLUTION OF THE SOUND-SYSTEM—*concluded*

Consonants.—Tolerated consonant groups.—Consonants dropped.
—Voiced and voiceless consonants.—H.—Assibilation.—Stump-
words.

Consonants

5.1₁. While the vowel-system has undergone very heavy, nearly
revolutionary, changes, consonants have, on the whole, proved
much more stable. Sound-development in English has thus
been totally different in its tendencies from that in French,
where final consonants have very often disappeared ; cp. the
two different treatments of such a word as *pots*, E. [pɔts], Fr.
[po]. English thus does not object to even very heavy heapings
of final consonants, many of them occasioned by the loss of
an earlier *e*, *e.g.* in *beasts, wasps, stretched* [tʃt], *judged* [dʒd],
lisped [spt].

5.1₂. Still, some alleviations of consonant-groups have taken
place in historic times. First, we shall mention some initial combinations which have been simplified, thus in *know, gnaw, write,
lisp* (formerly *wlispe*). Further, [juˑ] has been reduced to [uˑ] in
many combinations : always after *r*, as in *rude, prude, true, crew,
brew, drew, grew, fruit, threw*, and after *l*-combinations : *plume,
clue, glue, flew, sluice* ; generally also after [dʒ, tʃ] : *Jew, juice,
chew*. But otherwise the tendency has not been carried through
consistently ; after *l* and *s* there is a good deal of vacillation :
lute, lewd, sue, Susan. After [n, d, t] the omission of [j], in *new,
due=dew, Tuesday*, etc., is chiefly found in the pronunciation of
a great many Americans.

5.1₃. We must here also mention the reduction of *wh* [hw] to *w*,
through which *whale* and *wail, whet* and *wet, whine* and *wine*, etc.,
have become homophones. The older pronunciation has been
preserved in Scotland, Ireland, and great parts of the United
States ; in England it is insisted on in some schools, though rather

artificially. Very often it is not exactly two sounds [h]+[w], but rather a voiceless [w] (**2.6**).

5.1₄. The only initial consonant-groups that are tolerated in Present English are the following ones, most of them perfectly smooth :

[r] after most of the consonants : *bring, pride, draw, tree, grow, from, throw, shrink* ; but not after [s].

[l] after [b, p, g, k, f, s] : *blow, plum, glow, climb, fling, slow* ; but not after [d, t], though some people pronounce [dl, tl] instead of [gl, kl], neither after [þ, ʃ].

[w] only after [d, t, k, þ, s] : *dwell, twist, quite, thwart, swing.*

[j] after most of the consonants, chiefly before [uˑ] : *beauty, pew, due, tune, gewgaw, cure, mute, new, few, view, thews, suit, lute, hue* ; on the tendency to leave out [j], see **5.1₂**.

[ʃ] and [ʒ] only in [tʃ, dʒ] : *child, join.*

[p, t, k] only after [s] : *spy, sty, sky.*

The only *m*- and *n*-combinations (apart from [mj, nj]) that are found are [sm, sn] : *smile, snow.*

No combinations of [v], [ð] or [z] with other consonants are found initially.

The only initial groups of three consonants that are tolerated are the following, all of them beginning with *s* : [spr, str, skr, spl, skw, spj, stj, skj] : *spring, string, scream, split, square, spew, stew, skew.*

5.1₅. It will be easily understood that the natural tendency in English is to leave out the initial consonants of the Greek combinations *ps, pt, phth, ks* (*x*), *pn, mn* : *psalm, psychology, Ptolemy, phthisis, xylography* (pronounced as if beginning with *z*), *pneumonia, mnemonics.*

5.2. In the middle and end of words we have a certain number of cases in which consonants have been dropped, thus the consonant corresponding to German *ch* and spelt *gh* has disappeared, generally before *t* : *light, right, brought, bought, slaughter, caught,* but also finally in cases like *high, weigh, plough, through, thorough, borough.* In some cases, however, it was changed into [f] : *laugh,* *laughter, rough, enough, cough,* and others ; *draught* and *draft* are different spellings of originally the same word.

[w] has often been dropped after a consonant in medial posi- tion : *answer, conquer* (but kept in *conquest*), many place-names in *-wich* and *-wick,* e.g. *Greenwich, Warwick, -wark* in *Southwark* [sʌðək], which is now sometimes pronounced [sauþwək] from the spelling, *boatswain* and *coxswain* [bousn, kɔksn], *gunwale* [gʌnəl]. Cp. also the familiar forms *'ll* and *'d* (*'ud*) for *will* and *would.* On *rw* see **4.1₃**.

5.3₁. Among final groups that have been simplified, we have already mentioned *mn* (**3.2**). Similarly, original [mb] has become [m] : *lamb, comb,* etc., in which *b* used to be pronounced ; later a mute *b* was introduced into the spelling of some words that originally had only *m* : *thumb, limb.*

5.3₂. Between a back vowel and a consonant [l] has often dis- appeared. The oldest instances are *halfpenny* (*halfpence*) and *Ralph,* in which the old *a* was lengthened, so that the sound is now [ei : heipəni, reif], though the proper name is now often pronounced [rælf] from the spelling.

In those cases in which [l] was lost in later periods after *a,* we got [ɔ·] before [k] : *talk* [tɔ·k] ; but [a·] before a labial : *half, halve, psalm* ; thus also in *shan't=shall not.*

With *o* the result is [ou] : *folk, Holmes, Holborn* ; cp. also *won't* from the old form *wol* for *will.*

[l] is also dropped in *would, should* (*could*). It is well known that Scotch leaves out *l* in a great many other cases : *fu', a', ca'* for *full, all, call.*

On the weakening and loss of *r,* see **4.1-2.**

5.4. A final [n] was dropped in a very early period of the language. Most of the words that originally ended in *-n* have now no trace of that consonant. If English has, nevertheless, a great number of final [n]s, it is because it has been protected by a following vowel, either in the same word (where the vowel has subsequently become mute), or in the following word. The latter alternation is preserved faithfully in the two forms of the indefinite article : *an arm, an inn, an honour, an aim,* but *a* *name, a cup, a unit, a horse.* But the alternation between *mine* and *my*, *none* and *no*, which originally followed the same rule (cf. the old-fashioned *mine host*, where *h* was mute, and *none other*), has now been turned to a different grammatical use (**8**.3₅). In some words both forms survive though not used exactly in the same way : *maid, maiden, Lent, lenten, drunk, drunken, sunk, sunken* ; in others one form is more or less obsolete : *ope, open* ; thus in many participles : *broke, broken* ; *hid, hidden.*

The shortened form of the preposition *in* was formerly common, especially before the definite article *i' th'* ; *handicap* is from *hand-in-(the)-cap*. The corresponding form of *on* was *a*, the letter *a* representing the indistinct vowel [ə] ; hence we have frequent combinations like *aboard = on board, afoot = on foot, ashore = on shore*, and many others where *on* is no more used : *above, around, away, asleep, alive*, etc. Thus also with the verbal substantive : *set the clock a-going, burst out a-laughing, ride out a-hunting, go a-picknicking*, etc., where *a* is now omitted in polite speech.

5.5₁. Apart from the cases mentioned above, some consonants are liable to be dropped in rapid speech, especially in familiar combinations which are easily recognized and understood even if imperfectly pronounced.

When two identical sounds come together, one articulation is often sufficient. Thus when the adverbial ending *-ly* is to be attached to an adjective in *-le* : instead of *noble + ly* we say *nobly*, similarly *simply*, etc. ; though we write two *l*'s in *usually, actually*, etc., only one is pronounced. The *s* of the genitive is dispensed with in combinations like *for conscience' sake*.

An old reduction of two identical sounds to one is seen in *eighty* and *eighteen*, from *eight + ty* and *teen* ; cf. also *fortnight*, from *fourteen + night*.

5.5₂. In a sentence, too, when one word ends and the next one begins with the same sound, it is often unnecessary to articulate more than once. In *you've got to do it* or *next time* a phonetic illusion is produced, even if we pronounce only one [t], the hearer connecting the *t*-sound with what follows as well as with what precedes. Similarly [d] in *a good deal*, [s] in *yes sir*, [ð] in *with that*, [n] in *I can never forget it*, [m] in *some more tea*, etc. Even if the two sounds are only partially identical, we may in some cases dispense with one of them, e.g. *si(t) down, a grea(t) deal, nex(t) day*; cp. the reduction of *pb* to [b] in *cupboard, raspberry*, and of *kg* to [g] in *blackguard*.

5.5₃. But such reductions do not take place in less familiar combinations or when the comprehension would not be easy without each element being duly pronounced as such ; therefore we have real consonant-doubling in *penknife, unknown, cleanness, home-made, ill-looking, head-dress, book-case* (not two off-glides, but one long [k]-closure with a fresh impulse before the opening of the closure). In *wholly* the two *l*'s are pronounced to avoid misunderstanding with *holy*.

5.5₄. In some cases our alphabetical writing exaggerates a difference which, from the point of view of articulation, is very small indeed and acoustically is often hardly perceptible. Let us consider the two combinations [mt] and [mpt] : in the former the movements of the lips (opening), of the point (closing), and of the soft palate (raising) take place exactly at the same moment, while in the latter the soft palate is raised perhaps only a fraction of a second before the other movements are executed : no wonder, therefore, that there is in many languages a good deal of vacillation between the two groups. We now write *p* in *empty*, but *p* is often mute, and the old forms ME. *emty*, OE. *æmettig* show that *p* is intrusive, as it is in many words from Latin : *contempt, prompt*, etc. In *jumped* the feeling of connexion with *jump* will generally protect the [p] from being dropped.

An analogous case is *m(p)s*, where *p* is intrusive in *sempstress* by the side of *seamstress*, in *Thompson* by the side of *Thomson*, and in *glimpse*; cf. *presumption, Hampshire*, pronounced with or without [p] before [ʃ].

5.5₅. We have similar groups in which the middle stop may or may not be pronounced :

[n(t)ʃ] : *French, lunch*, etc.
[n(d)ʒ] : *strange, hinge*, etc.

[n(d)z] : *Windsor* ; in *stands, pounds,* etc., the connexion with
  stand, pound often protects [d].

[stn] or generally [sn] : *listen, hasten,* etc.; cf. also *mustn't*
  [mʌsnt].

[stl] or generally [sl] : *castle, whistle,* etc.

[stm] or generally [sm] : *Christmas, Westmoreland* ; in *postman,
  postmaster* [t] may be reintroduced from *post*; *nex(t)
  month.*

[f(t)n] : *soften* ; in *often* [t] is frequently introduced from the
  spelling.

[nƿs] or [ns] : *months, sevenths.*

Outside these groups [t] is omitted in familiar combinations
like *mus(t) go, can'(t) come, don'(t) know, half pas(t) five, jus(t)
before dinner* ; cf. also *perfec(t)ly.*

Voiced and Voiceless Consonants

5.6₁. Two main laws regulate voice or voicelessness in English
consonants, the first dependent on the position of the sound in
the end or middle of a word, the second dependent on stress.

According to the first law we have a voiced consonant in medial
and a voiceless consonant in final position ; this, however, concerns only fricatives, and it is important to remember that very
often a vowel which followed the consonant has since disappeared,
while the consonant which originally was voiced on account of
this vowel retains its voiced quality, though now in a final
position.

This explains the frequent alternations in the formation of
plurals, as in

  wife ǁ wives
  path [ƿ] ǁ paths [ðz]
  house [s] ǁ houses [ziz] **(20.2₃)**

and in substantives (adjectives) and the corresponding verbs, *e.g.*

  life ǁ live
  safe ǁ save
  breath ǁ breathe
  house ǁ house
  use ǁ use **(7.9)**

The feeling for the latter alternation has even been strong enough to produce some substantive forms like *belief* and *proof*, which formerly had the same voiced consonants as the verbs *believe* and *prove*.

5.6₂. According to the second law a consonant has been kept as voiceless after a strongly stressed vowel, but has been voiced after a weakly stressed vowel. In this way *off* has retained its [f], while the weaker form *of* is pronounced with [v]. A similar alternation in the case of *with* has now been levelled, the weak form [wið] being now nearly universal, though *therewith*, with strongly stressed *with*, has often [þ]. In the same way *s* is voiced in the habitually weak words *as*, *is*, *was*, *has*, and after weakly stressed syllables in *design*, *dessert*, *observe*, *possess*, *resemble*, and many similar words. In *resign* and *resolve* we have [z], but if new verbs are formed with a strongly stressed *re* (**4.6₂**) : *resign*, *resolve* =" sign or solve again," the sound is naturally [s].

5.6₃. This law explains the sound [z] in the frequent flexional endings found, *e.g.* in *princes* (also with different spelling *prince's*, *princes'*), *kisses*, *catches*, *bridges*. When the word ends in a non-hissing sound the vowel of the ending -*es* has disappeared, but we have the voiced *s*, *i.e.* [z], that belonged to the weak syllable, in *kings* (also with different spelling, *king's*, *kings'*, formerly *kinges*), *ladies* (*lady's*, *ladies'*), *ends*, *pills*, *comes*, etc. After a voiceless consonant, however, the *s* is naturally voiceless, *e.g.* in *dukes* (*duke's*, *dukes'*), *stops*, *beasts*.

The difference between *pence*, *hence* and *else* with [s] on the one hand, and *pens*, *hens* and *ells* on the other hand with [z], is due to the fact that the former words had become monosyllables at a time when *e* was not yet dropped in the ordinary plurals.

5.6₄. The combination [ks] has become voiced, *i.e.* [gz], after a weak syllable ; hence the alternation between voiceless and voiced consonants in words like *exhibition* ‖ *exhibit*, *exercise* ‖ *exert*. In *luxury* ‖ *luxurious* we have now [kʃ, gz] (**5.8₃**).

According to the same law *ch* in a weak syllable has become voiced [dʒ] in place-names like *Greenwich*, *Harwich*, and others,

which have retained the old spelling. *Knowledge, partridge,* and
a few other substantives had formerly *-ch.*

5.6₅. In some cases voice or voicelessness is determined by a
following stop : *gooseberry, husband* have [z] on account of the
voiced [b], and inversely, *newspaper, used to* have [s], and sometimes *have to* has [f] on account of the following voiceless [p, t].

H

5.7. *H* tends to disappear in weak forms of pronouns and
auxiliary verbs, not only in cases like *it* for *hit,* where the *h*-form
has totally disappeared, *'em* for old *hem* (not developed from
them), *I've* for *I have, you'd* for *you had,* etc., which are frequently
written, but also in the colloquial pronunciation of combinations
like *if (h)e took (h)is hat; you must (h)ave seen (h)im; we see
(h)er every day.*   Note the two forms with stressed and unstressed
pronouns : *it's good for him* [fə 'him, fɔr im], *we took it to her*
[tə 'həˑ, tu ə].

H is further lost in many compounds which are no longer felt
as such : *shepherd, Clapham, Durham, forehead, perhaps* (**4.1₃**).
H tends also to disappear between a stressed and an unstressed
vowel : *anni(h)ilate, ve(h)ement;* there is some vacillation between *an historical novel* and *a historical novel,* but before
stressed vowels [h] is not left out : *a history.*

The loss of [h] in educated speech in the cases mentioned here
has nothing to do with the general " dropping of one's haitches,"
which is found in all English rural dialects except the very
northernmost (Northumberland, Scotland) and in all the big
towns, and which is commonly looked upon as the surest indication of want of breeding.

Assibilation

5.8₁. This is the name of the development of new [ʃ, ʒ, tʃ, dʒ]
from combinations with [j].   It is chiefly, though not exclusively,
found between a stressed and an unstressed syllable.   It should
be noted that in such endings as *-ion* and *-ious, i* was at first a
vowel that formed a syllable in itself, and was thus often measured

in the practice of poets like Shakespeare, most frequently at the end of the line, where it is natural to slow down the movement; but even in his time the non-syllabic pronunciation was more common. This means the sound [-jǝn, -jǝs] in words like *opinion, odious.* Now, when such [j]s came after [s, z, t, d], it frequently led to assibilation. In many of these words we have an etymological spelling with *t* for [s], cp. French.

5.8₂. Examples of [sj] > [ʃ] :

mission, pension, nation, portion ; ocean, musician, Venetian.
vicious, ambitious, anxious.
special, social, partial.
ancient, patient ; patience, conscience.
Prussia, inertia ; species.
luxury.

In some words [sj] is found by the side of [ʃ] : *issue, tissue, sexual;* in learned words [sj] is preferred : *insulate, Lucius.*

Before a half-stressed vowel [ʃ] is found though *i* has not been absorbed : *associate, propitiate.*

Initially [ʃ] is recognized in *sugar* and *sure* only; in words like *suit, supreme,* as also after a weak first syllable, as in *assume,* we have [sj] (or [s], **5.1₂**).

5.8₃. Examples of [zj] > [ʒ] :

vision, fusion, occasion.
glazier, hosier ; but *easier* [iˑziǝ, iˑzjǝ] on account of *easy.*
measure, composure, azure.
usual, casual.

Before a stressed syllable *luxurious* [lʌgˈʒuǝriǝs] is the only example, but [-zju] is often heard.

5.8₄. Examples of [tj] > [tʃ] :

question, digestion.
Christian, righteous, also with [tj], *courteous* generally with [tj].
creature, future, nature ; in literary words often [-tjuǝ] :
    literature, legislature.
century ; fortune.
actual, punctual, virtue, virtual, virtuous often with [tj].

5.8₅. Examples of [dj] > [dʒ] :

soldier; immediately.
grandeur, verdure.
gradual, individual; educate, -tion.

In all these [dj] is frequent, and it is more frequent than [dʒ] in *cordial, tedious, India*, etc. ; in rarer words like *intermediate, tedium, assiduous* [dj] is the rule.

5.8₆. Assibilation may occur colloquially in rapid pronunciation of two subsequent words : *we shall miss you* [miʃ(j)uˑ], *God bless you; as usual, as yet* [əʒ(j)et] ; *don't you know* [dount-ʃəˈnou] ; *you bet your life; would you mind* [wudʒuˈmaind] ; *do you believe* may even become [dʒubiˈliˑv].

Stump-Words

5.9₁. While some of the sound-changes considered above have gradually led to shorter and shorter forms, many monosyllables have arisen through violent clippings. Such " stump-words " are frequent in pet-names, *e.g.* the old *Bess* for *Elizabeth, Meg* for *Margaret, Ed* for *Edward*, and more recent ones like *Di* for *Diana, Vic* for *Victoria, Mac* for *Macdonald*, etc. Outside proper names we find the same procedure, as in *mob* for *mobile, fad* for *fadaise, brig* for *brigantine*, which are no longer felt as abbreviations ; further, in such more recent stump-words as *pub* for *public-house, sov* for *sovereign, gov* for *governor, zep* for *zeppelin*, and the numerous shortenings in schoolboys', journalists' and printers' slang, which have partly at least come into existence through written abbreviations : *lab* for *laboratory, math* for *mathematics, gym* for *gymnasium* or *gymnastics, prep* for *preparation, ad* for *advertisement, par* for *paragraph*, etc.— all of them convenient short forms for what are felt to be too long and clumsy words.

It is rarer to find stump-words in which the ending has maintained itself : *bus* for *omnibus, phone* for *telephone*.

5.9₂. In this connexion we may mention also abbreviations consisting in reading the alphabetical names of the initials of words, *A.M.* for *ante meridiem, M.A.* for *magister artium, M.P.,* etc. In English as well as in other languages this method has in recent times been employed much more frequently than formerly, chiefly during and after the world war, which made combinations like *O.T.C.* for *Officers' Training Corps, G.H.Q.* for *General Head Quarters,* and others known in wide circles. In some cases the letters are read together without their alphabetical names, e.g. *Dora* for *Defence of the Realm Act, Waàc* for *Women's Army Auxiliary Corps, Wrens* for *Women's Royal Naval Service.*

SPELLING

Causes of unphonetic spelling.—French influence: *ch, g, c, ou, u, o.*
—Doubling of letters.—Differentiation of *i, j, u, v.*—Learned
spellings.

6.1₁. The traditional way of writing English is far from being
so consistent that it is possible, if we know the sounds of a word,
to know how it is to be spelled, or inversely, from the spelling
to draw any conclusions as to its pronunciation. The following
words in their traditional garb and in phonetic transcription
may serve as illustration :

though [ðou]—rhyming with *low*		
through [þruˑ]	,,	*true*
plough [plau]	,,	*now*
cough [kɔf]	,,	*off*
enough [i'nʌf]	,,	*cuff*

However chaotic this may seem, it is possible to a great extent
to explain the rise of all these discrepancies between sound and
spelling, and thus to give, if not rational, at any rate historical
reasons for them. A full account of all these anomalies would,
however, require a whole volume ; here we must, therefore, con-
tent ourselves with a succinct exposition of the chief facts that
have determined the present English spelling.

The alphabet used in England as well as in most European
countries is the Roman alphabet. Though this is better than
many Oriental alphabets, it is far from being perfect as a means
of rendering sounds, as it is deficient in signs for many simple
sounds (*e.g.* the initial consonants of *this* and *thick*, the final
one of *sing*) ; nor does it possess more than five vowel-letters,
where many languages distinguish a far greater number of vowels.

6.1₂. At first people could follow no other guide in their
spelling than their own ears : writing began as purely
phonetical. But soon they began to imitate the spellings of

others, whose manuscripts they copied, their teachers and their elders generally. As the spoken forms of words tend continually to change, this would mean that older, extinct forms of speech would continue to be written long after they had ceased to be heard. Such traditional spelling, which is found in all languages with a literary history, has become particularly powerful since the invention of the art of printing; in many respects, therefore, modern English orthography represents the pronunciation prevalent about that time or even earlier.

An equally important factor was the influence of French— later also of Latin—spelling. Norman scribes introduced several peculiarities of French spelling, not only when writing words taken over from that language, but also when writing native English words. Our present-day spelling cannot, therefore, be fully understood without some knowledge of the history of French.

6.2. The letters *ch* were used in Old French to denote the sound-combination [tʃ] as in *chaste, chief, merchant*; in English this spelling was used not only in originally French words, but also in native words like *child, much*. In French the stop [t] was later dropped, the sound [ʃ] only remaining; hence *ch* in some late loan-words comes to stand for [ʃ] : *machine, chaise* (which is the Modern French form of the same word that in the old form was taken over as *chair*), *chauffeur*.

In words from the classical languages *ch* denotes the sound [k] : *echo, chaos, scheme*. *Schedule* is pronounced with [sk] in America, with [ʃ] in England.

6.3₁. The sound-history of French also serves to explain some striking peculiarities concerning the use of the letter *g* in English spelling. Written French *gu* originally served to denote the combination of [g] with a following [u] or [w]; but this combination was later simplified in various ways. In the northernmost French dialects [g] was dropped, and English from those dialects adopted such words as *ward, reward, warden* and *war*. But in other parts of French it was inversely the [u]-sound that disappeared, and a great many words were adopted into English with this simple sound of [g], such as *gallop, garrison*; in some cases English kept the spelling *gu* though French now writes without the *u* : *guard, guarantee*. In both languages the spelling *gu* came to be extensively used as an orthographic device to denote the sound [g] before *e* and *i*, because in that position g was pronounced [dʒ], thus in *guide, guise* ; and in English this spelling was even transferred to a certain number of native words like *guess, guest, guild* (sb.), *guilt, tongue*, though it never obtained in some frequently used words like *get, give, begin, gild* (vb.).

In Old French the letter g stood for the sound-combination [dʒ], as Latin g [g] had developed in that way before [e] and [i] ; hence spellings like *gentle, giant, age, manage*, etc. Sometimes after a short vowel *dg* was written : *judge, lodge* ; thus also in native words like *edge, bridge* (**6.**7).

As with the corresponding voiceless combination [tʃ], see **6.**2, the stop in [dʒ] was later dropped in French ; hence g is in later loan-words pronounced [ʒ] : *rouge, mirage, prestige*.

6.3₂. Another Old French way of writing [dʒ] was *i*, later *j* ; hence we have English spellings like *joy, join, journey*. In *bijou* *j* has the later French value [ʒ].

6.4. In OE. the letter *c* was exclusively used for the sound [k], even before *e, i* and *y*, exactly as in Latin. But in French this Latin sound had become first [ts] and later [s] before *e* and *i* ; and this value of the letter *c* is consequently found in English, not only in French and Latin words, like *cease, centre, city, peace, pace*—even sometimes where French has *s* : *ace*, Fr. *as* ; *juice*, Fr. *jus*—but also in some native English words, e.g. *since, hence*. *Sc* is pronounced in the same way, e.g. *scene, science* ; it is written without any etymological reason in *scent* (from French *sentir*).

C is used for the sound [k] in *can, corn, cup, clean, creep* and many similar words, while *k* is written in *kiss, keep, think*, etc., and *q* before *u* : *queen*, etc. Instead of *ks*, *x* is written : *six*, etc., even in *coxcomb* and *coxswain* from *cock*.

6.5₁. French influence is responsible for the use of the digraph *ou* for ME. long [uˑ] as in *couch, spouse* (later Fr. *épouse*) ; sometimes also for short [u] : *couple, touch*. This was transferred to native words like *house, loud, out, our*, etc. When the long sound was later diphthongized (**3.**5), the spelling *ou* came to be very appropriate. As this diphthongizing did not take place in Scotch, *ou* is there still found for the sound [u·], as in *Dougall, dour, souter*, " shoemaker."

6.5₂. The simple vowel *u* was used for the short vowel as in *up, us, nut, full* (**3.**7), etc., and for the diphthong [iu] or [ju·], frequent in French words like *duke, use, due, virtue*, but also found in native words, e.g. *Tuesday, hue, Stuart* (the same word as *steward*).

But at a time when angular writing was fashionable, it became usual to avoid the letter *u* in close proximity with the letters *n, m*, and another *u* (*v, w*), where it was liable to cause ambiguity (five strokes might be interpreted *imi, inu, mu, um, uni, uui*, especially at a time when no dot was written over *i*) ; hence the use of *o* which has been retained in a great many words : *monk, money, honey, come, won, wonder, cover* (written *couer* before *v* and *u* were distinguished, **6.**8), *love*, etc.

A merely orthographic distinction is made between *son* and *sun, some* and *sum*.

6.6₁. In ME. vowels were frequently doubled to show length, and many of these spellings have been preserved, e.g. *see, deer, too, brood*, though the sounds have been changed so that they no more correspond to the short vowels of *set, hot*.

6.6₂. But neither *a* nor *u* were doubled in that way ; and instead of writing *ii* it became usual to write *y*. This letter, which in Old English served to denote the rounded vowel corresponding to [i] (=Fr. *u* in *bu*, German *ü* in *über*), has become a mere variant of *i* used preferably at the end of words, while *i* is used in the beginning and interior of words ; hence such alternations as *cry, cries, cried ; happy, happier, happiest, happiness ; body, bodiless, bodily*, etc. But *y* is kept before such endings as are felt more or less as independent elements, e.g. *citywards, ladyship, twentyfold, juryman*. After another vowel *y* is generally kept, e.g. *plays, played, boys* ; cf., however, *laid, paid, said* (but *lays, pays, says* : too much consistency must not be expected).

In some cases homophones are kept apart in the spelling : *die* (with *dies*, but *dying*, because *ii* is avoided)—*dye*, *flys*, ' light carriages,' but otherwise *flies* (sb. and vb.).

Further, *y* is written in many originally Greek words: *system*, *nymph*, etc.

Before a vowel, *y* is used as non-syllabic [i], *i.e.* [j], e.g. *yard*, *yellow*, *yield*, *yole*, *yule*, *beyond*.

6.7. Doubling of consonants has come to be extensively used to denote shortness of the preceding vowel, especially before a weak syllable, *e.g.* in *hotter*, *hottest* from *hot*, *sobbing* from *sob*. Instead of doubling *k*, *ch* and *g* [= dʒ] the combinations *ck*, *tch* and *dg(e)* are written, e.g. *trafficking* from *traffic*, *etch*, *edge*.

On account of the phonetic development, however, a double consonant is now written after some long vowels, *e.g.* in *roll*, *all*, *staff*, *glass*, which had formerly short vowels.

6.8. Though since the introduction of printing a great many minor changes have taken place without any great consistency, such as the leaving out of numerous mute *e*'s, only one important orthographic change must be recorded, namely, the regulating of *i* and *j*, *u* and *v*, so that now *i* and *u* are used for the vowels, *j* and *v* for the consonant sounds, while, for instance, the old editions of Shakespeare print *ioy*, *vs*, *vpon*, *fiue*, *fauour* = *joy*, *us*, *upon*, *five*, *favour*. The old use of *u* for the consonant explains the name of *w* : *double u*.

6.9. Scholars have introduced learned spellings in many words, e.g. *debt*, *doubt*, on account of Latin *debita*, *dubito*, formerly written as in French *dette*, *doute*; *victuals*, formerly *vittles*. In some cases the pronunciation has been modified according to the spelling; thus [p] has been introduced in *bankrupt*, earlier *bankeroute*, and [k] in *perfect*, earlier *perfit*, *parfit*. In recent years, with the enormous spread of popular education, combined with ignorance of the history of the language, such spelling-pronunciations have become increasingly numerous.

CHAPTER VII

WORD-CLASSES

Substantives. — Adjectives. — Verbs. — Pronouns. — Numerals. — Particles.—Provisional survey of inflexions.—Derivation of word-classes.

7.1. In dealing with linguistic subjects it is necessary to have names for the various classes into which words fall naturally, and which are generally, but not very felicitously, called " parts of speech." It is practically impossible to give exact and exhaustive definitions of these classes ; nevertheless the classification itself rarely offers occasion for doubt and will be sufficiently clear to students if a fair number of examples are given, as in the following lists.

Substantives

God, devil, man, Gladstone, John, Mary, American, friend, thief, army, animal, cat, plant, rose, bud, etc. (living beings and plants) ;

star, stone, mountain, house, room, road, book, picture, nose, etc. (things) ;

iron, air, water, tea, food, linen, etc. (substances) ;

lightning, gale, war, fight, walk, accident, death, echo, play, call, change, sleep, life, laughter, etc. (happenings, acts, states) ;

year, month, hour, inch, mile, pound, handful, bushel, shilling, etc. (measures, indications of quantity) ;

beauty, health, kindness, bitterness, poverty, etc. (qualities).

Some words may belong to two of these classes; thus *rain* sometimes means a substance, sometimes a happening. Nor are these sub-classes meant to be exhaustive : it would be difficult to tell in which of them to place such undoubted substantives as *time, space, form* and *cause*.

Many grammarians use the term *noun* for this class ; but *substantive* seems preferable.

7.2. Adjectives

beautiful, healthy, kind, long, poor, admirable, fast, dry, black,
    clean, busy, American, etc. (possessing such and such a
    quality : " qualifiers ") ;
numerous, many, few, much, etc. (" quantifiers ").

Little is sometimes a qualifier (*a little girl*), sometimes a
quantifier (*a little bread*).

It is worth noting that the " things " denoted by substantives
are characterized by several qualities which cannot all be
expressly indicated in the name itself, but that a qualifying
adjective serves to single out one quality, which may be ascribed
to several things.

7.3. Verbs

[I] go, take, fight, surprise, eat, breathe, speak, walk, clean,
    play, call.   ([I am in] activity.)
[I] sleep, remain, wait, live, suffer.
                ([I am in a] state.)
[I] become, grow, lose, die, dry.
                ([I am in a] process.)

Here again these sub-classes are not always easily distinguish-
able : is *love* an activity or a state ?

7.4₁. Pronouns

I, you, he, she, it (**Personal pronouns**).

The word " personal " is here taken in its specifically grammatical sense of " one of the three persons " (Chap. XV) : otherwise it would not be possible to include *it* among the personal
pronouns.

My, your, his, her, its (**Possessive pronouns**).

7.4₂. this, that, the, same, such (**Demonstrative pronouns**).
The is generally called " the definite article."

7.4₃. who, what, which (**Interrogative pronouns**, used in questions) ;

who, what, which (**Relative pronouns**).   The forms are the same as those of the interrogative pronouns; but their mutual spheres of application are different, as we shall see farther on.

7.4₄. one, an (a), some, any, either, all, both, every, each, none (no), neither (**Indefinite pronouns**).

An (*a*) is generally called " the indefinite article," and as such is classed together with *the* as an article.

7.4₅. Together with pronouns must be mentioned **pronominal adverbs**, which correspond to the various sub-classes :

Demonstrative : here, there; now, then; thus, so; therefore.
Interrogative and relative : where; when; how; why.
Indefinite : somewhere, anywhere, everywhere, nowhere; ever, never, always; somehow, anyhow.

7.4₆. The names here given to the sub-classes of pronouns are the traditional ones; a different classification will be found in Chap. XVI. The importance of these words in speech and in grammar is enormous, but nowhere is it perhaps so difficult as here to give a practicable definition or to say why all these words are classed together as " pronouns." They are less descriptive than most other words; they hint more than they denote exactly, and with regard to many of them it is characteristic that their full import in each sentence in which they occur can only be grasped from the whole situation or context : this is particularly true of words like *I* and *this*. The form of pronouns presents a great many irregularities; and in some of the following chapters (VIII, XIV, XV, XIX) we shall find distinctions with regard to pronouns to which there is nothing corresponding in other classes.

7.4₇. One, two, three, etc. (**Cardinals**).
First, second, third, etc. (**Ordinals**).

These two together are **Numerals**; they are by some grammarians taken as a sub-class under pronouns.

7.5₁. Particles

well, fast, long, gently, recently, again, yesterday, soon, rather, quite, perhaps, together, not, etc. (**Adverbs**, generally

serving to modify or specify some word or the sentence as
a whole) ;

at, in, through, for, of, etc. (**Prepositions**, indicating relations of
various kinds) ;

and, or, nor (**Co-ordinating conjunctions**) ;

that, if, unless, because, although, etc. (**Subordinating conjunctions**, serving to connect clauses .with the main sentence).

7.5₂. Some particles can be used in one capacity only, others
may be used now as adverbs, now as prepositions, and now as
conjunctions, others again in two of these capacities. Examples :

after :   Jill came tumbling after (adv.)
    tumbling after Jack (prep.)
    after we had left (conj.)

since :   they have lived happily ever since (adv.)
    ever since their marriage (prep.)
    since they were married (conj.)

in :   Is John in ? (adv.)
    in the house (prep.)

up :   he got up early (adv.)
    climb up the wall (prep.)

but :   no one but a fool would do that (prep.)
    not John, but his brother (co-ordinating conj.)
    there is no vice so simple but assumes Some marke of
        vertue on his outward parts (Sh., subordinating
        conj.)

The names of the parts of speech are taken from Latin, but students
of Latin should be warned against the etymological fallacy of taking these
names at their face value : a pronoun (Latin : *pronomen*) is not what stands
instead of a name or a noun (how would this apply to *who* or *nobody* ?) ;
an adverb (Latin : *adverbium*) need not belong to a verb (cf. *nearly ready*,
nearly everybody) ; nor need a preposition (Latin : *praepositio*) stand before
the word it governs (go the fools *among* (Sh.) ; What are you laughing *at* ?).
You might just as well believe that all blackguards are black or that turkeys
come from Turkey ; many names have either been chosen unfortunately
at first or have changed their meanings in course of time.

Provisional Survey of Inflexions

7.6. As the difference between the various word-classes manifests itself characteristically in their inflexions (*i.e.* formal modifications), it will be convenient here to give a preliminary list of the chief inflexions. This will have to be supplemented in following chapters, in which irregularities, etc., will be explained.

Substantives

wife : Genitive — wife's
Plural — wives
Genitive Plural — wives'

Adjectives and some Adverbs

long : Comparative — longer
Superlative — longest

Pronouns

Singular	Nominative :	I	he	she	who
	Objective :	me	him	her	whom
Plural	Nominative :	we	they		(who)
	Objective :	us	them		(whom)
	Singular :	this	that		
	Plural :	these	those		

Verbs

Base : drink, used as

(1) infinitive : I may drink, I want to drink.
(2) imperative : drink this!
(3) present indicative : I drink.
(4) present subjunctive : if he drink.

Third person indicative : drinks.
Preterit : drank.
Second participle : drunk.
Form in *-ing*, drinking, used as (1) first participle.
(2) gerund.

Derivation of Word-Classes

7.7₁. The reader will have noticed that some words were given as examples both of substantives and adjectives, others as substantives and verbs, and others again as adjectives and adverbs. This shows that in order to find out what class a word belongs to it is not enough to consider its form in itself; what is decisive is the way in which the word in connected speech " behaves " towards other words, and in which other words behave towards it. If we find that one and the same form is used now as a substantive, now as an adjective or verb, this does not mean that the distinction between word-classes is obliterated in English, for in each particular combination the form concerned belongs decidedly to one class only; but the form should not be looked at in isolation. This will be clear from the following examples and considerations:

7.7₂. Take the sentence

(1) The old beggar takes his hat and hobbles along.

Here *beggar* and *hat* are substantives, *old* is an adjective, *the* and *his* are pronouns, *and* and *along* are particles. Now, if we want to speak of more than one, the sentence becomes:

(2) The old beggars take their hats and hobble along.

Here *beggar* and *hat* are changed into *beggars* and *hats*: we express this by saying that these substantives form their plurals in -*s* (as in fact most substantives do). Inversely, *takes* and *hobbles* lose their -*s* in the plural; *his* becomes *their*, but the rest of the sentence is unchanged.

Next, if instead of speaking of the present time we want to speak of the past, the two sentences become

(3) The old beggar took his hat and hobbled along.
(4) The old beggars took their hats and hobbled along.

It will be seen that the change of time affects the verbs only (*takes* and *take* become *took*, *hobbles* and *hobble* become *hobbled*), but not the other parts of speech; further, that *took* and *hobbled* are alike in the singular and plural.

If now we apply these and similar tests to some of the words that were given above under two headings, we find that *fight* is a verb in *they fight*, because it becomes *he fights* and *he* (*they*) *fought*; but it is a substantive in *their fight* and *this fight*, because in the plural it becomes *their fights*, *these fights* and is not affected in form by the time in which the fights take place : *the present fight, a past fight.*

Walk, in the same way, is a substantive in *he takes a walk | they took a walk | two walks,* but a verb in *they walk, he walks, he walked* ; compare e.g. *he took two walks every day* and *he walked twice every day.*

Compare also :

His former love for her (substantive).
He loved her once (verb).

The two words *love* are related to each other as *admiration* and *admire.*

If we find the question

Will a change of air cure love ?

we have no hesitation in saying that *will* and *cure* are verbs, and *change, air,* and *love* substantives, though in other combinations *will* and *cure* may be substantives, and *change, air,* and *love* verbs.

7.7₃. Correspondingly, words like *clean* and *dry* are adjectives in *clean shirt, clean shirts, a dry coat, dry coats,* but verbs in *they clean their shoes* (cp. *he cleans his shoes, they cleaned their shoes*), *clothes dry in the sun* (cp. *the coat dries, dried*). Many other verbs are similarly formed direct from adjectives, e.g. *thin, slow (down), clear* ; thus also *busy* in *he busies himself, they busy themselves.*

7.7₄. With regard to those forms that may be either substantives or adjectives, the chief point to note is the plural, which is unchanged in adjectives ; compare, for instance, *two American* (adj.) *guests* and *two Americans* (sb.) *arrive* : this is parallel with *two Spanish guests* and *two Spaniards arrive.* *She eats a sweet* : here *sweet* is a substantive, because the plural is *sweets,* but in *a sweet girl* it is an adjective, because we say *sweet girls.*

Other substantives formed from adjectives are (here given in the plural) :

blacks, savages, privates (=private soldiers), *males* and *females, Liberals, evils, vegetables, halves.*

7.7₅. A few pronouns can be turned into substantives :

Some five hundred *nobodies* were assembled.
He fancies himself a *somebody*.
You must take a little *something* before you go to bed.
Lady, you are the cruell'st *shee* alive (Sh.).

7.7₆. Any word or part of a word or combination of words may be turned into a substantive if it is quoted as such (quotation substantives) :

Your *late* was misheard as *light*.
There should be two *l*'s in his name.
All the " *Thou shalt not's* " of the Bible.

7.7₇. *Long* and *fast* are adjectives in *a long day* and *a fast train*, but adverbs in *he walked long and fast*. Among other adverbs formed in the same way direct from adjectives may be mentioned *clean* (a clean shaven face), *half, early*.

7.8₁. This faculty of using one and the same form with different values, while the context shows in most cases unmistakably what part of speech is meant, is one of the most characteristic traits of English, and is found to a similar extent in no other European language. We may term such words " grammatical homophones " (Greek, *homo-*, " same," *phōnē*, " sound ").

Thus we can form innumerable verbs from substantives without change. The names of the different parts of the body are, of course, substantives, but from nearly each one of them a verb has been formed : *eye, nose* (you shall nose him as you go up the staires (Sh.)), *beard, shoulder, elbow* (one's way), *hand, finger, skin, foot* (it), etc. Other verbs formed in the same way are *ape, cook, husband, silence, time*.

Similarly a great many substantives are formed without any change from verbs, e.g. *build, cut, dress, embrace, gaze, glance, go, kill, visit*.

7.8₂. This has facilitated the development of a great many familiar phrases of the following type :

have a look (peep) at ; have a chat, wash, shave, swim, try ; have a drink, a smoke.

have a care, take care.
take a drive, ride, walk, rest.
give a glance, look, kick, push, shock, sigh, hint.
he made his bow to the hostess; make a plunge.

Such expressions instead of the simple verbs are in accordance with the general tendency of Modern English to place an insignificant (auxiliary) verb, to which the marks of person and tense are attached, before the really important idea: *do you write, does he write, he did not write, he has written, he will write,* etc. (**10.**4, **23.**3, **28.**6, etc.).

7.8₃. In this way we may even have three words of the same form derived from one another. Thus *smoke* is first a substantive (the smoke from the chimney), then a verb (the chimney smokes, he smokes a pipe), and finally a new substantive formed from the verb in the last sense (he likes a smoke after dinner). *Gossip* was at first a substantive meaning " godfather," this came to mean " an idle talker," and from this a verb was formed meaning " to talk idly " ; from this again we have a substantive, " idle talk." *Brush* (1) instrument, (2) verb, (3) a new substantive: *give your hat a brush*. *Wire* (1) metallic thread, (2) telegraph, (3) telegram.

7.8₄. In this connexion we may mention a frequent type of compounds in which (the base of) a verb enters as the first element, followed by an object or a particle. The resulting word may be a substantive, e.g. *pick-pocket, breakwater, stopgap, scare-crow* (*breakfast* with changed pronunciation, **4.**8) ; *lock-out, breakdown, drawback, shakedown, stay-at-home,* etc. Or it may be an adjective (in some cases rather a substantive used as an adjunct, **8.**5): *break-neck* (leaps of a break-neck character), *tell-tale* (a very tell-tale face), *lack-lustre, wash-hand* (a wash-hand stand), *do-nothing* (delicious do-nothing days), a *lean-to* pig-sty, a *tumble-down* shed, *lace-up* boots, a *sit-down* supper, a *go-ahead* nation, a *run-away* match, *go-to-meeting* clothes, etc.

These formations have become popular because they preserve the usual order (verb before object or particle), while with this order it would have been inconvenient or even impossible to use endings : one could not very well say *a picker-pocket* or *pick-pocketer, telling-tale* or *tell-taling*, etc.

7.9₁. It is not, however, possible in all cases to use the simple procedure described in the preceding sections when we want to form a word belonging to one word-class from one of another. Very often we have **formations with endings (suffixes)**, some of which go back to very early times, while others are taken over from Latin or French. Some examples of the most frequent modes of such formations may here be given.

Substantives from verbs :

bind : binding, draw : drawing.
act : action, describe : description, admit : admission.
treat : treatment, punish : punishment.
refuse : refusal, deny : denial, bury : burial.

Sometimes we have two substantives with slightly different senses :

build, building ; laugh, laughter ; move, movement (and motion) ; resolve, resolution ; exhibit, exhibition.

Substantives denoting agent :

bake : baker
act : actor
study : student

Verbs from substantives :

strength : strengthen
blood : bleed, food : feed
symbol : symbolize, organ : organize

Note specially the cases in which the substantive has voiceless and the verb voiced consonant (**5.**6), or in which the stress is different (**3.**4₄) :

life : live, belief : believe, proof : prove
breath : breathe, cloth : clothe
use : use, advice : advise, grass : graze
record : record

7.9₂. Substantives from adjectives:

kind : kindness, idle : idleness
false : falsehood, likely : likelihood
safe : safety, certain : certainty, real : reality, possible : possibility
true : truth, strong : strength
just : justice, ignorant : ignorance, innocent : innocence
constant : constancy, secret : secrecy
jealous : jealousy, fool : folly

Adjectives from substantives:

ice : icy, sleep : sleepy
child : childish, devil : devilish
friend : friendly, day : daily
care : careful, careless; art : artful, artless
trouble : troublesome, quarrel : quarrelsome
danger : dangerous, ruin : ruinous
nature : natural, music : musical

Adjectives from verbs:

interest : interesting
please : pleasant
act : active, talk : talkative
eat : eatable, admire : admirable

7.9₃. Verbs from adjectives:

short : shorten, soft : soften
real : realize, civil : civilize
full : fill, whole (originally *hal*) : heal

7.9₄. Adverbs from adjectives:

soft : softly, dry : drily

This ending serves to form adverbs from nearly all adjectives, except in the case of some short familiar words, where the same form is used both as adjective and as adverb. In many cases we have forms with and without -*ly* side by side. Sometimes a distinction is made more or less clearly between the two forms, *e.g.*

You must go direct to London | you must go to London directly ; he left directly after breakfast.

He works hard | he was hardly used; the form *hardly* is now
chiefly used in the sense " scarcely " : he hardly works.

High up in the air | a highly cultivated man.

He spoke loud enough to be heard all over the hall | he complained
loudly of their behaviour.

Pretty early | prettily dressed.

He said that right at the beginning | he said that rightly at the
beginning.

Just imagine what that will mean | he justly remarked. . . .

CHAPTER VIII

THE THREE RANKS

8.1₁. While the assignation of a word to one of the classes dealt with in the preceding chapter concerns the word in itself—a substantive remains always a substantive in whatever surroundings it may be found, and can therefore be marked as such in a dictionary—we now come to another classification which is somewhat similar in nature, but differs from the former because it concerns the mutual relations of words in combinations only, and is applicable not only to words, but also to groups of words as such.

Take the three words *terribly cold weather*. They are evidently not on the same footing, *weather* being, grammatically, most important, to which the two others are subordinate, and of these again *cold* is more important than *terribly*. *Weather* is determined or defined by *cold*, and *cold* in its turn similarly determined or defined by *terribly*. We have thus three ranks : " weather " is **Primary,** " cold " **Secondary,** and " terribly " **Tertiary** in this combination.

8.1₂. In this example we found a substantive as primary, an adjective as secondary, and a particle (an adverb) as tertiary ; and there is so far a certain correspondence between the three ranks and the three word-classes mentioned, as substantives, adjectives and adverbs habitually stand in this relation to one another. But, as we shall soon see, the correspondence is far from complete, and the two things, word-classes and ranks, really move in two different spheres. In some combinations a substantive may be secondary or tertiary, an adjective may be a primary, etc.

8.1₃. If we compare the two expressions *this furiously barking dog* and *this dog barks furiously*, it is easy to see that while *dog*

is primary, *this* secondary, and *furiously* tertiary in both, the
verb *bark* is found in two different forms, *barking* and *barks*;
but in both forms it must be said to be subordinated to *dog*
and superior in rank to *furiously*; thus both *barking* and *barks*
are here secondaries. There is, however, an evident difference
between the two word-groups, of which the latter can stand
alone as a communication in itself, while the former makes us
expect a continuation (*e.g.* this furiously barking dog belongs
to the butcher); cf. Chap. IX.

It is true that a tertiary may in some cases be further determined by a
word that is subordinated to it, and this again by a fifth word, as in *a not
very cleverly worded remark*; but this has no grammatical importance, and
we therefore speak here of three degrees only, reckoning *not* and *very* in
this example as tertiaries in the same way as *cleverly*.

8.2. As adjectives are generally secondaries, and adverbs
tertiaries, we see shiftings like the following, in which the
adverbs have the ending *-ly*:

absolute novelty	absolutely novel
utter darkness	utterly dark
awful fun	awfully funny
perfect stranger	perfectly strange
adj. + sb.	adv. + adj.
II + I	III + II

and similarly with verbs:

accurate description	describes accurately
frequent visits	visits frequently
severe judge	judges severely
careful reader	reads carefully
adj. + sb.	vb. + adv.
II + I	II + III

But in *an early riser* and *he rises early* there is no formal
difference between the adjective and the adverb.

We shall now go through a considerable number of examples
of words and word-groups employed in the three ranks, but it
will not be necessary to give examples of the most normal cases,
substantives as primaries, adjectives as secondaries, and adverbs

as tertiaries. In some cases the rank is indicated in the form of the word concerned, but that is not always the case.

On the rank of genitives, see 14.9.

PRIMARIES

Adjectives

8.3₁. Only exceptionally can an adjective be used in the singular as a primary if it denotes a living being : the Almighty | the accused ; cf. also the deceased.

But it may be freely used in this way to denote an abstract notion :

> To separate the known from the unknown.
> One must bow to the inevitable.
> He is always talking of the supernatural.

Cf. also such set phrases as :

> Hold one's own.
> Nothing out of the common.
> Sleep in the open.
> Get the better of something.

On the other hand, if the idea is quite concrete the rule is to add the word *thing* :

> This is the very latest thing.
> The only thing we know definitely is that the ring was stolen.

8.3₂. In a plural sense adjectives may be used as primaries to denote a whole class of living beings :

> England is a paradise for the well-to-do, a purgatory for the able, and a hell for the poor (Morley).
> The absent are always at fault.
> Let the dead bury their dead.
> They had to take care of their sick and wounded.

This is particularly frequent with those adjectives denoting nationalities which end in a hissing sound :

> the English, the British, the French, the Japanese, etc.,

generally with the definite article, but also with other pronouns : *we English*.

> The Swiss have their mountains, the French their Paris, the English their home. Happy English !

When individual members of the nation are meant, the plural in *-men* or the addition of *people* is generally used :

> These two Englishmen.
> He hated all the French people he met there.

These nationality-names are thus treated differently from those that may be both adjectives and substantives, *German*, *American*, etc. (**7.7₄**).

A common expedient when an adjective has to be used as a primary is the addition of *one* (**8.4**).

8.3₃. Quantifiers are frequently used as primaries :

> Much in that book was obscure.
> Much (most) of what he says is nonsense.
> Many (few) of the guests had seen him.
> He had enough to live on.

Adverbs

8.3₄. An adverb may in some connexions be a primary as the object of a verb, as in " We shall leave here to-morrow," and more frequently of a preposition : *from here* (which has super-seded *from hence* and the still older *hence* in the same sense : *hence* has been retained in literary English in a figurative sense), *from now, by then, for long*.

Pronouns

8.3₅. The personal pronouns *I*, *we*, *you*, etc., and *who* are used as primaries only ; thus also the compounds with *self*, *myself*, etc.

Possessive pronouns, with the exception of *his* and *its*, have separate forms as primaries, either in *-n* (*mine, thine*) or in *-s* (*ours, yours, hers, theirs*). Examples :

> Here is your hat, but where is mine ?
> Here is my hat, but where is yours ?

Mine is an old family = My family is an old one.
He is an old friend of mine.
You are all mine and my all (*all* first tertiary and then primary).

8.3₆. *None* [nʌn] is the primary form of *no*, as *mine* is that of *my*.

None of his brothers had any children.
None of your cheek, please!
Some have children, and some have none.
Shoes he had none.

Some and *any* are used as primaries, chiefly before *of* or referring to a substantive just mentioned, but also in the plural in speaking of persons:

Some of the man's money, if he had any, was due to us.
Did any of the crew survive?
Some are wise and some are otherwise.

Every is always a secondary.

The ordinary primaries corresponding to these pronouns are formed by the addition of *one* or *body* (in speaking of persons) and *thing* (neuter): *no one, nobody, nothing*, note the pronunciation [nʌþiŋ]; *some one, somebody, something*; *any one, anybody, anything*; *every one, everybody, everything*. *Someone, anyone* and *everyone* are often written together, but that is not possible with *no one*. On the sound of *-body*, see **4.7₂**.

The wise man can learn something from everyone, even from fools. The fool cannot learn anything from anyone, not even from a wise man.

Other pronouns, which are usually secondaries, can be used as primaries, e.g. *each, such, which*; *either, neither, both*; *other* as a primary (*another, the other*) has a plural in *-s*: *others*.

8.3₇. *What* as a primary is never used of a person (it is always neuter), and this is also as a rule true of *that, this* and *all* in the singular:

That'll do.
This above all: to thine own self be true (Sh.).
All is well that ends well.

But in the plural these pronouns may be used of persons :

Those who believe this are fools.
These are my sisters.
All send love to all.

The Prop-Word *One*

8.4₁. *One* is termed a prop-word when it has the important function of serving as primary on which to hang a secondary which, for some reason or other, cannot very well or conveniently stand alone as a primary.

In the following passage from *Hamlet* :

"Denmark's a prison." "Then is the world one." "A goodly one, in which there are many confines, wards, and dungeons; Denmark being one o' th' worst "—

we see first *one* standing by itself to represent the previously mentioned word with the indefinite article *a prison*, then preceded by the article and an adjective, and finally followed by a prepositional group ; by this means the clumsy repetitions " a prison," " a goodly prison " and " a prison of the worst (prisons) " are avoided.

One, of course, is originally a numeral, but when used as a prop-word its meaning is often more or less dissociated from that of the numeral, thus :

(*a*) When *one* is immediately preceded by *a* (which is originally a weakened form of *one*, OE. *an*) :

such a one | as good a one | too good a one;

(*b*) when we have the definite article :

This grey horse is stronger than the black one;

(*c*) when we have first the numeral and then an adjective with the prop-word :

German teachers had rather manage a dozen German boys than one English one (H. Spencer); and especially,

(*d*) when we have the plural *ones* :

Don't let us make imaginary evils, when we have so many real ones to encounter (Goldsmith).

This plural may also be used with a numeral :

Two grey horses and three black ones.

8.4₂. The secondary combined with *one* is very often an adjective, generally placed before *one*, but sometimes after it :

Stupid men are the only ones worth knowing (Jane Austen).

The secondary may also be a pronoun :

"Hand me this letter." "Which one? This one?" "Yes, that's the one."
You must get some other clothes—those ones aren't fit to be seen.
She had been in some prison, but what one she could not remember.

On *no one*, etc., see **8.3₆**, on *one* after a secondary substantive see **8.5₃**.

The secondary combined with *one* may be a (relative) clause :

He is of all men in the world the one I like best to talk to.
A house like the one where his uncle lived so many years.

Or it may be a prepositional group :

Open the drawer on the left—the one with the key in it.

8.4₃. In the examples given so far, the prop-word refers to some previously mentioned person or thing. It may also be used independently of such contextual reference, but then only of persons. Examples :

I stood like one thunderstruck (Defoe).
Madnesse in great ones must not unwatch'd go (Sh.).
Come, little ones.
Never the time and the place and the loved one all together ! (Browning).
She felt like one in a trance.
The Duchess was to be the one to bell the cat.

8.4₄. The development in Modern English of this prop-word makes it possible in some cases to see at once whether we have to do with a singular (*the great one*) or a plural (*the great ones*). If we say " Here are some envelopes, which do you want ? " the question may be made more definite by saying " which one do you want ? " or " which ones do you want ? "

It further renders the use of a genitive easy in cases where it would not otherwise be possible :

> Some ladies . . . this one's daughter had married beneath her rank.
>
> Many a poor one's blessing.
>
> It served as a bedroom for the two boys, also as the elder one's laboratory.

8.4₅. The use of *one* also serves to remove ambiguity in some cases : in the first example below, *European* without *one* would be taken as the substantive instead of the adjective :

> America is an older country than any European one (Wells).
>
> The middle one of the three windows was open.
>
> Go to the right : Go to the right one.
>
> A little : a little one.
>
> The evil : the Evil One.

8.4₆. The prop-word can replace the names of such things only as can be counted, therefore we say, *e.g.* ⟵

> I like red wine better than white.
>
> He had known good luck and bad.

Sometimes the lighter construction without *one* is preferred to the heavier with *one*; thus often with comparatives and superlatives, and when two adjectives stand close together :

> Two sisters : the elder took the younger by the waist.
>
> You haven't heard his latest.
>
> The old world and the new.
>
> It goes in at one ear and out at the other.

SECONDARIES

Substantives

8.5₁. Substantives are used as secondaries in the innumerable loose collocations in which each substantive preserves its stress and is therefore felt as a separate unit (**3.3₂**). Examples (the secondaries are here italicized) : *gold* coin, *stone* wall, *cannon* ball, *week* end, *parish* church, *lady* friend, *cock* pheasant, *London* papers.

These are different from such compounds in which one part is accentually subordinated to the other, and in which the pronunciation is often modified (**3.3₂**, **4.**8), e.g. *teatime, bricklayer,* *buttonhole, bedroom* ; *postman, waistcoat, Christmas, shepherd* from *sheep*.

Note the significance of word-order : *a garden flower* is a kind of flower, *a flower garden* a kind of garden ; cf. also *racehorse* and *horse-race*.

In " the London poor" *London* is a substantive used as a secondary, and *poor* an adjective used as a primary.

8.5₂. Collocations of a secondary and a primary substantive closely resemble combinations of an adjective secondary and a substantive, and this similarity leads to interesting grammatical consequences.

First we have these substantival secondaries co-ordinated with adjectives and even separated from their primaries :

> Her Christian and *family* name.
> He had given to local and *county* charities.
> He got into *money* and other difficulties.
> All national, *State, county,* and municipal offices.
> A *Boston* young lady.
> A *school* Latin dictionary.

8.5₃. Next the prop-word *one* (**8.4**) may be used with substantival secondaries :

> Two *gold* watches and a *silver* one.
> Give me a paper, one of the *Sunday* ones.
> That muslin dress is my best *summer* one.

8.5₄. Then the secondary may in some cases have an adverb before it, exactly as an adjective has : in " a division on strict party lines " the adjective *strict* qualifies *party lines*, which is treated as one unit, but in " a division on strictly party lines " *strictly* as a tertiary defines *party* (secondary) alone. Other examples of such adverbs :

> In purely Government work.
> On merely business grounds.
> From a too exclusively London standpoint.

The use of adverbs of degree is particularly noteworthy :

> The somewhat zigzag course of the narrative.
> In a more everyday tone.
> In the most matter-of-fact way.

8.5₅. In the case of some substantives, which were particularly often used in this way as secondaries before another substantive, the parallelism with adjectives has in course of time led to their becoming to all intents and purposes real adjectives, e.g. *chief* (from collocations like *chief justice, chief mourner*), *choice, commonplace*. Note the formation of superlatives like *chiefest, choicest*, and of adverbs like *chiefly, choicely*; cf. also the derived substantive *commonplaceness*. *Dainty* is originally a substantive meaning a delicacy, but now it is freely used as an adjective, from which are formed *daintier, daintiest, daintily* and *daintiness*.

8.5₆. In other cases the result of the isolation of a substantive used as a secondary in collocations is not an adjective, but a substantive, as when *a copper* is used = " a copper boiler " or " a copper coin " (with the plural *coppers*), *a canary* = " a canary bird," *a return* = " a return ticket " (we'd better take returns), *a buttonhole* = " a buttonhole bouquet," *a sixpenny* = " a sixpenny magazine," etc.

Pronouns

8.6₁. Examples of those that have a special form for the primary use (**8.3₅**) :

My (our, your, her, their, no, some, any, every) book.

And of those that have the same form for primary and secondary use :

His (that, this, what, which, each, either, neither) book; all, both books.

The two so-called articles are pronouns which are never used as primaries : *the* book, *a* book.

Adverbs

8.6₂. The use of adverbs as secondaries is comparatively rare ; examples :

The above remark.
The off side.
In a far-off country.
In after years.

Note also the pronominal adverbs *then* and *hither* :

The then government.
The hither shore.

TERTIARIES

Substantives

8.7₁. An isolated substantive is seldom used as a tertiary :

The sea went *mountains* high.
Lady Cecily, *part* pleased, *part* amused, *part* sympathetic.

Some substantives, used in this way, are now reckoned rather as adverbs :

Come *home*.
I bought it *cheap*.

8.7₂. Composite expressions consisting of substantives and other words are often used as tertiaries :

He lived there *several years*.
I slept *all Sunday afternoon*.
She died *last night*.
I shall be back *this day week*.
He would not look *my way*.
She lives *next door*.
I am not *a bit* tired.
I feel *a great deal* better.
A wall, *five feet* high.
He stood, *sailor-fashion*, on the deck.
We always travel *third class*.
Talking *face to face*.
They went out *arm in arm*.

Adjectives

8.7₃. As tertiaries we must recognize the following :

In *extreme* old age.
They are grown up *amazing* fine girls (Jane Austen).
Uncommon pretty company (Thackeray).
Silver had *terrible* hard work getting up the knoll (Stevenson).

But in the first example *old-age* may be considered one compound substantive, which is then determined by the secondary *extreme.* In the other cases literary English now generally prefers adverbs in *-ly*.

Compare, further, such fixed combinations as *new-laid eggs* and *new-mown hay* with the free combination *the newly appointed minister*; both *new-married* and *newly married* may be said.

The unchanged adverbs mentioned in **7.7₇** differ from the cases here mentioned in so far as they may be used with verbs (*he walks fast,* etc.), while adjectival tertiaries are only found before other adjectives and participles.

Pronouns

8.7₄. *The* is tertiary before a comparative :

The sooner, the better (**22.6₂**).

None is tertiary especially before the just mentioned *the* and *too*:

None the less surely.
None too sure.

No must also be considered a tertiary in some combinations, though its rank is sometimes doubtful :

To the no small delectation of a little crowd.
It ought to have happened just so and no otherwise.
She had to go, whether or no she wanted it.
He was no more wounded than I was.

Similarly *any* in

He was never wounded any more than I was.

Instead of *something*, which was formerly used as a tertiary, we now say *somewhat* :

He was somewhat paler than usual.

All as a tertiary :

You will be all the better for a drop of whisky.
The all-important question is whether he can prove his alibi.

8.7₅. When *either, neither,* and *both* are tertiaries, as in

Either he or she must be guilty.
Neither he nor she is guilty.
Both he and she are guilty

these words are generally termed conjunctions.

Stressed *that* is used as a tertiary in vulgar speech : I was that sleepy. But unstressed *that* [ðət] as a tertiary is the conjunction, as in " I say that he is mad " (**33.1**). On the relative *that* [ðət] see **34.2**.

Rank of word-groups

8.8₁. While the distinction between substantives, adjectives, etc. (word-classes, parts of speech), concerns single words in themselves, word-groups as such may be employed in the same ways as single words in different " ranks," and then have to be termed primaries, etc., according to circumstances. The rank of the group is one thing, the rank within the group another. Thus the group *Sunday afternoon*, which contains a secondary *Sunday* and a primary *afternoon*, may as a whole be

a primary : Sunday afternoon was fine,
a secondary : a Sunday afternoon concert, or
a tertiary : he slept all Sunday afternoon.

8.8₂. A preposition with its object may in itself be used as a primary, when it is made the object of another preposition : from *behind the tree* | from *over the way* | since *before the war* | up till *within about twenty years* | young ladies of *from sixteen to twenty-six years of age*.

But instead of saying " he ran *to in* the room," which we might expect on the analogy of these combinations, we say " into the room," combining the ideas in another way, and similarly " the cat jumped on to (sometimes written *onto*) the table " (i.e. *to* some place *on* the table).

We shall meet rank-distinctions of word-groups again in Chaps. **XXIX-XXXV.**

JUNCTION AND NEXUS

Adjunct and adnex.—Restrictive and non-restrictive adjuncts.—
Relation between adjunct and primary.—Adjuncts of composite
names.—Apposition. — Participles. — Extraposition. — Nexus. —
Dependent nexus.

9.1. A secondary can be joined to a primary in two essentially
different ways, for which we use the terms **Junction** and **Nexus.**
As separate names for the secondary in these two functions we
shall use the terms **Adjunct** and **Adnex** respectively.

9.2$_1$. In a junction the joining of the two elements is so close
that they may be considered one composite name for what
might in many cases just as well have been called by a single
name. Compare thus:

A silly person : a fool.
The warmest season : summer.
A very tall person : a giant.
An offensive smell : a stench.

9.2$_2$. Adjuncts may be either restrictive or non-restrictive.
The former kind gives a necessary determination to its primary,
which it specifies so as to keep it distinct from other things or
beings having the same name; e.g. *a red rose* as distinct from
a white rose. The addition of a non-restrictive adjunct does not
serve that purpose; it is more emotional, whereas a restrictive
is purely intellectual. Examples:

No, my poor little girl!
Beautiful Evelyn Hope is dead!

We shall meet the same twofold division in the chapter on Relative
Clauses (**34.1**).

9.2$_3$. When we say *young Burns*, we may either think of the
contrast between two persons of the same name, one young and
one old, or of one person only, considered in his youth as con-

trasted with his later years—or finally, *young* may be used
without any thought of contrast as a more or less superfluous
flourish to the name.

The Lower Danube or *the Upper Rhine* means one part of
each of these rivers; the adjuncts are thus used differently from
the use in *the lower* (or *upper*) *lip*.

9.3₁. Here we have already seen that the logical relation
between adjunct and primary is not always the same, and not
always so simple as in *a red rose* which means the same thing as
a rose that is red. This will be still more clear through an
analysis of the following combinations:

An early dinner.
An early riser.
The early Victorians.

First class.
First offenders are not punished severely.

Comparative anatomy.
We owed our comparative safety to the fog.

A perfect copy.
He spoke with perfect ease.
They are perfect strangers.

A young lady.
In his young days.

Conscientious work.
Conscientious objectors.

A born orator.
In all their born days.

A married woman.
Their married life was very happy.

A criminal neglect of duty.
The criminal courts.

A deaf-and-dumb teacher (one who is d.).
A deaf-and-dumb teacher (one who teaches the d.).

A lunatic girl.
A lunatic asylum.

In *New Englander, Pacific Islanders* the adjective qualifies only
the beginning of the next word (cp. *comparative safety*).

9.4. With composite names the adjunct sometimes belongs to the nearest substantive only ; this is the case in the following examples in spite of the different spelling :

Everyday speech (*speech* is defined by *everyday,* and *day* by *every*).
An all-night sitting.
A public schoolboy.
The dirty clothes-basket.
Smith & Co., old and new booksellers.

But if we hear a man mentioned as *the old bookseller,* we naturally take *old* as defining *bookseller,* not *book.* Similarly in

A new tooth-brush.
A beautiful parish church.
A green garden table.
His big schoolboy handwriting, etc.

In the expression *a first-rate second-hand bookshop, second-hand* goes with *book,* but *first-rate* with the whole combination *second-hand bookshop.*

The man who advertised a " superfluous hair-remover " would have done better to put the hyphen between *superfluous* and *hair.*

9.5. With regard to genitives we notice corresponding phenomena : in *her mother's heart* the adjunct *her* belongs to the whole expression *mother's heart* (cp., on the other hand, *the heart of her mother*). Similarly in " Interrupted by *a loud visitor's knock* at the front door." In *a haggard, old man's smile* the word *haggard* qualifies *old man's smile,* which is felt as one whole.

Apposition. Extraposition

9.6₁. In such composite denominations as *John Smith, Dr Smith, Mr Smith, Miss Smith, Miss Lydia Smith,* etc., the words preceding the family name are to some extent similar, though perhaps not exactly parallel, to the adjuncts dealt with in the beginning of this chapter. The elements are joined together in a somewhat looser way in *my brother Charles ; the Brontë sisters ; the celebrated explorer, Sven Hedin ; the river Thames ; London town,* etc.

It is difficult to distinguish such combinations from others, for which we have the grammatical term " apposition " : In *St John the Baptist* we say that *the Baptist* is in apposition to *St John.* Similarly in *his father, the renowned physician; Bradley the lexicographer, not the philosopher,* etc.

9.6₂. Consider the series :

We were all of us drunk.
We were most of us drunk.
We were none of us drunk.
The poets are not all alike.
They neither of them looked up.

In the last of these sentences we may speak of restrictive apposition. Compare further :

Give these boys a shilling each,

in which *each* is in apposition to *these boys.*

9.6₃. Participles are very often placed in apposition, either after or before the word they qualify :

He came back, utterly exhausted, from his long ride.
She went out, having first locked the drawer carefully.
Thus musing, in a wood I sate me down
Alone, continuing there to muse (Wordsworth).
And so, having noted down our names and addresses, the police-
man dismissed us.
I thought you would know, being a friend of the family.

(Note that *being,* used in this way, always indicates cause or reason, not time).

9.6₄. The connexion is, of course, quite normal in

Looking up the river, we saw a great many small boats.

But it is different in sentences like the following :

Looking up the river, the character of the scene was varied (Scott).
He felt himself gently touched on the shoulder; and looking
round, his father stood before him (Dickens).
Arrived there, his first act was to kneel down (Hardy).
Thus loaded, our progress was slower (Wells).
And knocking at the gate, 'twas open'd wide (Byron).

In such cases grammarians speak of "unattached participles," and point out how these may often lead to misunderstandings. There are, however, some stock expressions in which unattached participles are perfectly legitimate, see, *e.g.*

> Strictly speaking, he ought to have been punished.
> Talking of Johnson, what has become of his youngest daughter?
> The letter must have been very long, judging by the time he was upstairs writing it.
> His knowledge of Greek is wonderful, considering his age.

9.6₅. A word or group of words is often placed by itself, outside the sentence proper, in which it is represented by a pronoun; we then speak of "extraposition":

> For the raine, it raineth every day (Sh.).
> Charles Dickens, *he* was a novelist!
> He was a great novelist, that Charles Dickens.
> It is unexampled, I think, that calm creative perspicacity of Shakespeare (Carlyle).
> It was a wonderful invention, the Universal Thrift Club (Bennett).
> That woman that cannot make her fault her husband's occasion, let her never nurse her childe (Sh.).
> That priest who entered, do you know his name?
> Inferiority complex—what exactly does that mean?

There will be occasion to speak of extraposition in other places of this grammar (see preparatory *it* **16.1₆**, etc., predicatives **13.1**, relative clauses **14.3₂**, **33.4₆**).

Nexus

9.7₁. We shall now look at the second way in which a secondary can be joined to a primary: we shall call this **Nexus,** and for the secondary in these combinations we shall use the term **Adnex.**

If we compare *the red door* and *the barking dog*, on the one hand (junction), and on the other *the door is red* and *the dog barks* or *the dog is barking* (nexus), we find that the former kind is more rigid or stiff, and the latter more pliable; there is, as it were, more life in it. A junction is like a picture, a nexus is like a drama or a process. In a nexus something new is added to the conception contained in the primary: the difference between that and a junction is seen clearly by comparing, *e.g.*

The blue dress is the oldest.
The oldest dress is blue.
A dancing woman charms.
A charming woman dances.

9.7₂. In examples like " the door is red " and " the dog barks "
the nexus is independent and forms a whole sentence, *i.e.* it
gives a complete bit of information. But it is important to
notice that a nexus may also be dependent, and in that case does
not give a complete piece of information. The simplest instances
of this are found in the so-called clauses, which resemble
sentences in their construction, but form only part of a communication, *e.g.*

I see *that the door is red*.
I know *that the dog barks*.
She is afraid *when the dog barks*, etc.

But the same relation between a primary and a secondary
obtains also in various other combinations, in which we are
therefore entitled to speak of a dependent nexus. These will
be considered in some detail in Chaps. XXIX-XXXII; here
we shall give only a few examples to show their intrinsic
similarity to dependent clauses:

I paint the door red (paint it so that afterwards it is red).
I hear the dog bark (cp. hear that he barks).
I make the dog bark.

Very often a substantive in itself contains the idea of a
(dependent) nexus. Examples of such nexus-substantives:

The dog's *barking* was heard all over the place.
I saw the King's *arrival* (cp. I saw that the King arrived).
On account of her *pride* (cp. because she was proud).

See for further details Chaps. XXX, XXXI.

CHAPTER X

SENTENCE-STRUCTURE

Subject and predicate. — Object. — Word-order. —Inversion. — Amorphous sentences.

10.1₁. In such a simple sentence as *the dog barks*—and naturally also in clauses like *that the dog barks* or *when the dog barks*—we call *the dog* **Subject** and *barks* **Predicate,** and say that *barks* is predicated of the dog. The same terms are used also in more complicated utterances; in

> *the big dog that my brother bought yesterday in London* barked furiously at the butcher,

the first ten words (italicized) form together the subject, and the rest the predicate. In

> *the cat and the dog* do not agree very well

there are not two grammatical subjects, but *the cat and the dog* together is the subject of the sentence, as will be seen from a comparison with the synonymous expression

> *they* do not agree very well.

Any primary (see Chap. VIII) may be the subject of a sentence.

On gerunds, infinitives and clauses as subjects, see Chap. XXXI ff.

10.1₂. Very often a sentence contains more than one primary connected with the same verb, but only one is the subject. In

> Charles took a ticket

we call *Charles* the **Subject,** and *a ticket* the **Object** of *took*.
In the sentence

> Charles gave his daughter a ticket

we have even two objects; *the ticket* is the direct and *his daughter* the indirect object.

In " Charles saw his daughter and her husband " there is only one grammatical object (though denoting two persons; cp. " saw them "); in " Charles gave his daughter and her husband their tickets and a few pounds " there are two grammatical objects, each consisting of two parts joined by means of *and*.

10.2₁. How are we to find out what is the subject? This is done most easily by taking the verb in the form in which it is found in the sentence, and asking Who (or What) followed by it :

> Tom beats John.   Who beats?   Tom.
> John is beaten by Tom.   Who is beaten?   John.

The subject is different in these two sentences, though both indicate the same action, and though the agent in both cases is Tom. In the former we have an active, and in the latter a passive verb, see Chap. XII.

> Charles gave his daughter a ticket.   Who gave?   Charles.
>   Charles therefore is the subject.
> Fire destroyed the building.   What destroyed?   Fire.
> The building was destroyed by fire.   What was destroyed?   The
>   building.

10.2₂. What is said in the preceding paragraphs is merely an aid to our grammatical analysis ; but a much more important question is : What means does the English language possess to enable the man in the street, who is no grammarian and has no need of learned terms like subject and object, to understand the meaning of sentences? If he hears a sentence like " John saw Henry," it is, of course, necessary for him at once to know who was the seer and who was seen. How is this effected?

10.2₃. Some pronouns have different forms—**case-forms**— according as they stand as subject or object, *e.g.* :

> I saw her.   I gave her the ticket.
> She saw me.   She gave me the ticket, etc.
> See on case-distinctions, Chap. XIV.

10.2₄. But such formal differences are not found with all pronouns even :

> You saw nobody.
> Nobody saw you.

And substantives and adjectives have in English no endings or similar formal distinctions to show their role within the sentence, such as are found in many other languages and were to some extent found in Old English. If English has been able to do away with such formal means, it is because it has developed a tolerably fixed **word-order** which in the great majority of cases shows without fail what is the subject of the sentence.

10.2$_5$. No grammatical rules of word-order can, however, be strictly observed in all cases ; there is a certain freedom in that respect, and much depends on what is at every moment uppermost in the mind of the speaker. He will always tend to pronounce first what is most actual to him ; and, on the other hand, he may sometimes on purpose—more or less consciously—hold back an idea so as to produce a greater effect if its appearance is prepared in the right way. There are thus two emphatic places, first and last.

We shall now consider the chief grammatical uses of word-order.

10.3$_1$. When we hear the sentences :
John saw Henry, and
Henry saw John,

the word-order gives us the key to the right understanding. The normal word-order in English is :
Subject—Verb—Object ; we may write this as an abbreviated formula :

$$S—V—O$$

It will be seen that this order is regularly followed even where there are formal criteria to decide which is the subject and which the object, as is the case with some pronouns (**10.2$_3$**). On the other hand, it is evident that it is not so necessary to follow this order if there is only one primary in the sentence ; hence the order V—S is comparatively more frequent if there is no object than if there is one.

In a statistical investigation of word-order in a series of representative nineteenth-century writers, it was found that the order S—V—O was used in from 82 to 97 per cent. of all sentences containing all these three members, while the percentage for Beowulf was 16 and for King Alfred's prose 40. This shows a great growth of regularity in the development of a thousand years.

10.3₂. In some cases the subject may be separated from the verb by an adverb :

You never can tell.
Charles always (usually, sometimes) took a walk before breakfast.
Charles wisely refrained from further remarks.
They simply would not leave us alone.
He naturally expressed his thanks (=it was natural that he . . .).

But a descriptive adverb follows the verb ; it may often be regarded more or less as an afterthought :

He expressed his thanks naturally (=in a natural way).

10.4₁. In certain generally well-defined cases the subject is placed after its verb (V—S). This word-order is called **Inversion.**
This is, first, the rule in questions :

Had the man no money ? (V—S—O).

But, as we shall see in Chap. XXVIII, the subject is in most questions placed before the really important verb, and only a comparatively insignificant auxiliary—denoted v—is placed first to mark the question as such ; the formula then is

$$v—S—V—O :$$

Could John see Henry ?
Did John see Henry ?
Had John seen Henry ?

10.4₂. Note the difference between a question and an exclamation :

How old is he ?
How old he is !
What an ass he is !

In long literary exclamations we may have inversion :

What a piece of worke is a man ! (Sh.).

10.4₃. The same word-order, V—S or v—S—V, is found in some clauses without any conjunction :

Mr Darnley has offered us his assistance, should any be needed.
Even had she been alive, we should not have seen her (**35.**3).

10.4₄. In short sentences inserted in quotations the subject may come after *says* and *said*, especially if the subject is a substantive (a personal name) ; but not so often after other verbs :

> No, said he (No, he said), I will never do it.
> No, he whispered, I will never do it.
> You were right, said Smith, and without you we should have made a fearful mess of it.

10.4₅. Next, in wishes, the old order V—S is seen in such a fixed formula as :

> Long live the king !

But, as a rule, we have a similar compromise as in questions, the auxiliary *may* being placed before, and the real verb after, the subject :

$$v—S—V$$

> May the king live long !

Note the difference in :

> " The war may come," says one party.   " Yes," says the other; and secretly mutters, " May the war come !" (Lowes Dickinson).

Such a wish as *God bless you !* has the normal word-order.

10.4₆. Sometimes inversion is occasioned by the fact that some grammatically inferior member of the sentence is placed in the beginning to attract attention ; the subject is then more easily thrown into relief if it comes last :

> Crack goes the whip !
> Bang came another shot.
> Out rushed the man and his wife (but with an unstressed pronoun : Out they rushed).
> Gloster, 'tis true that we are in great danger.
> The greater therefore should our courage be (Sh.).

10.4₇. This order (V—S, or generally v—S—V) is particularly frequent when the sentence is introduced negatively :

> Never did I see the like.
> Not till then did I realize the danger of the situation.
> (He knew nothing about it.)   No more did his wife.
> Scarcely had he entered the room, when he broke out in insults.

Little and *only* are in this respect treated as negatives :

> Little did we think that we were never to see him again.
> Only on one occasion did he speak to me of his mother.   (But : On one occasion he spoke to me . . .).

10.4₈. Note the difference in meaning according as the verb or the subject is placed last when *so* comes first; in the latter case it implies " also " as the subject is thrown into relief :

" You must go to bed now." " So I must, and so must you."
So the physician said in his prospectus, and so said all the citizens in the city (Stevenson).

Thus also with *no more* :

" I am afraid he did not turn up." " No more he did." " No more did his brother."

The object may be similarly stressed at the end :

" He lov'd his mother dearly." " So did he mee " (Sh.).

10.4₉. If there is no verb, it may sometimes be doubtful whether a word is meant as subject or as object, thus after *than* and *as* :

He likes his father better than (just as much as) his mother (cf. **14.2**).

Perfect clearness can here be obtained by the insertion of a verb :

. . . than his mother does, or, than he does his mother ;

even the word-order *than does his mother* is clear : *his mother* is subject, because there is no subject before *does*.

This inversion is pretty frequent in literary style :

Tennyson liked Society no better than did General Gordon.

Word-order is often regulated by considerations of balance in the sentence. Compare thus :

Among the guests were the Prime Minister and his children.
Among the guests the Prime Minister and his children were particularly noticed.

10.5. With an imperative it is generally unnecessary to add the subject :

Come! Take that! (V—O).

When the subject is expressed, we have remnants of the old order (V—S) in such set phrases as *Mind you* and *Praise ye the Lord !*

But otherwise the normal word-order (S—V—O) is followed here in modern colloquial speech :

> Never you mind !
> You take that seat, John, and someone fetch a few more chairs !

With a negative we have the order v—S—V—O :

> Don't you begin it !

10.6₁. The subject is left out colloquially in some set phrases :

> (I) thank you.
> (God) bless you !
> Confound it !
> (It) serves him right.

10.6₂. In familiar speech even more than the subject may be dropped in the beginning of a sentence if the meaning is obvious :

> (Have you) got a match ?
> (I shall) see you again to-morrow.
> (I am) sorry. (It was) my mistake (**13.4₂**).
> (It will) serve him right.

10.7₁. The object is, as already stated, normally placed after the verb. But it may sometimes be placed in the beginning, chiefly for the sake of contrast, and then we have the order O—S—V, *e.g.* :

> Talent, Mr Micawber has ; capital, Mr Micawber has not (Dickens).
> Things base and vile, holding no quantity.
> Love can transpose to forme and dignity (Sh.).

Thus also the ironical :

> Love ! A lot you know about it !

After a negative (cf. **10.4₇**) we have O—v—S—V in

> Not a word did he say in her favour.

Exceptionally a poet may use the order S—O—V, as Tennyson does in

> God the traitor's hope confound !

—but then there is no danger of any one's taking *the traitor's hope* as the subject.

The order V—O—S in

> Early in 1661 took place a general election (Macaulay)

is only justified, because *took place* is a set phrase, but

> Early in 1661 a general election took place

would be more natural.

10.7₂. An interrogative or a relative pronoun must be placed first, but the word-order, assisted by *do* (**28.6**), precludes any ambiguity :

> What picture surpasses Mona Lisa?
> What picture does Mona Lisa surpass?
> This picture, which surpasses Mona Lisa.
> This picture, which Mona Lisa surpasses.

If the famous oracular answer, " The Duke yet lives that Henry shall depose " is ambiguous, it is only because it is in verse, where one expects inversions : in ordinary prose it could be understood only in one way, as the word-order would be reversed if *Henry* was meant as the object.

10.8₁. When *here* and *there* (meaning at this and at that place) are put first, we generally have normal word-order if the sentence contains a full verb :

> Here the gamekeeper found the dead body.
> There Scott wrote all his best novels.

Inversion, however, takes place with short verbs in sentences like :

> Here comes the old lady.

This is the rule in the case of the insignificant verb *is*, if the subject is stressed :

> Here is your coat, and there are your gloves.

An unstressed pronoun precedes the verb :

> Here it is.   There they are.

10.8₂. Inversion is always found when unstressed *there* has lost its local meaning and is pronounced [ðə], see **4.9₄**; we call this " preparatory *there* " :

> There was no one there (note the two *there*s in the same sentence).
> There came a time when he did repent.

Where there's a will, there's a way.

"There's nere a villaine dwelling in all Denmarke But hee's an arrant knave." "There needs no ghost, my lord, come from the grave, To tell us this " (Sh.).

10.8₃. When clauses, gerunds and infinitives, especially infinitives followed by one or more complements, are to be the subject or object of a sentence, it is generally found convenient not to place them in the usual position for a subject or object, but to use the pronoun *it* there and then place the clause or infinitive in extraposition (**16.1₆**).

10.9. Alongside of the sentences considered so far, in which we are able to recognize a nexus between a subject and a predicate, we have other kinds of sentences which cannot be thus analysed. Let us call them **amorphous sentences.** They consist of only one member, though this may contain more than one word. While the sentences of complete predicational nexuses are (often, at any rate) intellectual and formed so as to satisfy the strict requirements of logicians, amorphous sentences are more suitable for the emotional side of human nature. When anyone wants to give vent to a strong feeling he does not stop to consider the logical analysis of his ideas, but language furnishes him with a great many adequate means of bringing the state of his mind to the consciousness of his hearer or hearers.

Such amorphous sentences range from sounds which are not otherwise used in ordinary speech, such as the click (suction-stop) of compassion, annoyance or impatience conventionally, but imperfectly, written *tut* or *tck*, through single ordinary speech sounds like [ʃ·] to enjoin silence (conventionally spelled *hush*), or sound-combinations like *hm!* or *ha ha!* and conventional "interjections" like *alas! hullo!* or *hurra!* to single words or word-combinations capable of being used also in the first class of sentences.

As examples of such amorphous or one-member sentences may serve : Yes! | Goodbye! | Thanks! | Thanks awfully! | What! | Dear me! | Heavens! | Of course! | Nonsense! | Silence! | Waiter, another bottle! | Your health! | Poor fellow! | An aeroplane! | This way, ladies! | Off with his head! | Out with your suspicions! |

Why all this fuss? | Hence his financial difficulties! | O, these women!

On account of the emotional character of amorphous sentences the actual meaning of each often depends to a very great extent on its tone. *Yes* may, according to circumstances, mean " I gladly agree with what you say," " I reluctantly agree with what you say," " What do you want? " or " Please go on! " *John!* may mean, among other things, " Come here at once," " How delightful to see you! " " Can it really be John? " " I'm ashamed of you," etc.

In most amorphous sentences no ingenuity would suffice to say what exactly is " left out " or what could be supplied in order to make them into sentences of the recognized type consisting of a subject and a predicate. No explanation by means of ellipsis is therefore available, and it is best to acknowledge amorphous sentences on the same footing as other sentences.

We may finish this chapter by the following definition.

A sentence is a (relatively) complete and independent unit of communication (or—in the case of soliloquy—what might be a communication were there someone to listen to it)—the completeness and independence being shown by its standing alone or its capability of standing alone, *i.e.* of being uttered by itself.

CHAPTER XI

RELATIONS OF VERB TO SUBJECT AND OBJECT

Agent and sufferer.—Double-faced verbs.—Split subjects.—
Object.—Instrumental.—Result.—Cognate.—Same verb different
objects.— Prepositional phrases.— Reflexive.— Reciprocal.— Indirect object.—The *to*-phrase.—Transitive and intransitive.—
Objects after adjectives.

11.1$_1$. As has been seen already from the examples given above,
the **subject** cannot be defined by means of such words as active
or agent.   This is further evident when we consider the meaning of several verbs, which denote anything but action, *e.g.*

He suffered torture.
He lost his father in the war.

Some verbs can in some connexions denote an action, in
others a suffering on the part of the subject :

He broke a twig.
He broke his leg.
He burned the papers.
He burned his finger.
Charles had his hair cut.
King Charles the First had his head cut off.

11.1$_2$. Some verbs are " double-faced " in a curious way :

The garden swarms with bees = bees swarm in the garden.
This stream abounds in fish = fish abound in this stream.

Compare further :

The place was crawling with Indians.
Her face was streaming with tears.
The young officer who was in charge of the prisoners.
The prisoners who were in the charge of the young officer.
I was in sight of the shore.   The shore was in sight.

11.2$_1$. If we analyse sentences like

He happened to fall.
He is sure to turn up.
He is believed to be rich,—

there can be no doubt as to the grammatical subject : it is *he*. But notionally the matter is not so simple : we cannot in the usual way ask : " Who happened ? " " Who is sure ? " " Who is believed ? " We must either complete these questions by adding *to fall*, etc., or else we must ask : " What happened ? " " What is sure ? " " What is believed ? " We thus discover that the notional subject is really a complete nexus, in which *he* is the primary, and *fall, turn up*, and *be rich* respectively is the secondary (adnex). We may express this in an unidiomatic way by saying that the notional subject, which is thus split in two, is *he-to-fall*, etc. Cf. **29.1₁** and **32.5**.

11.2₂. If now we consider such a sentence as

The path was easy to find,—

we see that *the path* is the subject of the sentence, but at the same time it is, as it were, the object of *to find* (to find the path was easy). Similar constructions are seen in

His face was so ghastly to see that I grew alarmed.
Some girls are jolly to watch when they run.
A happy man or woman is a better thing to find than a five-pound note (Stevenson).
Little remains to add.

11.3₁. An **object** is a primary which is intimately connected with the verb of the sentence (or clause), though less intimately so than the subject. After finding the latter as described in **10.2₁**, we may proceed to find the object by asking *Whom*, or *What* with the subject and the form of the verb actually used ; thus we find the objects of the two sentences :

She eats an apple every morning : What does she eat ? an apple.
The mystery puzzled us a great deal : Whom did the mystery puzzle ? us—

while *every morning* and *a great deal* are tertiaries.

11.3₂. On account of the infinite variety of meanings attached to verbs no simple definition can be given of the relation of the object to the verb, such as " the receiver of the action " or " the person or thing directly affected by the action " ; this will

be seen from the following examples, in which the object is
italicized :

> They murdered *the chief*.
> Mother cut *the pie*.
> The boy saw *the moon*.
> The boy wanted *a bad hiding*.
> We left *London*.
> We missed *the train*, etc.

11.3₃. In many cases the object expresses that by means of
which something is done (**instrumental object**) :

> They threw *stones*.
> Mary nodded *her head*.
> She shrugged *her shoulders*.
> He pointed *his forefinger* at Arthur.
> He struck *his hand* upon his knee (= struck his knee with his
> hand).

11.3₄. An **object of result** is found not only in such cases as

> The architect built *a house*,
> John wrote *a letter*,

but also in many cases in which the same verb may be used with
other objects ; compare thus the following list, in which the
object of result is placed in the second column :

I dig the ground.	I dig a grave.
She lights the lamp.	She lights a fire.
He paints the door.	He paints portraits.
He eats an apple.	Moths eat holes in curtains.
We picked flowers.	We picked a quarrel.
The sailors worked the pumps.	He worked his passage to America.

11.3₅. A subdivision under the object of result is the so-called
cognate object, as in

> I dreamt a curious dream.
> Mowgli laughed a little short ugly laugh (Kipling).
> I would faine dye a dry death (Sh.).

Another subdivision is found when a verb comes to mean
" express by -ing " :

> She laughed her thanks.
> Sir Charles nodded approval.

11.4₁. Some examples may be given to show that one and the same verb may very often take different kinds of objects or stand in different relations to its objects :

Enter a house | enter one's name in a list.
Run a race | run a risk | run a business.
Pass the bridge | pass an examination | pass the time | pass round this picture.
The clergyman married Mr A and Miss B | Mr A married Miss B.
Fight the enemy | they fought many battles | people do not fight cocks nowadays.
Hang curtains, criminals | hang the walls with pictures.
Plant roses | plant the garden with roses.
Pay the driver | pay five shillings | pay the bill.
Present young ladies with flowers | present flowers to young ladies.
Wrap her in the cloak | wrap the cloak round her.
Help him on with his coat | Kate was helping soup from an enormous tureen | she couldn't help laughing.
Serve one's country | serve the guests | serve coffee.
Ask questions | ask one's way of a passer-by | ask a passer-by to show one the way | ask him about his intentions | What did he ask for the motor ? | ask him to dinner.
Answer a letter, a question, the bell | answer the teacher | he answered nothing.
Turn the handle | turn prose into verse | turn a corner.
Wait their turn | wait dinner.
Speak French | his eye spoke his admiration of her | speak a — vessel.

11.4₂. Not a few verbs are used sometimes with an object, sometimes with a prepositional phrase. In some cases the meaning is completely changed (*call a person, call on him*; *he has not tasted food today*; *the food tastes of ginger*) ; in others the act is more complete when there is no preposition :

Strike him | strike at him.
We know him | we know of him.

With some verbs the difference is not so easily definable :

Confess a crime | confess to a liking for something.
I don't believe a word of it | he believes in God.
Watch a person | watch over a person.

Meet a person | meet all claims | meet with him | meet with an
   accident.
Attend school | attend to one's work.

11.4₃. When an auxiliary verb stands by itself, it may take
an object as if a full verb had been expressed :

Though I do hate him as I do hell paines (Sh.).
She fondled the thing in her arms as a mother would a child.
I could no more stir the canoe than I could the other boat.
He flung the message into the fire, as he had a thousand like it.

Reflexive

11.5₁. When the subject and object are identical, we use for
the latter a so-called reflexive pronoun, formed by means of
self, e.g. *I defend myself.*   The pronouns are the following :

(I) myself	(we) ourselves.
(thou) thyself ⎫	(you) yourselves.
(you) yourself ⎭	
(he) himself ⎫	
(she) herself ⎬	(they) themselves.
(it) itself ⎭	
(one) oneself (rarer one's self).	

A few verbs are always used reflexively :

She prides herself on her good looks.
He absented himself from all committee meetings.

11.5₂. There is a tendency to get rid of these pronouns whenever no ambiguity is to be feared :

I washed, dressed and shaved, and then felt infinitely better.
He is training for the race.
He drew back a little.
The army retired in good order.
The disease spread rapidly.
You must prepare for death.

11.5₃. Sometimes a difference is made, or may be made,
between the fuller and the shorter expression ; *behave oneself*
is often used of good manners and breeding, while *behave* is

used of action generally: the troops behaved gallantly under fire.

> He settled himself comfortably in an easy-chair | they settled in Australia.
> No opportunity offered | He offered himself as an interpreter.

Sometimes there is an element of exertion in the reflexive use : *We kept ourselves warm by walking to and fro* is more deliberate than *we kept warm*, etc.; cf. *the soup did not keep warm* very long. *He proved himself a fine fellow* emphasizes his endeavours, while *he proved a fine fellow* merely means that people saw that he was.

It is natural that the tendency to use verbs without the reflexive pronouns is stronger in English, where these pronouns are heavy and cumbersome, than in other languages where the corresponding forms are short and light (French *se*, German *sich*, etc.).

11.5$_4$. The reflexive pronouns are also used after prepositions :

> He looked at himself in the glass.
> He lives by himself in an old cottage.

But if the preposition has a purely local meaning, the simple forms without *self* are used :

> Shut the door behind you!
> I have no change about me.
> She stood, looking straight in front of her.
> They had the whole afternoon before them.

Reciprocal

11.6$_1$. To express mutual action or relation we have the so-called reciprocal pronouns *each other* and *one another* for all persons :

> We (you, they) do not love each other (or, one another).

The distinction sometimes insisted on that *each other* should refer to two only and *one another* to more than two " is neither of present utility nor based on historic usage " (H. W. Fowler).

11.6$_2$. Here we find the same tendency to do without the object in some familiar instances :

We meet occasionally.
They kissed and parted.
They married in haste and repented at leisure.

Direct and Indirect Object

11.7$_1$. Some verbs are frequently or even regularly combined with two objects : in " They offered the butler a reward " *the butler* is an **indirect** and *a reward* a **direct object.** While some languages (*e.g.* German, Old English, Latin) have one case-form, the accusative, for the direct, and another, the dative, for the indirect object (case-forms, which, by the way, serve also other functions), Modern English makes no such distinction in form. Why, then, are we entitled to have different names for these two kinds of objects?

The direct object is more essential to the verb and more closely connected with it than the indirect object, in spite of the seemingly privileged position of the latter immediately after the verb in most sentences. In " they offered the butler a reward " it is possible to isolate the direct object (*they offered a reward*), but not the indirect object (*they offered the butler*). *A reward* is the object of *offered*, but *the butler* is the object of *offered a reward*. It is, therefore, quite natural to ask " What did they offer? " but not " Whom (or To whom) did they offer? " without mentioning the object. Thus also in the passive we can say " A reward was offered," but not " The butler was offered " without saying what; nor can we ask " Who was offered? " though it is possible to ask " Who was offered a reward? " as well as " What was offered? " Hence we may say that in " A reward was offered the butler " *a reward* is the subject of *was offered*, but in the equally possible turn " The butler was offered a reward " *the butler* is the subject of the whole combination *was offered a reward*, but not really of *was offered* by itself.

We shall see below (**11.7$_4$**) that it is in most cases (though not in all) possible to substitute a group with the preposition *to* for the indirect object.

11.7₂. The chief classes of verbs that can take a direct and an indirect object are the following :

Give and synonyms and the opposite :

> Give papa my best love !
> He left his sister a hundred pounds.
> Pay the driver five shillings.
> We must buy her some clothes.
> I can refuse you nothing.
> They grudged us every little advantage.

Verbs of motion implying giving and the like :

> Kindly pass me the mustard.
> He would bring his little boy home a box of bricks.
> The landlady dropped the Countess a respectful curtsey.
> He bore his cousin no ill-will.

Wish, intend, cause, etc.

> I wish the government all possible success.
> They meant us no harm.
> The delay caused us a good deal of trouble.
> Will you do me a great favour ?

Verbs of *communication* :

> He told us the most fantastic stories.
> He always wanted to read me his latest poems.

In all these examples the indirect object is a person, as indeed is nearly always the case ; instances like the following are much rarer :

> He allowed his imagination full play.
> This was possible, though we had never given it a thought.

11.7₃. As will appear from all the examples given hitherto, the rule, which is almost universal, is to place the indirect before the direct object. Exceptions are only found in the case of weak pronouns, chiefly *it* (and *them* used of things, thus as the plural of *it*) :

> Let me tell the story, as mother told it us.
> My books ? Why do you never come and let me show them you ?

But even here many people would prefer the opposite order or, to be perfectly clear, use the *to*-phrase : *told it to us, show them to you.* In England one often hears *give it me* ; Americans nearly always say *give it to me.*

The *to*-phrase

11.7₄. The preposition *to*, which indicates a movement in the direction of someone, has naturally come to be used as a more emphatic or distinct expression of the relation otherwise indicated by the indirect object, as in *bring it to me, give (show) it to your father,* etc. The *to*-phrase has been constantly growing in frequency since the first feeble beginnings in Old English, and it has been extended to many cases where the local meaning of the preposition is totally obliterated, as with *deny* :

Give to dogges what thou denyest to men (Sh.).

The weakening of the local meaning of *to* is the same as with the infinitive (**32.**1).

Sometimes the *to*-phrase is preferable or even necessary instead of an indirect object without the preposition, thus when a word is placed first, or when a group of words would be too long to be conveniently placed before the direct object, or finally when the direct object is not expressed :

To him they showed everything, to me nothing.
The man to whom my father gave me, and to whom I gave myself.
You should give the tools to those who can handle them.
She gave largely to hospitals.
Give none offence, neither to the Jews, nor to the Gentiles (AV.).

11.7₅. While *to* would not be possible in

They played us a good many tricks,
Will you keep me company to-night?
It gave her some uneasiness,

on the other hand *to* is indispensable in some set phrases :

Give rise to suspicion, give birth to a son, pay attention (heed) to, make love to.

There are also a certain number of verbs, chiefly of Latin origin, which are nearly always combined with *to*, e.g. *ascribe, attribute, dedicate, describe, introduce, mention, propose, reveal, refer, suggest.*

A parallel use of *to* is found with substantives and adjectives, where the local meaning of the preposition is equally obliterated: *a pleasure, a great help, a calamity to someone, it is interesting, obvious, helpful, injurious to everybody*, etc. Compare also *It seems to me* | *What is that to you?*

Transitive and Intransitive Use of Verbs

11.8₁. We speak of a verb as **transitive** if it has an object, and **intransitive** if it has none. The same verb is very often used both transitively and intransitively, when the meaning of the object is evident from the context; see, for instance:

Transitive:	Intransitive:
He plays the violin.	He plays extremely well.
He left London.	He left yesterday.
He lends money.	I neither lend nor borrow.
Smoke cigars.	She does not ṣmoke.

Many verbs are used thus intransitively in special idiomatic meanings, e.g. *pull* (= row), *strike* (work), it does not *pay*, that will *do*, *put* to sea, the fire *caught* rapidly, he *takes* after his father, etc.

11.8₂. Verbs of motion and change are particularly frequent in this double employment as transitive and intransitive, *e.g.*

Move a stone.	The stone moves.
Change the subject.	The fashion changes.
Roll a ball.	The ball rolls.
Turn the leaf.	The current turns.
Begin the play.	The play begins at eight.
End the discussion.	The meeting ended at ten.
Pass the wine.	The train passed.
The soldiers burned everything that would burn.	

When such verbs are used thus intransitively, we very often think of a thing as moved of itself or through an inward impulse, see, e.g., *the stone rolled down the hill*, as different from *the stone was rolled down the hill*. Cp. further:

The carriage stopped: she looked up; it was stopped by Mr Weston.

If it does not change of itself, it will have to be changed.

Shut the door.	The door will not shut.
Open the door.	The door opened, and a stranger entered.

11.8₃. Parallel with *open* we have a similar double use of many verbs derived from adjectives :

Clear up a difficulty.	The weather clears up.
Cool one's enthusiasm.	The earth cools down.
Their company wearied her.	She wearied of their company.
He filled his pockets.	His eyes filled with tears.
The sun ripens the apples.	Apples ripen in the sun.

11.8₄. While in the case of the verbs first mentioned (*play*, etc., **11.8₁**) there can be no doubt that the transitive is the original and the intransitive the derived use (cp. also the originally reflexive and reciprocal verbs, **11.5₂**, **11.6₂**), it is not always clear with verbs of this class which use is the original and which the derived. *He rolls the ball* may be conceived as = " he makes the ball roll, causes the ball to roll." We may therefore speak of the transitive *roll* as the causative of the intransitive *roll*. There are many other verbs which are evidently at first intransitive, so that the transitive verb must be considered a causative, *e.g.*

Intransitive :	Transitive :
Corn grows.	To grow corn | grow a pair of moustaches.
The dinner bell rang.	He rang the bell.
He worked hard.	He worked his servants hard.
He dined with us.	We dined him.
The box stood on the floor.	He stood the box on the floor.

11.8₅. In two cases we have separate verbs for the intransitive and the corresponding transitive (causative) use :

Intransitive :	Transitive :
sit, sat, sat.	set, set, set.
lie, lay, lain.	lay, laid, laid.

But even apart from the vulgar confusion of *lie* and *lay* (which was formerly considered venial : Byron in a famous passage writes " There let him lay ") the distinction is not carried through quite consistently : *set* is intransitive in *the sun sets | set out for a journey | he sits down and sets to work*, and on the other hand, *sit* is often used causatively =" make to sit " (as in " taking Paul in his arms, and sitting him on another little table," Dickens), because *set* so often means " put, place " in general, not merely in a sitting posture.

11.8₆. The same double-sidedness as in many of the verbs here considered (*roll*, etc.) is found in some originally transitive verbs, which are used intransitively in some combinations, *e.g.*

> His plays won't act, and his poems won't sell.
> The mud will brush off when it is dry.
> The words would not form on her lips.
> None of the babies photographed well.
> This dress washes better than the blue one.
> Overcoats that would not wear out.

The meaning here is nearly the same as in the passive of the same verbs; yet there are certain differences. It is not possible to say, in speaking of a single act of selling, " this house sold yesterday "; and if we say, " his books sell very well," we think to some extent of the books as active themselves, rather than of the activity of the bookseller. We indicate in such a sentence something that is felt as characteristic of the subject; therefore the verb generally requires some further descriptive term :

> The meat cuts tender.
> His scientific papers read like novels.

11.8₇. Often the pseudo-activity of the subject is shown by the use of the verb *will* :

> The figures will not add.
> The suit-case would not lock.
> 　　*Cf.* also : Riches tend to accumulate.

11.9. Verbs are not the only words that can take objects. There are a few adjectives which can be thus constructed :

> He is not *worth* his salt.
> I will make it worth your while to obey me.
> His stuff is not worth reading.
> He looks *like* an actor.
> That is just like you.
> What is she like ?

There is nothing like doing a thing at once.
The sisters live *near* each other.
His firm came near being ruined last year.
Always wear wool *next* your skin.
I sat in the chair next the fire.

(In some of these phrases *to* may be inserted.)

When a particle takes an object it is called a preposition
(**7.**5), or a conjunction if the object is a clause.

CHAPTER XII

PASSIVE

Formation of the passive.—Why is this turn chosen ?—The subject of a passive verb.—Converted subject.

12.1. One and the same idea can often be expressed in two different ways, by means of an active, and by means of a passive construction. The English passive is formed with an auxiliary, generally *be*, but often also *get* or *become* (**24.**1₆), and the second participle : " Tom beats John " (active) and " John was beaten by Tom " mean essentially the same thing and yet they are not in every respect synonymous, and it is therefore not superfluous for a language to have both turns and thus be able to shift the point of view.   As a rule the person or thing that is the centre of interest at the moment is made the subject of the sentence, and therefore the verb is in some cases put in the active, in others in the passive.

12.2. In the vast majority of cases the choice of the passive turn is due to one of the following reasons :

(1) The active subject (what would be the subject if we had chosen the active turn) is unknown or cannot easily be stated :

Her father was killed in the Boer war.
The city is well supplied with water.
I was tempted to go on.
The murderer was caught yesterday, and it is believed that he will be hanged.
She came to the Derby not only to see, but just as much to be seen.

In " the doctor was sent for " neither the sender nor the person sent is mentioned, because they present no interest to the speaker.

(2) The active subject is self-evident from the context :

He was elected Member of Parliament for Leeds.
She told me that her master had dismissed her. No reason had been assigned ; no objection had been made to her conduct. She had been forbidden to appeal to her mistress, etc.

(3) There may be a special reason (tact or delicacy of senti-ment) for not mentioning the active subject; thus the mention of the first person is often avoided, in writing more frequently than in speaking :

> Enough has been said here of a subject which will be treated more fully in a subsequent chapter.

In none of these cases is the active subject mentioned : over 70 per cent. of passive sentences found in English literature contain no mention of the active subject.

(4) Where it is indicated (" converted subject ") the reason why the passive turn is preferred is generally the greater interest taken in the passive than in the active subject :

> The house was struck by lightning.
> His son was run over by a motor car.

(5) Or the passive turn may facilitate the connexion of one sentence with another :

> He rose to speak, and was listened to with enthusiasm by the great crowd present. (*Cf.* also the last example under 1.)

12.3. The **subject of a passive verb** is what in the active would be an object. But if in the active there are two objects, only one of them can be made the subject; the other object is " re-tained " as such : in other words, a passive verb can have an object.

But which of the two objects is made the subject of a passive sentence? Originally only the direct object could be thus used, *e.g.*

> The property that was left her by her husband.
> Justice shall be done everybody.
> Had time been permitted him, he would have disclosed every-thing.

12.4₁. But during the last few centuries there has been a growing tendency to make the indirect object the subject in the passive. The explanation is that the greater interest felt for persons than for things naturally leads to the placing of the indirect before the direct object. We saw this in the active

(They offered the butler a reward); consequently the order in the passive becomes :

The butler was offered a reward.

This order is seen, for instance, in

Genius, demanding bread, is given a stone after its possessor's death (Shaw).

12.4₂. In these sentences there is nothing in the form to show which is the subject and which the retained object; but as it is an almost universal practice in English to have the subject first, *the butler* and *Genius* cannot be felt as anything else than subjects; and a natural consequence is that pronouns are put in the nominative in sentences like :

He was given a lodge to keep (Stevenson).
Thou art granted space (Sh.).
Yet here she is allow'd her virgin crants (Sh.).
He would be denied the benefits of the last sacraments (Sterne).
You will be spared the suffering and I the virtue (Shelley).
We were shown a room (Goldsmith).

Milton writes :

Some other hour of the day might be taught them the rules of arithmetic.

But now we say :

In the afternoon they might be taught arithmetic.

The new construction has had to fight its way against the opposition of many grammarians, who thought more of Latin rules than of the natural tendency of their own language. So much is certain that it facilitates convenient combinations like the following :

Brothers who have all either bought or been left estates (Tennyson).
He (Gray) was offered, and declined, the office of poet-laureate (Gosse).
I think the house may be made comfortable and given the air of a gentleman's residence (Jane Austen).
You've been given fair trial and found guilty (Galsworthy).

12.5. In such a sentence as

Everybody laughed at Jim,

laughed, of course, is intransitive; *Jim* is " governed by " or, as it may also be termed " the object of " the preposition *at*. But the whole may also be analysed in another way, *laughed at* may be called a transitive verb-phrase having *Jim* as its object. In this way we come to understand how it is possible to turn the sentence into the passive :

Jim was laughed at by everybody.

Other similar passive sentences are :

This must be looked into.
Foch was looked upon as the saviour of France.
The bed had not been slept in.
Ile not be juggel'd with (Sh.).
She was quite ready to be fallen in love with (Jane Austen).
The doctor was speedily sent for.

12.6. Even phrases containing a transitive verb with its object followed by a preposition may be thus turned into the passive :

The original purpose was gradually lost sight of.
She will be taken good care of.
He was taken no notice of, but his sister was made much of.
I hate being found fault with.

This liberty is found with such set phrases only as those here exemplified.

12.7. The **converted subject** of a passive sentence, *i.e.* what would have been the subject if the idea had been expressed in an active form, is now regularly indicated by means of the preposition *by* :

The city was destroyed by the French.

But the old preposition was *of*, which is still found, chiefly after verbs denoting mental states : *beloved, scorned, admired,* etc.

Of all forsaken, and forsaking all (Dryden).

PREDICATIVES

Extraposition.—Quasi-predicatives.—Real predicatives.—Link-verb.—No verb.—Predicatives of becoming.—What can be a predicative ?—Article or no article with substantives as predicatives.—Predicative left out.

13.1. In such sentences as *he was quiet* | *he seemed quiet, he became quiet,* we call *quiet* a predicative. The predicative gives a description of the subject, while the verb in itself expresses no adequate thought without being complemented by this addition. In *The more fool he !* the predicative *the more fool* is even connected with the subject *he* without any verb. We shall now see that sentences of this kind may be considered the last link of a long series beginning with descriptions which stand really outside the sentence as an afterthought (in " extraposition," **9.**6_5).

Clear examples of extraposition are :

There he sat, a giant among dwarfs.

(This may even be written :

There he sat. A giant among dwarfs !)
Mont Blanc appears,—still, snowy, and serene (Shelley).
Heere I stand, your slave, a poore, infirme, weake, and dispis'd old man (Sh.).

13.2_1. From such instances the transition is easy to others in which the description forms an essential part of the sentence, while the verb has still its ordinary full force ; very often we may transcribe by means of *be* with a predicative. Here we may speak of quasi-predicatives :

We parted the best of friends = we were the best of friends when we parted.

When sorrowes come, they come not single spies, But in battalions (Sh.).

She had left them a merry, kittenish child. She returned a full-grown woman.

He went cabin-boy on board an Indiaman.

The snow was falling pretty thick.

Still waters run deep.
His remarks passed unnoticed.
They were born poor, lived poor, and poor they died.
Time hung heavy on our hands.
I believe in marrying young.

13.2₂. Transitional cases, in which the verb loses something of its original meaning and is approximately an " empty " word :

The natives go naked all the year.
She stood godmother to his child.
She wished she had stood firm.
He stood about six feet high.
John will act best man for me.
It is no use coming the high and mighty over me.

13.3₁. Finally, we have undoubted predicatives as necessary complements to the verb ; thus with *seem* and *appear*, and verbs that mean " appear to some special sense " :

Her black dress that had seemed so smart in the village now
    appeared almost shabby.
This proved a big mistake.
That which we call a rose, By any other name would smell as
    sweete (Sh.).
Custom stales all good things, but how delicious they taste at first !
That sounds promising.
The carpet feels soft.
The room strikes nice and warm in coming in.
The moon shines bright.
Tennyson looked the poet he was.

Note the difference between *he looked angry* and *he looked angrily at her.*

13.3₂. Predicatives are used with verbs which mean " be as it was, be still " :

Keep (remain, continue) quiet.
Rest, especially with *assured, contented, satisfied.*

Outside these categories there are a few verbs that can take predicatives in special senses :

He shammed dead (but in *sham death* we have an object).
He pleaded guilty to the offence.
They fight shy of him.

13.3₃. While all these verbs have a meaning of their own, even when they are used with a predicative which is more essential to the meaning of the whole than the verbs, this cannot be said of the completely colourless verb *be*, which is hardly ever used by itself (God alone is = exists | Let me be!), but is most often used with a predicative. It then serves to connect this with the subject as what is technically termed a **copula** or **link-verb**, as in *I am glad to see you.*

13.4₁. In some cases we have predicatives without a verb, thus in exclamatory questions (literary) implying a comparison :

Who so smooth and silky as Mr Murdstone at first! (Dickens).

A peculiar grammatical phenomenon is seen in " sentences of deprecation " : a subject and a predicative are placed together without a verb in such a way that the connexion between them is as it were brushed aside at once as impossible ; the negative meaning is indicated by the same intonation as in questions, often in an exaggerated form and often given to the two members separately :

He a gentleman ! Why, his grandfather was a tradesman (Defoe).
She a beauty ! I should as soon call her mother a wit (Jane Austen).

The two members may be joined by means of *and* :

Of course he'll come. A sailor and afraid of the weather ! [= " How can a sailor be afraid of the weather ? "]

13.4₂. Next we have isolated predicatives as in emotionally coloured exclamations, in which it is obvious from the whole situation what one is talking about :

Splendid ! How delightful !
What a nasty smell !

This is frequent in such stock phrases as :

Sorry, my mistake (**10.6₂**).
Just my luck !
All the more reason for you to marry again.

13.4₃. *No matter* (= " it is of no importance ") is often used in this way before an interrogative clause :

Something must be fixed on. No matter what, so long as something is chosen.

No matter how wild or extravagant the assertion, there are always
people ready to believe it.

He had to do what he thought right, no matter what the consequences.

This may even be found after a preposition :

At no matter what risk, the thing must be accomplished quickly.
In the presence of no matter whom (Bennett).

13.44. *And* is often used before such an isolated predicative :

They went away in despair, and no wonder.
Of course they died ; and a good thing too.
Anyway they are gone, and a good riddance.

13.45. A peculiar type of contemptuous exclamatory sentences
consists of a predicative followed by what may be considered a
relative clause. (Note the ironical adjectives in some of the
examples) :

A good, honest trade you're learning, Sir Peter ! (Sheridan).
A pretty mess we shall be in by then !
A confounded nuisance women are !
But the things these girls would say !
The hypocrite that he felt himself as he said this !

13.46. A frequent construction in colloquial speech consists
in placing the predicative first and then the subject without any
verb. This word-order is generally due to a strong emotion ;
very often the predicative is pronounced without the speaker at
first intending to let anything else follow ; if then the subject
comes, it is as a kind of afterthought or tag :

Thrice blessed they that master so their blood (Sh.).
Far from me such shifts and palliatives.
Quite serious, all this, though it reads like a jest.
Pretty encouragement this for a lover !
Awful rotters, those undergraduates !
How splendid of you to think of that !
Needless to say, he never mentioned that afterwards.

In these two sentences the infinitive with *to* is the subject.

Funny you should have thought of that.
How true, that there is nothing dead in this Universe (Carlyle).

In these two the subject is a clause.

13.4₇. This pre-order of the predicative is particularly natural if it is accompanied by one of the words which demand the first place, such as (1) an interrogative word, (2) one of the "indefinite relative" words, (3) *the* with comparatives to indicate difference :

(1) What a beastly and pitiful wretch that Wordsworth (Shelley).
What a nuisance their turning us out of the club.
How horrid of you to smile !

(2) Life is life still, whatever its pangs.
He would have greeted any summons, however unreasonable the hour.

(3) The fewer men, the greater share of honour (Sh.).
Now am I in Arden, the more foole I (Sh.).
(Without *the* : "I don't understand a word of it." "More fool you ! ")

13.5₁. In all the cases hitherto mentioned we have **predicatives of being.** But there is another class, **predicatives of becoming ;** the underlying notion is " begin to be."

The number of quasi-predicatives is not very great in this class :

She fell an easy prey to his power of seduction.
His words fell flat.
The man had risen superior to his environment.
She has turned out quite a pretty girl.
She blushed (flushed, flashed) crimson with anger.
I commenced carpenter. I renounced it and commenced poet (Cowper).
Their friendship was already wearing thinner.
I didn't expect he would cut up so rough.

13.5₂. Ordinary predicatives are found with *become* and its synonyms :

He is growing old now.
She got sleepy.

Verbs of motion with weakened meaning :

I shall go mad if you don't stop that noise.
Her cheek went red as a rose.
Politeness came natural to him.
How came they acquainted (=How did they become acquainted)?

She ran wild with joy at the idea.
Our stores run low.
He fell silent.
She turned pale.
Are we turn'd Turkes? (Sh.).
The door burst (blew, flew, slid) open.
He broke loose from his bad companions.

On predicatives after passives, see **29.1₇**.

What can be a Predicative ?

13.6₁. As predicatives we find (1) adjectives, (2) pronouns, (3) substantives, (4) adverbs and prepositional groups.

Of these adjectives require no particular mention here. Pronouns as predicatives are seen, *e.g.* in *That's it* | *Who is he?* On the case-form after *it is* (*I* or *me*), see **14.3₄**. Possessive pronouns as predicatives take the primary form : *This seat is mine*.

Numerals are frequent as predicatives : *They were five in number*. A separate use is seen in

She is twenty, but looks seventeen (*i.e.* years old).

13.6₂. Substantives as predicatives generally have either the indefinite or the definite article :

He is a rascal (**17.2₄**; in the plural : They are rascals).
There is no doubt that Brown was the thief.
This is the book you were looking for.
These are the books you were looking for.

The definite article may be used in the predicative to denote one that has the typical characteristics of the class in question in a high degree (**16.6₃**).

But there are certain well-defined cases in which a substantive predicative has no article.

First, if it is a mass-word :

This is cotton, not wool (but, of course, This is the cotton you
    were looking for).
It would be great fun to baffle them.

Next, if a degree is indicated by means of *enough* or some other adverb :

> He is not philosopher enough to judge of this.
> We were asses enough to give Heligoland to Germany.
> He is more coxcomb than fool.

This should be compared with such expressions of quantity to denote degree as *He is much (somewhat) of a vagabond | He is enough of a philosopher to judge of this.* We have three possible expressions :

> He was less statesman than warrior.
> He was less a statesman than a warrior.
> He was less of a statesman than (a) warrior.

Third, if the substantive is followed by a prepositional group (with *to* or *of*), which gives a sufficient determination :

> He became Bishop of Durham.
> It was clear that the Prime Minister would be master of the situation.
> He was secretary to Lord Salisbury.
> He was heir to a fortune of two million dollars.

Sometimes the necessary determination is given by the context; whether I say " when Edward III was King " or " when Edward III was King of England," the meaning is the same. " He is a captain " means " he is one of the officers called captains." " He is Captain," *i.e.* of the particular ship or football team we are talking of.

13.7. Abstract substantives may be used as descriptive predicatives in a way that is peculiar to English ; *is* here seems to approach *has* in meaning. Examples :

> When I was your age I knew better.
> What colour are her eyes?
> She turned lead-colour.
> You are just the height I like.
> I have forgotten what relation Agnes is to you.
> He is not our sort. (This leads to the colloquial *He is a good sort* = " a good fellow ").
> It is not the least use crying; it is no good crying.
> What consequence is that to you?

13.8. Adverbs or prepositional groups may be predicatives; very often they mean practically the same thing as adjectives :

He is well, is in good health—he is healthy.
He is alive—he is living.
He is at liberty—he is free.
It is at an end—it is ended.
He is in love with her—he is very fond of her.

Hence such collocations as : he is young and in perfect health
those who are either poor or poorly.
Examples after other verbs than *be* :

He looked very well (in perfect health, on the point of death).
Don't come unless you feel up to it.
The insects came all alive as soon as you touched them.
His clothes have gone sorrowfully out-at-elbows.
When she met him, everything else became of no account.

But *well* is not a predicative in *she sings well*, where it describes her manner of singing; similarly the prepositional groups mentioned above are different from others, in which the pre-position has its local meaning : *He is in Rome, at Oxford.* Note that *at home* may be used in both ways : He is not at home (local) | He feels perfectly at home in France (predicative).

13.9. A predicative may be left out after the simple *be*, if it is sufficiently clear from the context :

Is he rich? Yes, he is. (Yes, he is; immensely.)
He was angry, but I was not.
This was very useful to him, as it had been to his father.

In other cases we must use representative *so* (**16.**3₅).

CHAPTER XIV

CASE

Cases in pronouns.—Nominative and objective.—After *than* and *as.—But, save, except.*—Case after *let.*—Relative attraction.—Predicative.—Objective in independent position.—*Himself.*—*Who.*—Second person.—Cases in substantives.—Common case and genitive. — Group-genitive. — Difficulties with pronouns.—The meaning of genitive.—Restrictions in the use of the genitive.—Lifeless things.—Measures.—Genitives as primaries.—Genitive after *of.*

Cases in Pronouns

14.1. In some pronouns, but in no other word-class, we find a distinction between the two " cases," **nominative** and **objective** :

Nominative	I	we	he	she	they	who
Objective	me	us	him	her	them	whom

By the side of *them* there is a colloquial form *'em*, from an old *hem*, which existed before the adoption of *them*.

The nominative is used as the subject and the objective as the object :

I (we, he, she, they) loved him (her, them, me, us), etc.

The objective is also used as indirect object and as object after prepositions :

He gave me (us, him, her, them) a shilling.
He spoke to me (us, him, her, them).

In these cases there can be no doubt ; but outside them things are not so simple, and there is often a good deal of natural hesitation : indeed the right use of these case forms is one of the knottiest points in English grammar.

14.2$_1$. We shall now go through some of the most important instances in which people do not feel certain which form to use.

Than is (or may be) a conjunction, and conjunctions have no influence on the case of words following them. We may form such a sentence as :

I like him better than he me (=than he likes me).

But such combinations with two members after *than* are very rare ; generally only one person or thing is compared (cf. **10.4₉**). It is quite natural to say, *e.g.*

You seem to have suffered more than I.
I like *her* no better than *him* (stress on *her* and *him*),

with the case form of the subject and object respectively. It is likewise natural to add *does* for the sake of clearness in

I like her no better than he does,

if the comparison is between *I* and *he* as subjects. Further, as there is no difference in form in a substantive following after *than* :

Mary is bigger than John.
I never saw anyone stronger than John,

and as we may hesitate between

I never saw anyone stronger than him (agreeing with *anyone*)

and

I never saw anyone stronger than he (than he is),

there is a strong inducement to use the objective after *than*, and thus to treat *than* as a preposition, especially if the verb in the main sentence is not transitive so that no misconception can arise. Sentences like

He is bigger than me,

are not only nearly universal in colloquial speech, but are found in many writers of repute :

A stone is heavie, and the sand weightie : but a fooles wrath is heavier then them both (AV.).
Our cousin, who was himself in little better circumstances than me (Goldsmith).
He was a good bit older than me (Lamb).
She was neither better bred nor wiser than you or me (Thackeray).
He is wiser than us all (Kipling).

Than is always treated as a preposition in the combination *than whom*, which is found in Shakespeare, Milton, Pope, etc., but has hardly ever been colloquial. Note that here the addition of *is* is impossible.

Belial came last, then whom a spirit more lewd Fell not from Heaven (Milton).

14.2₂. *As* likewise is a conjunction :

> I like him as well as he me.
> You seem to have suffered as much as I.
> I like her just as well as him, etc.,

parallel with the above-mentioned sentences with *than*. But we find here again a strong tendency to treat *as* as a preposition, and thus to use the objective in

> Is shee as tall as me ? (Sh.).
> You are not as good as me (Fielding).

After *such as* the nominative is often used, as a verb (*am, is, are*) is easily supplied :

> Happiness is not for such as I.
> For these, and such as we our selves (Marlowe).

14.2₃. The three synonyms *but, except* and *save* are originally prepositions and thus require the objective :

> Nobody else went but (except, save) me.

As, however, the word after these prepositions is felt as parallel with the subject of the sentence, the nominative has been in frequent use for centuries (and then *but*, etc., must be termed conjunctions) :

> Nobody else went but (except, save) I.
> No one but I ever showed him any regard.
> That no man might draw short breath to day But I and Harry Monmouth (Sh.).
> There were no other passengers that night, but we four (Dickens).
> Who but he was responsible ?
> Does any one indeed exist except I ? (Mary Shelley).
> Every one is worthy of love, except he who thinks that he is (Wilde).
> Not a man depart, Save I alone (Sh.).

14.3₁. The feeling that some word is notionally the subject of the verbal idea, is sometimes strong enough to make a speaker or writer put it in the nominative in spite of the grammatical construction which requires the objective ; thus after *let* :

> Let fortune go to hell for it, not I (Sh.).
> Let He who made thee answer that (Byron).
> Let love be blamed for it, not she, nor I (Tennyson).

Let us make a covenant, I and thou (AV.).
Let us be candid, you and I (Modern novel).

In the last two sentences we see how the feeling for the construction is strong at once (*let us*), but weakened after some time.

14.3₂. It is pretty frequent to begin a sentence with such words as *he that* (especially if the relative is the subject of the clause), even if it is afterwards found necessary to insert a pronoun in another case :

Hee that rewards me, heaven reward him (Sh.).
Hee that is without sinne among you, let him first cast a stone at her (AV.).
Cf. **9.**6₅ and **33.**4₆.

14.3₃. Inversely, a writer may begin with a pronoun in the objective because he is thinking of a relative clause in which it is the object, without at once realizing that it is afterwards required as the subject of the main sentence :

Him I accuse the city port by this hath enter'd (Sh.).
I [know] better then him I am before knowes mee (*Id.*).
Our noble Arthur, him Ye scarce can overpraise, will hear and know (Tennyson).

In **14.**2₃, 3₁, 3₂ and 3₃ we have instances of what is termed relative attraction—a grammatical phenomenon which is well known in Greek and other languages.

14.3₄. Relative attraction is also responsible for the distinction which many people will make in the case after *it is* :

It is I am in fault, is it ? (Thackeray).
It was I who was fond of her, not she of me.
It was her I was fond of, not him.
'Tis not thy wealth, but her that I esteeme (Marlowe).

Even apart from such cases as the last-mentioned (where the objective is used because the word is to be the object in a relative clause) it is and has long been natural to use the objective in the predicative :

It is me (him, her, etc.).
What would you do if you were me ?
That's mee, I warrant you (Sh.).
Be thou, spirit fierce, my spirit ! Be thou me, impetuous one (Shelley).

The reason evidently is that a predicative is felt as a kind of object ; it has the same position after the verb as the object, and there are other signs, too, that show the parallelism between these two grammatical categories (thus the possibility of a relative clause without a pronoun : " I am not the man I was," in the same way as in " I am not the man he wanted," etc.).

14.4₁. On the whole, the natural tendency in English has been towards a state in which the nominative of pronouns is used only where it is clearly the subject, and where this is shown by close proximity to (generally position immediately before) a verb, while the objective is used everywhere else.

A few quotations will show this use of the objective in an independent position :

> What could I do with Fanny ?   Me ! a poor helpless widow (Jane Austen).
> "Oh !" she [Queen Victoria] instantly replied, " *he* [Peel] began it, not *me* " (Strachey).
> Lord Raingo : We've had our little differences, you and me (Bennett).
> Another fellow, probably him who had remained below, came to the door (Stevenson).
> He could scarcely restrain the blush of the evildoer.   And him sixty ! (Bennett).
> Me ! Marry a poor girl ?   No, not me !
> Dear me !

14.4₂. If it is now the rule to say *himself* everywhere, even where people in old days said *he self*, the reason is the same ; similarly *themselves* :

> He saw it himself.
> They saw it themselves.

14.4₃. The same influence has been at work, but with a different result, in the interrogative pronoun *who*. This is always placed first and is nearly always followed immediately by the verb of the sentence ; therefore the form *who* is generalized, so that it is now practically the only form used in colloquial speech.   This has been so for at least three centuries, as shown

by innumerable quotations from Shakespeare and other Elizabethan dramatists :

> Who did you meet there?
> Who is that letter from? (=pedantic "From whom is that
> letter?").
> Who have ye there, my lordes? (Marlowe).
> Who didst thou leave to tend his Majesty? (Sh.).
> Pray you, who does the wolfe love? The lambe (Sh.).
> Who should I see there but the most artful procuress (Addison).
> Who can he take after? (Sheridan).
> But he didn't know who he was talking to (G. Eliot).

Grammarians have been so severe in blaming this that now
many people feel proud when they remember writing *whom* and
even try to use that form in speech.

14.4$_4$. In the relative pronoun, too, the form *whom* tends to
be displaced by *who*, but the tendency is not so strong as with
the interrogative pronoun, evidently because the relative as
object is not followed immediately by the verb.

It is, namely, well worth noticing that the only places in which
whom is still naturally used are those in which it comes immediately before the subject of the following verb : *than whom*
(14.2$_1$) and sentences like the following :

> Ferdinand whom they supposed is droun'd (Sh.).
> I met a man whom I thought was a lunatic (E. F. Benson).
> Let Gilbert's wife be whom she might (G. Eliot).

But then such sentences are often blamed as incorrect.

14.5. In this survey of the cases of pronouns we have left to
the end those of the second person. The old forms are :

	Singular	Plural
Nominative	thou	ye
Objective	thee	you

Thomson's use of *thee* in

> The nations not so blest as thee

must be explained according to **14.2$_2$**.

In the Middle Ages people began to use the plural forms in
addressing one person, at first respectfully to superiors, then

politely to equals, and finally to everybody. The old singulars
continued in use in some dialects and were for religious reasons
preserved among Quakers, though generally in such a way that
thee was used everywhere, most often combined with the third
person of the verb : *thee has* for *thou hast*. The old distinctions
have been kept alive in religious and poetic language ; but in
everyday life only one form survives, *you*, without any case or
number distinction.

Cases in Substantives

14.6₁. In substantives we have two cases, a **common case,**
corresponding to both nominative and objective in pronouns,
and a **genitive.**

The regular way of forming the genitive is by adding the
s-ending with its threefold pronunciation (**4.6, 5.6₃**).

> [iz] after sibilants (hissing sounds) [z, s, ʒ, ʃ] : *James's, prince's,
> judge's, witch's.*
> [z] after voiced non-sibilants : *boy's, man's, lady's, king's.*
> [s] after voiceless non-sibilants : *Smith's, count's, duke's,
> bishop's.*

14.6₂. This ending may be added to plurals, but only to such as
are not formed by means of the *s*-ending. We thus get in some
substantives the possibility of four, in others of three, distinct
forms, but in the great majority of words only two forms are
distinguished in sound, though it has been, since the eighteenth
century, habitual to make an artificial distinction in writing by
means of an apostrophe, which is placed before *s* in the genitive
singular and after *s* in the genitive plural :

Singular	common case	man	child	thief	boy	lady
	genitive	man's	child's	thief's	boy's	lady's
Plural	common case	men	children	thieves	boys	ladies
	genitive	men's	children's	thieves'	boys'	ladies'

Cf. number **20.**2.

The genitive plural of those words in which it is not distinct
from the genitive singular is used very seldom indeed : we do
not say *my aunts' husbands, our friends' jewels, these doctors'*

opinions, the servants' faces, but *the husbands of my aunts, the jewels of our friends, the opinions of these doctors, the faces of the servants.* Genitive plurals are, however, frequent in such more or less set phrases as may be considered compounds, e.g. *schoolboys' clothes, girls' friendships, a lovers' quarrel,* and in expressions of measures, etc. (**14.8₇**). On the spelling *a printer's error, many printers' errors, lady's* (or *ladies') maids,* see **21.6₄**.

14.6₃. A genitive is formed not only from substantives, but also from a few pronouns : *one's, some one's, no one's, any one's, every one's, somebody's, nobody's, anybody's, everybody's* ; further, from *he* : *his,* from *it* : *its,* and from *who* : *whose.* In other cases we have special possessive pronouns corresponding to the genitive (on the double series of forms, see **8.3₅**) ; but most pronouns (e.g. *this, that, each*) have no genitive or possessive.

If in juridical language genitives are formed like *the deceased's will* or *the accused's innocence, deceased* and *accused* must be considered substantives ; similarly in

A paralytic's senseless arm.
A black's skull will hold as much as a white's (Ruskin).

Note that in the last cases the substantival character is also shown by the possibility of forming a plural (*the blacks* and *the whites*).

But no genitive can be formed from such primary adjectives as *the poor, the Portuguese, the Swiss, the French,* etc.

14.6₄. While we have the full genitive in *James's wife, St James's Park, Keats's poems, Chambers's Journal,* the ending is left out in other names—chiefly classical—ending in a sibilant :

Phœbus' steeds.
He has done Hercules' share.
St Agnes' eve.
Pears' soap.

Note especially *for conscience' sake, for goodness' sake* (on account of the following *s*) ; before *sake* the *s* is also sometimes left out, even if the word does not in itself end in *s* : for *brevity sake, for fashion sake.*

The Group-Genitive

14.7₁. The *s* is appended to a group of words if it forms a sense unit :

> All the other people's opinions.
> Today is the heir-apparent's birthday.
> The King of Denmark's court.
> A doctor of divinity's gown.
> The man of the world's respectability.
> He said that in plenty of people's hearing.
> At about a quarter of a mile's distance.
> My daughter-in-law's jewels.
> The commander-in-chief's office.
> A man about town's chambers.
> Everybody else's rights are my wrongs (Dickens).
> Credulity is belief in somebody else's nonsense.
> At her lord and master's sudden return.
> My wife and childrens ghosts will haunt me still (Sh.).
> Beaumont and Fletcher's plays.
> We had an hour and a half's talk.
> In a year or two's time.
> The test of a man or woman's breeding is how they behave in a quarrel (Shaw).
> Mr What's-his-name's stupid remark.

We may speak of *Adam and Eve's children*, but not of *Tom and his brother's children* instead of *Tom's and his brother's children*.

Very rarely an ambiguity may arise from constructions of this kind, as in the well-known puzzle :

> The son of Pharaoh's daughter was the daughter of Pharaoh's son.

The group genitive offers (theoretically) the possibility of distinguishing the four cases in

> My son-in-law arrives.
> My son-in-law's arrival.
> My sons-in-law arrive.
> My sons-in-law's arrival—

but the last-mentioned form will practically never occur.

14.7₂. The reason why the two *s*-endings are thus treated differently is the same that has led to the retaining of such irregular plurals as *men* and *wives*, while the genitive ending is always added to the unchanged word : *man's, wife's*. If we put a word in the plural, the change affects this word only : its relation to the rest of the sentence remains the same. But the function of a genitive is that of closely connecting a word or a unit of words with the following word : therefore the *s* is always wedged in between the two and is felt as belonging nearly as much to the word following it as to the preceding one. It is even more important that the *s* should come immediately before the governing word than that it should come immediately after the word which it turns into a genitive case. Hence *the King of Denmark's castle* as against the *Kings of Denmark*, etc.

14.7₃. Shakespeare writes

This same scull, sir, was Yoricks scull, the kings jester,—

with the common case in apposition to the genitive, and the same form may still be found, especially in somewhat long combinations :

I bought it at Smith's, the bookseller in Trinity Street.

Otherwise : " at Smith, the bookseller's " or " at Smith's, the bookseller's." Anyhow, the *s* must always come last if there is a governing word to follow : " at Smith the bookseller's office."

14.7₄. With pronouns the group genitive (possessive) offers some peculiar difficulties. The following constructions, found in good English writers, may not all be acceptable to everybody :

It went to all our hearts.
You youngsters' business is your own pleasure.
Hopeless resignation had settled on some of their faces.
It is none of our faults (=the fault of none of us).
Without meaning to hurt either of your feelings.
I would not be in some of your coats for two pence (Sh.).
My minde hath bin as bigge as one of yours (Sh.).
It does not matter whose ever it is.
To represent yours and her very humble servant.
To cut your and each other's throat.
Trifle with your own and others' hearts.
For your sake and my own.

Of is used to avoid such difficulties in :
> The power of us the tribunes (Sh.).
> For the happiness of them all.
> For the sake of me and my husband.

The Meaning of Genitive

14.8₁. Genitives, and similarly possessive pronouns, indicate not only possession in the strict sense of that word, but any kind of intimate relation :

> John's house, wife, children, servants, uncle, master, enemies, life, opinions, work, books (not only those he owns, but those he has written), portrait (one representing him), etc., and similarly :
> my house . . . portrait.

From such combinations as *Tom's life and death* we are easily led to *Tom's actions, Tom's presence* and other cases of subjective genitive, which cannot be separated from the objective genitive (**30.**4, **31.**2 and 3).

14.8₂. A genitive makes the meaning of the whole combination definite : *my friend's brother* means his only brother or the one brother we have just been speaking about ; *my friend's brothers* means all his brothers, or all those indicated by the context or by the whole situation. Thus also *Dr Arnold's pupils* is definite when we say

> Dr Arnold's pupils were always diligent.

But the *of*-phrase is preferred in

> We were pupils of Dr Arnold :

because the predicative is indefinite, so that this means the same as

> We were some of Dr Arnold's pupils.

Restrictions in the Use of the Genitive

14.8₃. The use of the genitive is in English comparatively restricted, and a prepositional group with *of* is very extensively used in virtually the same sense :

> This clergyman's young wife=the young wife of this clergyman.
> Your neighbour's house=the house of your neighbour.

The *of*-combination has so far prevailed that there are very few cases where a genitive cannot be replaced by it, and it is even used to supplant a possessive pronoun in such stock phrases as *not for the life of me.* *Of* is often employed to avoid tacking on the *s* to too long a string of words, as in

> He is the son of the well-known politician whose death was announced the other day.
> Will Wimble's is the case of many a younger brother of a great family (Addison).
> The wife of a clergyman of the Church of England (Thackeray).
> On the occasion of the coming of age of the youngest son of a wealthy member of Parliament,—

where most people will resent the iteration of *of*'s less than they do the repeated *s*'s in

> He is my wife's first husband's only child's godfather.

Cf. **14.6₂** on the genitive plural.

While the *s*-genitive is placed before, the *of*-combination comes after the word they determine.

14.8₄. The genitive is chiefly used with the names of human beings. With names of animals the *of*-phrase is generally preferred : *the head of our white horse* is better than *our white horse's head, the feathers of this bird* better than *this bird's feathers.* The genitive is, however, frequent in combinations like *a fox's tail, an owl's nest, a cat's paw,* which may be considered a kind of compound (= the tail of a fox, etc.).

We also say

> I saw something white with long ears like a cat's (to avoid the clumsy : those of a cat).

With names of lifeless things the *of*-phrase is the rule :

> In the middle of the town.
> At the bottom of the page.
> At the end of her power.
> The hospitals of London.
> The door of the room.
> The roof of the house.
> The foot of a mountain.

Such combinations as *a ship's doctor* (*carpenter*) must be considered compounds (cf. *statesman*, which is written as one word).

The genitive of lifeless things is used before *sake* : *for variety's sake*, and in a certain number of traditional fixed combinations :

> At his wit's (or wits') end (From the Bible).
> Know something at one's fingers' ends.
> From week's end to week's end.
> Out of harm's way.
> I was never in luck's way long.
> To his heart's content.

These may be regarded approximately as compounds.

14.8₅. When a country is thought of politically as a living being, the genitive is frequently used :

> England's interests in India.
> We should be at Russia's mercy.
> He was his country's pride.

In these cases we also speak of a country as *she* (**19.6₅**). If the country is looked upon from a purely geographical point of view, *of* is used : *the boundaries of Switzerland*, etc.

Note also the genitives in :

> An entire understanding of Heaven's ways (Ruskin ;=God's).
> Nature's purpose in giving wings to bats.

14.8₆. Poets use the genitive very often where *of* would be used in prose :

> In my minds eye (Sh.).
> After lifes fitful fever (Sh.).
> Thou know'st not golds effect (Sh.).
> To know mortal nature's nothingness (Byron).
> And the sorrow's crown of sorrow is rememb'ring happier things (Tennyson).

In the same way in higher literary style :

> We talk much of money's worth (Ruskin).
> Setting out upon life's journey (Stevenson).

Some journalists are inordinately fond of this genitive.

14.8₇. The genitive is, however, idiomatic in indications of measure (of space and time) :

> At a boat's length from the ship.
> A stone's throw from the house.

The door stood open, though only by a hair's breadth.
A good day's work.
A two hours' walk.
The seven years' war.
I had a good afternoon's rest (but in a different sense : afternoon
tea).
Our last year's supply.
He gave six months' notice.

A genitive of words denoting time is also found in

Today's post.
Yesterday's news.
Let us consult upon to morrowes business (Sh.).

A time-indication is rendered vague by the use of the genitive
followed by *time* : an hour's time ; I'll be back in three weeks'
time, etc.

Genitives as Primaries

14.9₁. The proper sphere of a genitive is that of an adjunct (a
secondary). But a genitive may also stand as a primary, thus
very frequently when a substantive has just been mentioned :

Render unto Cesar the things which are *Cesars* : and unto God
the things that are *Gods* (AV.).
His own fortune was lost; *his dead wife's* remained.
Threads that seemed no thicker than *a spider's*.

14.9₂. But no substantive is previously mentioned in cases
like the following idiomatic uses of the genitive :

I bought this at *the grocer's*.
St Paul's is one of the principal sights of London.
A fellow of *St John's*.

Note the use of an adjective belonging to a substantive which
is not expressed :

The empty appearance which *a well-managed* confectioner's
always has at night.

14.9₃. The genitive is also a primary in combinations like
" an old friend of *Tom's*," and the same is true of the possessive
pronoun in " that old friend of *yours*." In this idiom *of* makes

it possible to combine two ideas which cannot be immediately joined, for it is impossible to say " an old Tom's friend " or " a Tom's old friend," etc. Examples with other pronominal adjuncts :

> Any friend of my son's is welcome here.
> This is no fault of Frank's.
> That long nose of Tom's.
> That tender heart of hers.
> This life of ours (where Shakespeare has the archaic " this our life ").
> What business is that of yours? (Here *of yours* belongs to *what business.*)

By means of this idiom we may make a distinction between " a portrait of the king " (representing him) and " a portrait of the king's " (belonging to him), and similarly between " an impartial estimate of Tennyson " and " an impartial estimate of Tennyson's."

Some of the examples given show conclusively that *of* cannot here be taken in its partitive sense (as in *some of us*) : it is in fact appositional, as it is in *the City of Rome* (= the City which is Rome), *the three of us* (= the three who are we), *a stripling of a page* (= a stripling who is a page), *that clever little wretch of a Rebecca, her old sharper of a father*, etc.

PERSON

Three persons.—Substitutes for pronouns.—Indirect speech.—
Vocative.—Imperative.—Verbs.—Difficulties.—Generic person.

15.1. When in grammar we speak of the three persons, we mean the distinction between :

the speaker : the first person,
the person (or persons) spoken to : the second person, and
what is neither speaker nor spoken to : the third person.

It is easy to see that this grammatical terminology has nothing to do with the ordinary use of the word person : " the horse runs " and " the sun shines " are in the third person, and if in a fable we make the horse say " I run " or the sun say " I shine," both sentences are in the first person.

15.2$_1$. The distinction applies primarily to the " personal pronouns " : first person *I*, second person *you* (and the old *thou*) ; to the third person belong not only the personal pronouns *he, she, it*, but everything else : *the man* goes, *who* goes, *everybody* goes, etc.

The plural *we* means I (the speaker) + someone else or some others. It is therefore often necessary to specify who else is included : *we gentlemen, we Yorkshiremen, we Europeans*, etc. In **27.4$_2$** we shall see an occasional distinction according as the person addressed is or is not included. On the plural of the second person see **14.5**.

Some of us, most of us is, strictly speaking, in the third person ; therefore we should say

Most of us lost their heads.

But it is, at any rate, excusable, if the speaker includes himself, to say :

Most of us lost our heads.

Similarly with *most of you*.

15.2₂. Various motives (modesty, pride, jocularity) may lead to the use of substitutes for *I*, such as *yours truly*, *your humble servant* (from the subscription in letters), *this child*, *the present writer*, or one's proper name, as in

> Speake, Cæsar is turn'd to hear (Sh., = "I am").

Present company may be used instead of *we* or *us*.

Similarly we have substitutes for the second person : the paternal *we* (" How are we this morning? ") and especially deferential words like *your excellency, your worship, your Majesty,* —further *my darling* (" Is my darling ill? "), and, the most curious of all, *it* in addressing a child; this is used even by Lady Macbeth in addressing her husband.

15.3. In indirect speech persons are naturally shifted according to circumstances : " I hate you " thus may become " He said that he hated me," or " her," or " You said that you hated me," etc.

15.4₁. Any name may be made into the second person, as in
> Come here, John !
> I beg your pardon, Miss Langton.
> What do you think, Dr Cassell?
> Anything else, sir?

Here we say that *John, Miss Langton, Dr Cassell* and *sir* are vocatives, but in English the vocative is not, as in some languages, a separate case.

15.4₂. Any imperative is virtually in the second person, even if seemingly addressed to a " third person," as in
> Oh, please, someone go in and tell her.
> Go one and cal the Jew into the court (Sh.).

This is shown by the addition in
> And bring out my hat, somebody, will you (Dickens).

Someone, one, and *somebody* in these sentences mean " one of you present."

15.5₁. In many languages the distinction between the three persons is found not only in the pronouns (primaries), but also in the verbs (secondaries), where it does not logically belong.

This was the case to a great extent in Old English, but has
generally been given up in Modern English, where we say
indiscriminately :

I, we, you, he, they can, may, must, will,—called, spoke, etc.,

thus with most auxiliaries and with all preterits.

The only survivals of personal distinctions in verbs are the
following :

In the present tense the third person singular of most verbs
ends in -s (**23.**1$_4$).

From the verb *be* we have in the present the forms *I am, you
are, he is* (plural *are* in all persons).

The present subjunctive (**27.**3) is always like the base and
thus does not add -s in the third person.

In the second person we have forms in -t or -st with the old
pronoun *thou* : *art, wert* or *wast, wilt, shalt, canst, mayst, do(e)st,
didst, couldest* or *couldst, speakest, callest, calledst,* etc.

The auxiliaries to express futurity and conditioned unreality
generally vary according to the person : *I shall go, I should go,*
but *you (he) will go, would go* ; see Chaps. XXV and XXVI.

15.5$_2$. How great an advantage is gained from the freedom
from personal inflexions in the vast majority of English verb-
forms can best be appreciated by comparing the ease with
which sentences are formed like :

Neither my brother nor I saw it.
Neither my brother nor I can have seen it—

and the difficulty in saying

Neither my brother nor I am (? is, ? are) rich.

A few quotations will show how various writers have cut this
Gordian knot :

Nor God, nor I, delights in perjur'd men (Sh.).
Neither she nor I were wet (Charlotte Brontë).
Neither you nor I is the ideal man (Walpole).

Similar difficulties are seen in the following sentences :

And none but thou shalt be my paramour (Marlowe).
Heaven, and not wee, have safely fought to day (Sh.).
I am a poet, who mean nobody any harm (Cowper).

> The presumption that I, the person who now write and think, am
>   that one mind (Shelley).
> It is you yourself that is hunted down (Stevenson).

With the last sentence compare " It isn't you that is wrong,
but John," in which the third person in the verb may be justified
by the fact that the meaning is " the person that is wrong, is
John, not you," cf. on *it is*, **34.1₄**.

15.5₃. After *your excellency* and the other substitutes for the
second person the verb is put in the third person, but after
myself, yourself it is generally made to agree with the person
meant : *myself am, yourself are*.   Still, Shakespeare sometimes
has the third person : *my self hath, your self is*, because *self* was
felt to be a substantive with the possessive pronoun as an
adjunct (formerly written as a separate word).

15.6₁. We may use the term **" generic person "** for what
vaguely comprises all persons (French *on*, Scandinavian and
German *man*).   In English *one* is used in this sense, often as a
kind of disguised *I* :

> One would think she was mad (One is tempted to think . . .).
> One might have expected a politer answer from him.
> Why, may one ask ?
> One may smile, and smile and be a villaine (Sh.).
> One must always be on one's best behaviour there.
> One must make one's discoveries for oneself, mustn't one ?

In cases like the last two sentences, Elizabethan writers often
continued generic *one* by means of *his, himself, he*, and this is
still done in Scotland and America, *e.g.*

> I know, the more one sickens, the worse at ease he is (Sh.).
> One does not stickle about his vehicle (Carlyle).
> One always does himself and his audience an injustice when he
>   speaks merely for the sake of speaking (Amr.).

This generic *one* is weakly stressed and is distinct from the
stressed *one* in cases like :

> One danced with his sister, and another with his cousin.

Colloquially *a fellow, a chap*, etc., Scotch *a body*, have often
the same generic sense as *one* :

> What is a fellow to do under such circumstances ?
> Gin (if) a body kiss a body, need a body cry ?

15.6₂. Instead of the formal *one* the personal pronouns, *we* and *you*, are often used in familiar speech with the same meaning of generic person ; an emotional colouring is particularly strong in *you* with its more or less apparent appeal to the person spoken to :

> We live to learn.
> You never can tell.
> Could you expect more than that?
> You cannot eat your pudding and have it.
> [=One . . . one's . . .]

15.6₃. Parallel to this use of *you* =" one " we have an indefinite use of *your* with no real reference to the person addressed, very often with a tinge of contempt :

> Your marriage comes by destinie, your cuckow sings by kinde (Sh.).
> None of your live languages for Miss Blimber (Dickens).
> Some young aristocrat, one of your idle insolent rich.

CHAPTER XVI

DEFINITE PRONOUNS

Division of pronouns.—Pronouns of contextual indication (Personal pronouns).—Ambiguities.—Unspecified. *they*.—The *self*-pronouns.—*It*.—Preparatory *it*.—Unspecified *it*.—Emphatic *it*.—Pronouns of pointing: *this, that, yon*.—Representative *that*.—Indefinite *that*.—*Hereafter*, etc.—*Thus*.—*So*.—The definite article.—Demonstrative *the*.—The article of complete determination.—Words without article.—Proper names.—Times and dates.—The typical.—Distributive.—Languages.—Diseases.—No article.—Repetition.—The article of incomplete determination.—Adjectives with proper names.—The pronoun of identity (*same*).—The pronoun of similarity (*such*).

16.1₁. In this and the following two chapters we shall take each pronoun separately and deal with such questions as do not find their natural place in other chapters (Case, Person, Number, Question, Clause). The classification here adopted differs in some respects from that in **7.**4. Relative pronouns have been classed among definites : *who* in *the man who knows* is just as definite as *he* and differs from it chiefly by serving to connect a clause to the main sentence. On the other hand, *who* in *Who knows?* is indefinite and the only difference from *somebody* lies in the request for an answer.

Pronouns are divided into the following classes.

A. Pronouns of definite indication :

1. Pronouns of contextual indication. (Personal pronouns, **16.1.**)
2. Pronouns of pointing. (*This, that, yonder, thus, so,* **16.**2–3.)
3. The definite article. (*The,* **16.**4–8.)
4. The pronoun of identity. (*Same,* **16.**9.)
5. The pronoun of similarity. (*Such,* **16.**9₄.)
6. Pronouns of connexion. (Relative pronouns, Chaps. XXXIII and XXXIV.)

B. Pronouns of indefinite indication :

1. The pronoun of indefinite unity. (*One,* **17.**1.)
2. The indefinite article. (*An, a,* **17.**1₂–5.)

3. The pronoun of difference. (*Other*, **17.**6.)
4. The pronoun of discretion. (*Certain*, **17.**7.)
5. The pronoun of unspecified quantity. (*Some*, **17.**8.)
6. The pronouns of indifference. (*Any, either*, **17.**9.)
7. Indefinite pronouns requesting a solution. (Interrogative pronouns, **28.**5.)

C. Pronouns of totality:

1. Positive. (*All, both, every, each*, **18.**1–4.)
2. Negative. (*No, none, neither*, **18.**5.)

The definitions implied in these names do not cover all the various uses of each pronoun, but only the most typical ones. In some places it has been thought expedient to treat pronominal adverbs together with the corresponding pronouns.

Pronouns of Contextual Indication
(Personal Pronouns)

16.1$_2$. The indication contained in *I, we, you* is always quite definite, determined by the situation.

The same is true of *he, she, they* in the great majority of cases : the situation and the context show exactly what is meant in each sentence in which these words occur.

This is true even in such seemingly ambiguous cases as :

Jack was very respectful to Tom, and took off his hat when he met him.

Jack was very rude to Tom, and knocked off his hat when he met him—

his hat referring in one sentence to Jack's and in the other to Tom's.

Similarly there is really little danger of misunderstanding *it* in :

If the baby does not thrive on raw milk, boil it.

Nevertheless, it is best to be very careful about one's pronouns.

In the spoken language, stress often removes any doubt as to the meaning ; thus *he* must be stressed twice in :

Shelley is the very reverse of all this. Where Wordsworth is strong, he is weak ; where Wordsworth is weak, he is strong (Mill).

Theoretically, a sentence like :

John told Robert's son that he must help him—

is capable of six different meanings.

16.1₃. Instead of referring back to some one previously mentioned *he* is defined by a following relative clause in

He who can't keep a penny will never have many—

where *he* is virtually synonymous with *anyone*.

Today the plural of this *he who* is *those who* rather than *they who*.

16.1₄. *They* is used without any reference to previously mentioned persons (" unspecified *they* ") in

They say that he drank himself to death.

16.1₅. The *self*-pronouns (which we have seen in the reflexive function in **11.**5) are used to point a contrast :

The Kaiser himself believed in an early victory.
Never leave to others what you can do yourself.
There was no one present but my brother Jack and myself.
I wasn't quite myself, your Lordship, when I beat her.
A girl who has no one to think for her is obliged to think for herself.

16.1₆. *It* generally refers back to something previously mentioned :

I took the book from the table and placed it on the shelf.
Where is the horse? It is in the stable.
He took the bottle from out the cupboard : I saw it myself (*i.e.* his taking the bottle).

But *it* has also another very important function, namely as " preparatory it " to represent a whole group of words which it would not be convenient to put in the place required by the ordinary rules of word-order without causing ambiguity or obscurity. The group itself (an infinitive with its complements, a clause, etc.) then comes afterwards in " extraposition."

This *it* may be the subject.

It is wrong to lie.
It rests with you to decide.
It was splendid that you could come to-day.

It occurred to me that he might be ill.
It seems to me that he must be wrong.
It is curious how often one sees them together.
It is strange the number of mistakes he always makes.
It is no use trying to evade the question.
It does not matter whether he sees us or not.

Or it may be the object, or part of the object :

We have it in our power to do great harm or great good.
I think it wrong to lie.   I look upon it as wrong to lie.
I always make it a rule to verify all quotations.
He thought it a pity that Mary should be absent just then.
I think it rather dangerous your venturing out there.
I looked upon it as very awkward that he changed the subject
just then.
You must see to it that the children get up in time.

16.1₇. In all sentences mentioned so far *it* refers to something
specified, whether a thing, an action, or an idea.   But in a great
many cases *it* is used in such a way that it is not possible in this
way to point to something specifically referred to.   Examples
of this " unspecified it " occur in the first place in sentences
descriptive of natural phenomena :

It rains (snows, freezes, clears up, etc.).
It is cold today.   It has been cloudy all day.

Next, of time :

It is half-past six.
It was a long time before he came to.
It is Sunday tomorrow.

And of space :

How far is it to Charing Cross ?
It is a long way to Tipperary.

16.1₈. Further, in a great many idiomatic phrases as the
object of verbs :

We must have it out some day.
That is coming it rather strong.
I say, you are going it !
I will give it him hot.
If you are found out, you will catch it.

This use of *it* is particularly frequent with verbs that are

derived from substantives without the addition of any ending :
here it serves to mark out the verbal function distinctly :

> We can walk it quite easily (bus it, cab it, foot it).
> To lord it, queen it.
> We would sleep out on fine nights; and hotel it, and inn it, and
> pub it when it was wet.
> Ile devill-porter it no further (Sh.).

Finally, this unspecified *it* is found in numerous prepositional
phrases, *e.g.* :

> Make a day of it.
> Make a clean breast of it.
> There is nothing for it but to submit.
> You are in for it.

A comic effect is produced by the two meanings of *it* in

> He never opens his mouth but he puts his foot in it.

16.1₉. From the use in children's games, where " John's it "
means that he is the one who is to catch the others, etc., we
have the derived emphatic usage in recent slang, where *he's it*
(sometimes written with a capital *It*) means that he is (or imagines
himself) a very important personage.

Pronouns of Pointing

16.2₁. English has (or had) three demonstrative pronouns for
three different distances from the speaker :

> this that yon (yonder).

These may be said to correspond roughly to the three persons,
I, you, and he. Correspondingly we have the three adverbs of
place :

> here there yonder (yon),

while for time we have only two adverbs :

> now then.

Yon is obsolete and *yonder* obsolescent in Standard English
(and this is even more true of the third form *yond*), so that we
have now two categories only, *this, here, now* for what is nearer,
and *that, there, then* for what is farther away.

It is worth noting that the vowels in *this* and *that*, *here* and *there* agree with the general tendency found in many languages to denote " near " by high-front vowels and " far " by lower and more retracted vowels, cp. French *ici* and *là* and the play of the vowels in *zigzag*, *tittle-tattle*, *riff-raff* and many similar popular formations.

16.2₂. The first use of *this* or *that* is to point at what is nearer or farther away in space ; they are often accompanied by a pointing gesture :

> First on this side, then on that.
> I like this cake better than that one.
> You must do it like this.

Sometimes *this* may stand by itself= " this place " :

> Get out of this, please !

Note *this* in introducing a person :

> This is my sister Ann,—

and *that* in sentences like :

> Come here, that's a good boy.

16.2₃. In speaking of time *this* refers to the present, though not in the narrowest sense : *this morning* and *this evening* mean " the morning and evening of today " ; the former therefore may refer to the past, and the latter to a future time.   Similarly *this spring*, *this autumn*= " the spring, the autumn of this year." Cf. further :

> He has been dead this fortnight (these two years).
> I have not seen your mother this long time.

(In these two we have a past time extending to the present.)

> I shall not be ready this half-hour yet.
> One of these days he will be famous.

(In these, inversely, a future time extending from the present.)

With certain prepositions *this* may be used by itself (as a primary)= the present time :

> Long before this he was a respected citizen.
> They must have arrived by this.

16.2₄. *This* often refers to what is following, and *that* to what precedes :

> This above all : to thine owne selfe be true (Sh.).
> To be, or not to be, that is the question (Sh.).
> This is what he said : "How could he be such a fool!"
> "How could he be such a fool!" That was what he said.
> Is that all?

That, similarly referring to what precedes, is also seen in combinations like :

> "I rather like Jack," she said as soon as that young gentleman had left the room.

Note also the supplementary description in :

> I had to bolt, and that at once.
> I had only seen her once, and that six years ago, when we were children.
> For years, and those the most critical of her life, she lived at Oxford.
> I met Mr Bennett yesterday,—the father, that is, not the son.

Here we may mention the recent (originally American) idiomatic use of *at that* in a restrictive addition :

> It is only a snapshot, and a poor one at that.
> Then a nigger will be lynched—probably the wrong nigger at that.

16.2₅. The idea of pointing (demonstrative, properly, or deictic, as learned grammarians say) is totally obliterated when *that* is purely representative of something previously mentioned :

> He had squandered away his own fortune and that of his younger sister.
> And pity from thee more dear Than that from another (Shelley).
> Her face was now sadly different from that which we used to admire at home.
> The dialects of America are not so widely apart as those spoken in the mother country.

That serves to represent (more or less emphatically) a previously mentioned action, or to stand for a predicative (even if the subject is in the plural) :

> Did he work in the fields?—Yes, he did that occasionally.
> The Duke hath banished me.—That he hath not (Sh.).
> In sooth Ile know your business, Harry, that I will (Sh.).

And look at him now, old, not exactly feeble yet—no, not that
yet, not quite.

All men my brothers ? Nay, thank Heaven, that they are not !

Cf. below *so*, which is weaker.

16.2₆. Nor has *that* (*those*) any demonstrative force when it
stands before a relative clause or other similar adjunct, *e.g.*

That man that hath a tongue, I say, is no man
If with his tongue he cannot win a woman (Sh.).

Never tell a woman that which is not interesting enough to magnify
into a secret.

(Instead of this neutral *that which* we most often say *what*.)

Those that think must govern those that toil (Goldsmith).

Interpreters for the benefit of those unacquainted with the
language of the country.

16.2₇. *That* and *those* may even be indefinite and mean nearly
" something, some people " before a relative clause, especially
after *there is, there are* :

There was that in her manner which prepared us for what was
coming.

But I have that within, which passeth show (Sh.).

There are those who believe it, though others are more sceptical.

16.2₈. A similarly indefinite meaning results when *this and that*
joined together means various (things, etc.) ; in the same way
here and there means " at various places," and *now and then* " at
various times." An extension is seen in : *this, that, and the
other* (thing, etc.).

16.2₉. Alongside of prepositional groups such as *after this,
after that, in this, in that,* etc., we have compounds like *hereafter,
thereafter, herein, therein,* etc. The only one of these compounds
that is frequently used in colloquial speech is *therefore.*

16.3₁. Corresponding to *this* and *that* we have the two " pronominal adverbs " *thus* and *so*. *Thus* has a stronger demonstrative force than *so*, and generally indicates manner, = " in
this way," either with back-reference or pointing to what follows.
In two derived senses it indicates consequence (= " therefore,
accordingly ") and, more rarely, degree, chiefly in the combination *thus much.*

16.3₂. The uses of *so* are much more varied and cannot all be dealt with here. If used of manner *so* is weaker than *thus* ; see, for instance, its use at the end of an enumeration : . . . *and so on.*

It so happened that John was absent that day.
I don't care for the so-called classics.

16.3₃. In the beginning of a sentence *so* often comes to mean " therefore, accordingly " :

He was ill, so he could not come.

16.3₄. *So* often denotes degree or extension, (*a*) with back-reference, (*b*) with reference to something following :

(*a*) So far, everything was all right.
He got so far, but not further.
So much for his ancestors. Now as to his education . . .
He cannot come. So much the better.
He looks upon literature as so much rubbish, and upon friends as so many encumbrances.
Only a mile or so.

(*b*) The weather was not so bad as we expected.
He was so excited that he forgot his manners.
I got up so early that I was able to catch the first train.
I got up early so as to be able to catch the first train.

In familiar speech *so* is often used without supplement and thus comes to mean pretty much the same thing as " very " :

I'm so glad you've come at last.
We saw ever so many mummies at the Museum.

16.3₅. *So* is very often representative of something previously mentioned. Thus it stands for a predicative :

Is he rich? Yes, immensely so.
He was not angry at first, but became so after a little while.
She is pretty well, and we hope she will keep (remain) so.
There is nothing either good or bad, but thinking makes it so (Sh.).
They had many scruples, only they did not call them so.

So represents a whole idea (nexus) after such verbs as *think, suppose, expect, say,* etc.

We shall see him there, at least I hope (expect, believe, think) so.
Is he ill? I am afraid so.
I didn't know he would come. Why, I told you so.

Compare also such sentences as :

He puzzles me very much.　Why so?
He comes here very seldom, and if so, never without good reason.
He admired Jane very much.　Not so his brother.

16.3₆. Representative *so* placed first serves to confirm a previous statement :

He seems a clever fellow.　So he is.
The rain has stopped.　So it has (So I see.　So it seems).

If in this case the verb follows immediately after *so*, the implication is ' also ' (**10.**4₈) :

He is very poor, and so are all his brothers.

16.3₇. Note also *do* with *so* to represent a previously mentioned verb :

He had promised to pay, but he failed to do so (he hasn't done so, he couldn't or wouldn't do so; instead of doing so he left the country).

So, however, is only used after the infinitive, participle, and gerund of *do*, otherwise this verb suffices in itself :

He had promised to pay, but he didn't (he never does).

Nor is *so* used after the auxiliaries if these stand alone :

He has promised to pay, but he can't (won't, etc.).

The Definite Article

16.4₁. *The* may be considered a weakened *that*. A remnant of the *t* is seen in the dialectal form *the t'other* (originally *that-other*).

As *the* is phonetically a weaker *that*, its meaning also is weakened : instead of pointing out it serves to designate or single out. *The* is generally called the definite article : a better name would be the defining or determining article.　It has really two distinct functions, that of determining in itself, and that of determining in connexion with a following word or words containing the essential specification.　We therefore speak of **the article of complete,** and **the article of incomplete determination.**

In a few combinations *the* seems to have a comparatively full demonstrative force ·

> Lend you money?   No, I shall do nothing of the kind (=of that kind).
>
> I am occupied for the moment (=for this moment, which is not said).
>
> Compare the Scotch : *the day*= today.

16.4₂. The article has the emphatic form [ði·] in cases like this :

> He was one of the first, if not *the* first, to use a typewriter.

This emphatic *the* has often the meaning ' the best, the proper, the real ' :

> Fox used to say, " I never want *a* word, but Pitt never wants *the* word."

Though *the* has virtually the same meaning in the familiar sayings :

> That's the thing.
>
> You wanted one particular key : is this the one ?—

there is no necessity to mark this by emphatic pronunciation.

The Article of Complete Determination

16.4₃. The chief use of the article is to indicate the person or thing that at the moment is uppermost in the mind of the speaker and presumably in that of the hearer too.   Thus it recalls what has just been mentioned :

> Once upon a time there lived an old tailor in a small village.   The tailor was known all over the village as " Old Harry " . . .

Or else the whole situation is sufficient to show what is meant :

> Shut the door, please.
>
> Which way is the wind?
>
> He is on the river every Sunday [if spoken in London, the Thames is meant].
>
> Our children are not allowed to play in the street.
>
> The doctor said that the patient was likely to recover.
>
> Who is to take the chair to-night?

While *king* in itself may be applied to hundreds of individuals, living and dead, *the king* is as definite as a proper name : if we

are in the middle of a story or a conversation about some particular king, then it is he that is meant, otherwise it means ' our
king,' the present king of the country in which we are living.
But the situation may change, and then the value of the definition
contained in the article changes automatically. " The king is
dead. Long live the King ! " In the second sentence the same
two words refer to the legal successor of the man who was
mentioned in the first.

The necessary specification is similarly obvious in combinations
like *the sun, the moon, the City*, etc.

16.5₁. The article is used more sparingly in English than in
many other languages ; it is used chiefly when the word without
it would not be easily understood as sufficiently specialized.
There is therefore a strong tendency to do without it in many
cases where the individualization is self-evident. Examples are
father, mother, baby, uncle, nurse, cook and other names of persons
in familiar intercourse ; further, names of meals :

> Breakfast is at eight.
> He came immediately after lunch.
> I am afraid we shall be late for dinner.

But the article is necessary in other cases, for instance in
speaking of the quality of a meal :

> The dinner was a very frugal one.

16.5₂. Names of public institutions are used without the
article if their purpose is thought of rather than the actual
building :

> Go to church (but : we walked to the church and there took the
> bus).
> School is over.
> He was sent to prison for his offence.
> Scrooge's name was good upon 'Change (Dickens).

In the same way *town* is used without the article after certain
prepositions (stay in town, go into town, return from town) when
we speak of the town to which the person concerned stands in

personal relation : otherwise, for instance, when a town has been mentioned more incidentally the article is required :

He came to the town in the morning.

A similar rule obtains with regard to the use of the article with *bed* (go to bed, stay in bed, etc.) and *table* (we were still at table when he arrived), but on the other hand :

He found the purse in the bed, and not on the table, as we expected.

Compare also :

He went to sea (*i.e.* became a sailor).
He went down to the sea and sat there for an hour.

16.5₃. As a rule, proper names need no article, as they are definite enough in themselves. But it is impossible to draw a hard-and-fast line of demarcation between proper names and common names : it might be said that the articleless words mentioned in the last few paragraphs are treated in this way because they stand as a kind of proper name. The more a composite name of a locality is felt to be chosen quite arbitrarily, the more undoubted is its right to be treated as a proper name ; hence we have no article in names like *Gower Street, Gloucester Square, Shaftesbury Avenue,* etc. Nor is there any article in *Newcastle, New York, New South Wales, Great Britain, British East Africa,* and similar geographical names. On the other hand, *the Dover Road* has the article, because the name is still felt as meaning the road leading to Dover. But *Finchley Road* and *Edgware Road* in London generally have no article though they really lead to Finchley and Edgware. In such cases convenience plays a part, and consistency is not to be expected. *Tower Bridge* generally, and *London Bridge* and *Westminster Bridge* always, do without the article. Similarly, *Regent's Park* in London, *Central Park* in New York; but Londoners hesitate between *Green Park* and *the Green Park.* If *the Strand* and *the Mall* in London keep their article, it is probably because, unlike other names of streets, they are not composite. On the use of the article when an adjective qualifies a proper name that is complete in itself, see **16.8₄.**

It is only natural that there should be some inconsistencies in the use of the article or no article where a word might or might not be considered a proper name; compare thus the following instances :

God—the Lord.
Satan—the Devil.
Scripture, Holy Writ—the Bible.
The divell can cite Scripture for his purpose (Sh.).

16.5₄. When a plural is formed of a proper name, the article is required because it ceases to be a proper name in the fullest sense : *the Plantagenets, the Stuarts, the Tullivers* (cf. the possibility of speaking of *a few Tullivers*). In the genitive the article is the only audible sign of the number : *the Miss Tullivers' arrival*, as against *Miss Tulliver's arrival*.

In accordance with this rule we have the article with geographical names with plural form : *the West Indies, the Netherlands, the Alps, the Hebrides*, etc.

16.5₅. English titles prefixed to a name have no article : *Mr Smith, Dr Johnson, King George*, etc. But *Lady* sometimes takes the article, and so do some foreign titles : *the Archduke Ferdinand, the Czar Peter*, etc. This, of course, is different from the use of the article in *the historian Green* as distinguished from *the philosopher Green* or *Green the philosopher*; cf. *St John the Baptist*—where the substantive is not a title.

16.5₆. In the names of countries, imitation of foreign usage is sometimes stronger than the English practice of having no article : *the Tyrol, the Sudan*; in some cases the article may be due to the ellipsis of a common name which was formerly always added : *the Sahara* (desert), *the Crimea* (peninsula). *The Congo* may have the article because the name originally denotes the river.

The names of oceans have the article because they are still felt as adjectives to which the word *Sea* or *Ocean* may be added : *the Baltic, the Atlantic, the Pacific*. River-names have the article : *the Thames* (cf. the frequent addition : *the Thames river* or *the river Thames*), *the Severn, the Rhine* (cf. German *der Rhein*) ;

except in such names of towns as *Newcastle-on-Tyne, Stratford-on-Avon.*

16.5₇. The ellipsis of a common name accounts for the use of the article in cases like *the Bedford* (hotel), *the George* (inn), *the Holborn* (restaurant), *the Shaftesbury* (theatre), *the Marshalsea* (prison), *companion of the Bath* (order), *the Cornhill* (magazine), etc. In this way a distinction is made between the town *Bedford* and the person *George*, on the one hand, and the houses named after them, on the other hand.

16.6₁. Names of periods of time and dates are often used without the definite article :

> March was a cold month.
> He was married in June 1920 (but : in the June of 1920).
> If winter comes, can spring be far behind (Shelley).
> He will be here before Christmas.

On Sunday generally means ' next Sunday ' or ' last Sunday,' and like these expressions has relation to the present time, but when a more remote period is referred to, the article is used :

> He arrived on a Thursday, and already on the Saturday he could report that everything had been settled.

Similarly, *the next Sunday* and *the last Sunday* have not the same reference to the present time as *next Sunday* and *last Sunday*.

If we say *night came* or *day broke* without the article, it may be because *night* and *day* are here looked upon as mass-words (**21.**1) ; cf. " Twilight was coming on," and further, *all day, all night* (but : *all the evening*). We say *at night*, but *in the evening*.

16.6₂. On the use of *the* with superlatives and the difference between *most* and *the most*, see **22.7₄** and **22.8₂**.

The use of *the* with a predicative has been dealt with in **13.**6.

16.6₃. The article in *to play the fool, act the lover*, etc., originates from the old character-plays, where it was usual for one actor to have always the same kind of parts. Similarly with *look* :

> I made shift to look the happy lover.

This leads to the use of the definite article to denote ' the typical ' whatever it is, chiefly in the predicative :

> He is quite the gentleman.
> She was the perfect girl, the perfect companion.
> Mr Lecky is always the historian, never the partisan (MacCarthy).
> Eustacia was no longer the goddess but the woman to him, a being to fight for, support (Hardy).
> Cecil Rhodes, an almost unique combination of the financier and the idealist.

This perhaps explains the current idioms :

> He is not quite the thing today.
> We have to do the civil to him.

16.6₄. In the chapter on Number (**21.5**) we shall see the use of words in a generic sense with and without the article in the singular and in the plural.

It is perhaps to be explained from the generic use that we say :

> He plays the violin (the piano, flute, etc.).

But if the object of the play is the name of a game, there is no article :

> He plays football (chess, etc., thus also cards).

Here *football*, etc., is perhaps to be considered as a kind of mass-word.

16.6₅. The distributive use of *the* (= each) may be considered a kind of generic singular :

> It sells at ten shillings the bushel.
> He punished me ; not two or three times in the week, nor once or twice in the day, but continually.
> We buy them by the hundred.
> She sat by the hour by his bedside.

16.6₆. The names of languages are generally used without the article :

> He talks (writes, understands) French.

Here the language is considered a mass-word. But it is customary to say " translated from the French," probably because one says " from the French of Maupassant," etc. Cf.

also " What is the French for cauliflower ? " (=the French word or expression).

16.6₇. With names of diseases there is a good deal of vacillation ; but " he suffers from gout (measles, scarlatina, etc.) " is nowadays more usual than the addition of the article. Note, however, the slangy plurals, *the creeps, the horrors, the dumps,* and others. The indefinite article may also in some cases be used : I had quite a headache yesterday.

16.7₁. The tendency to brevity in set phrases probably accounts for the want of the article, first, in a great many prepositional combinations like

>   At bottom ; at sea ; out at elbows ; at last (*at* may stand phonetically for older *atte,* from *at the*).
>   By way of answer.
>   In fact ; take the matter in hand ; in course of time ; in case he comes.
>   He looked out of window.
>   On account of ; what on earth ; set on edge ; make his hair stand on end ; on shore ; on tiptoe ; on top of.
>   Go to press ; put to sea ; all is fish that comes to net.

Walk up (down) hill is indefinite, but *he walked up the hill,* if the definite hill in question is meant.

16.7₂. Secondly, in such phrases consisting of a verb and its object as

>   Lose sight of ; lose heart, patience, courage.
>   Cast (weigh) anchor.
>   Keep house.

16.7₃. In the third place, in many phrases consisting of two (or three) parallel members :

>   From beginning to end ; from end to end ; from north to south ; live from hand to mouth.
>   Without looking to right or left (but : he looked first to the right, then to the left).
>   Let me tell you, as man to man.
>   Making money hand over fist ; he took the coin between thumb and finger.
>   Hand in hand ; arm in arm ; face to face.

Husband and wife ought to stand on an equal footing.
Thus father and son were left together.
Not enough to keep body and soul together.

16.7₄. As a rule, it is enough to place the article once with two or more parallel words, especially if they belong closely together :

The Prince and Princess of Wales.
The French and English languages.
The bride and bridegroom were coming out of the church.
Through the length and breadth of England.
The method, patience, and ingenuity which he brought to the task.

If the two words designate one and the same person, the article is, of course, not repeated :

He became the teacher and protector of the young man.

On the other hand, if a contrast is meant, two articles are required :

Struggles between the Calvinists and the Papists.

The Article of Incomplete Determination

16.8₁. We shall here deal with those cases in which the definite article is not in itself sufficient to determine what we are speaking about. Under this category may be reckoned all combinations in which the substantive has an adjective (*the grey horse*, etc.) ; thus very often with superlatives and ordinals (*the eldest boy* ; *the fifth girl in the third row*, etc.).

The clearest instances are, however, found when the supplementary determination follows after the substantive, thus with a prepositional group and with a relative clause :

The man in the moon.
The view from the upper storey.
The day before yesterday.
The book you lent me.
The boy who showed us the way.
He is not the fool we thought him.

A genitive or possessive pronoun is enough to determine a word, e.g. *Shelley's death* ; *my father* (**14.8₂**). It may be said that such a group as *my son* is not definite enough, because I may have several sons ; if, however, we look at the way in which such groups are actually used in ordinary language, we see that, for instance, the sentence " My son arrived yesterday " is perfectly definite and concerns only that son who is determined by the context (if we have been speaking of one particular son) or by the situation.

On the other hand, if instead of a genitive we use the *of*-phrase, the article is required just as in the other prepositional groups just exemplified :

> The death of Shelley.
> The house of the eldest son of the Bishop (= the Bishop's eldest son's house).

16.8₂. Note the difference between the two sentences :

> About that time he was starting business.
> About the time he was starting business he became engaged.

While " about that time " is a complete indication of time, the definite article in the latter sentence is only the article of incomplete determination, which has to be supplemented by the clause " he was starting business " to form a complete indication of the time of his engagement. In other words, " about that time " corresponds to " then," " about the time " to " when."

16.8₃. The addition of some qualifying restriction makes it necessary to have the article with words which otherwise are used without it, thus mass-words, proper names and analogues.

> The gold that is kept in the cellars of the great banks.
> History is his subject, especially the history of the Reformation.
> When he came back, he was a broken man, quite different from the Lecky we had known in his youth ; and the England he now saw was not the same as the England he had left twenty years before.
> The God you worship is not the god of our fathers.
> A lower deep, To which the Hell I suffer seems a Heav'n (Milton).
> In the following June, the June of 1914.

16.8₄. When an adjective is put before a proper name in order to distinguish two or more bearers of the same name, the article is required, as in *the younger Pitt* over against *the elder Pitt*, or *the new Turkey* when contrasted with Turkey as it was before.

> Paris now is very different from the dirty Paris of the Middle Ages.

In other cases the general tendency is to do without the article before a proper name preceded by an adjective, especially if this is of an emotional or ornamental character. We see this, not only in standing epithets like *Immortal Shakespeare, Rare Ben Jonson, Merry Old England, Perfidious Albion,* but also in combinations like :

> Dear little Mary was ill yesterday.
> Her championship of poor harmless Mr Dick (Dickens).
> In good old Queen Victoria's time.
> In dusty, sooty, ever noisy Liverpool (Carlyle).
> Beautiful Evelyn Hope is dead (Browning).

We may even say *fashionable London,* meaning the fashionable part of (the population of) London.

Young Burns may mean either a different person from *old Burns* (in which case we should expect the article according to what was said above), or if applied to the one individual indicated by the situation or context, it means that man in his youth or with some emphasis laid on the fact of his being still young.

(Cf. such composite proper names as *Neu York,* above **16.**5₃.)

16.8₅. Fashion requires the article before certain honorific adjectives : *the Honourable John Burns, the Right Reverend Edward Smith,* even *the most noble the Marquis of Bagwig.*

The Pronoun of Identity

16.9₁. *The same* is the ordinary pronoun of identity—identity either with something mentioned immediately before or stated in various ways by means of what follows :

> Shakespeare died in 1616. In the same year Cervantes, too, died.
> A happy New Year ! The same to you.

16.9₂. Cervantes died in the same year as Shakespeare.

> I want the same wine as usual.
> I want the same wine as I had yesterday (or : the same wine that, or which, I had yesterday).

It was the same man who was afterwards assassinated.
In the same place where we stayed last year.

Incomplete identity is denoted by *much the same*.

16.9₃. Mutual identity may also be implied as in

Shakespeare and Cervantes died in the same year.
All the planets travel round the sun in the same direction.
Rich or poor, that was all the same to him.
What she did not like, was a quiet life, the same thing day after
  day.

A fuller expression of this is *one and the same*, in which we
might say that *one* as indefinite neutralizes the definite article;
thus in

He is always humming one and the same tune.   Cf. *one* **17.1.**

The Pronoun of Similarity

16.9₄. *Such* may refer, first, to something just mentioned :

With politicians, journalists or such important personages.
Such, then, were the conditions under which he took the reins of
  government.
His love for Mary, if such it may be termed, did not prevent this
  infidelity.
People kill one another by the thousand.   Such is life !
He was president of the board and as such had a decisive vote.

Such may be preceded by an indefinite pronoun :

With a carriage-and-pair, or some other such conveyance.
He took taxis, whenever any such were available.
Honest money-lenders ?   There are no such persons !

16.9₅. Secondly, *such* refers to something following, pretty
much in the same way as *the same* :

This offers no difficulty for such as you (on the case, see **14.2**).
Let me have men about me, that are fat,
Sleeke-headed men, and such as sleepe a-nights (Sh.).
We are such stuffe as dreames are made on (Sh.).
I am not such a fool that I believe every word he says (or such a
  fool as to believe . . .).

Such as frequently introduces examples of a class :

Eminent Bolshevists, such as Lenin, Trotzky and Stalin.

16.9₆. The meaning of quality is often obliterated, so that *such as* comes to mean " the . . . (sg.) that " and especially in the plural " those . . . that or who " :

He used such power as he possessed for the benefit of mankind.
Such as heard him were full of admiration.

16.9₇. On the other hand, there is often no real comparison, and *such* (pronounced emphatically) comes to mean ' very great ' (cp. the use of *so*) :

He is such an admirer of you !
Don't be in such a hurry !
Such a long sermon='so long a sermon.' In the plural only *such long sermons* is said, not *so long sermons*.

16.9₈. There is likewise no comparison when *such*, and especially *such and such*, is used instead of a specific indication which the speaker or writer will not or cannot use (cp. *certain, so and so*) :

You spurn'd me such a day ; another time You cald me dog (Sh.).
We met on such and such a day, at such and such a place.

CHAPTER XVII

INDEFINITE PRONOUNS

Indefinite unity (*one*).—Indefinite article.—Place of indefinite article.—Pronoun of difference (*other*).—Pronoun of discretion (*certain*).—Pronoun of unspecified quantity (*some*).—Pronouns of indifference (*any, either*).

The Pronoun of Indefinite Unity

17.1₁. In **15.**6 we have seen the use of *one* to express the 'generic person.' Here we shall give examples of various pronominal uses which are easily explained from the numerical value of *one* :

> She was now a free agent—if she had not formerly been one.
> (This leads up to the use of *one* as a prop-word, **8.**4.)
> Then must you speake Of one that lov'd not wisely, but too well (Sh.).
> Rain or sunshine, that is all one to me.
> (Cp. *one and the same*, **16.**9₃.)
> At last, one fine morning, we started for home.
> One day you are sure to repent of this.
> He mentioned as his source an English lady, one Miss Arundel (= a certain M.A.).

In the last few examples *one* approaches the function of the indefinite article.

The Indefinite Article

17.1₂. *An* (before vowels), *a* (before consonants) is what is traditionally termed 'the indefinite article'; a better name would be 'the article of indetermination.' It is historically a weakened form of *one*.

an aim	a name
an heir	a hair
an M.P.	a unit

A has the value of the numeral *one* in a few combinations :

> In a word; at a blow; Rome wasn't built in a day.
> She does not care a fig for him—not one fig (Thackeray).

Not one hapenny, not a hapenny, shall she ever hae o' mine (Fielding).
For a day or two = for one or two days.
They all, to a man, voted for the Liberal candidate.

In some set phrases the indefinite article means "one and the same," *e.g.* :

Birds of a feather flock together.
Three at a time.
These foyles have all a length (Sh.).
We are of a mind once more (Sheridan).

17.2₂. The indefinite article is used not only in introductory remarks like those exemplified in **16.4₃**, where we expect further information, but also in a great many other cases where the singular of a noun is required, while no identification is possible or important, though the matter is not sufficiently indifferent to warrant the use of *any* :

He wanted to sit quietly in an easy-chair with a good book.
Let us go to a restaurant and have a good dinner.
He had on a blue shirt and a green tie.
He spent a week in a small village.
A small group of scientists admired him greatly.

If *to a degree* has come to mean ' in a high degree, extremely,' this must be explained by the omission of some necessary complement like " which can hardly be expressed " :

His second marriage was irregular to a degree.

17.2₃. We may collect here some examples of the indefinite article in idiomatic expressions which in other languages often have no article ; they show the English disinclination to bare (naked) substantives with a concrete meaning :

He took a fancy to the boy.
She takes an interest in his work.
He takes a pride in all his children.
I have a (great) mind to leave at once.
With a view to being useful.
He has quite a genius for invention.
Walking always gives one an appetite.
She is in a fever ; in a passion.
We were in a (great) hurry.
I am not in a position to help you.

He is under an obligation to obey orders.
He is at a loss to understand their behaviour.
I wish you a merry Christmas and a happy New Year.
Our hens lay on an average six eggs a day.

17.2₄. As a natural consequence of the fact that a predicative is generally indefinite (because " he is a rascal " means ' he is one of the class of rascals ') most substantives as predicatives are provided with the indefinite article.   Some exceptions have been mentioned above (**13.6, 16.6₃**).   Examples of the regular usage :

He was (became, remained) a sailor.
He died a bachelor.
He proved a trusty friend.
She was an only child.
'Tis pity though, in this sublime world, that
Pleasure's a sin, and sometimes sin a pleasure (Byron ; in prose we
    say now : " it's a pity ").

The indefinite article is seen also in the analogous cases :

We look upon him as a fool.
We consider him a fool.
I make it a rule to examine everything for myself.
She had been rapidly growing into a tall, handsome girl.
I felt myself suddenly raised from a boy to a man.

No article is used in a predicative placed as in this sentence :

She has more sense than Mary, child though she is.

17.2₅. As stated above (**16.6₂**), a superlative regularly requires the definite article.   Thus it is impossible to say, *e.g.* " a best book, a cleverest remark."   But if the superlative enters into a fixed combination with a substantive, it is possible to have the indefinite article before it :

I had a best suit that lasted me six years.
His novel was evidently not a best seller.
I like to go to a first night.

17.2₆. In the generic use we may say that *a* means ' any,' or, perhaps rather, that one (cat) is taken as representative of the whole class :

A cat is not so vigilant as a dog.
A cat may look at a king.

Thus also in comparisons :

As grave as a judge ; as deaf as a post.

The indefinite article approaches the generic use in cases like these :

He likes a smoke after dinner.

17.2₇. *Of a* is used before a time-indication to denote the habitual ; here the article has nearly the meaning of *any* :

He rises early of a morning (but : He rose early in the morning, in speaking of one particular morning).
It was his custom of a Sunday to sit close by the fire.

17.3. In some combinations *an, a* is used distributively, approaching in meaning to ' each.' Here it is explained as being historically = *on* (cf. the old " his hair stood an end "), but is now felt as the indefinite article :

He lives on sixpence a day.
He goes to London once or twice a year.
Love will come but once a life (Tennyson).
It costs two shillings a pound (also : the pound).

17.4₁. If we find no article in combinations like the following with *never* (or with *ever* and other expressions if implying *never*), the reason seems to be that we are speaking really of the whole class ; it is thus a kind of generic singular :

Never was man less suited to lady than this burly lord.
For there was never yet philosopher That could endure the tooth-ake patiently (Sh.).
Was ever man so crossed as I am ?
Nature and Love ! What more could poet ask ?

It is different when *never a* (*man*) comes to mean simply *no* (*man*) with total obliteration of the temporal meaning (hence dialectal *ne'era, narra*) :

And again he uttered never a word.

17.4₂. While *little* and *few* are negative terms, *a little* and *a few* are positive ; compare thus :

From him we expect little more than a pun.
From him we expect a little more than a pun.
There are few mistakes in his papers (praise).
There are a few mistakes in his papers (blame).

17.5₁. The indefinite article naturally precedes an adjective (*an old man*, etc.). There are, however, some exceptions to this rule. *How* and *however*, like other interrogative and relative words, come first and attract the adjective : similarly with *so, as, too* and *no less* :

> How great a crime had been committed, was not discovered till next day.
> However dark a night.
> We could not do it in so short a time.
> He is as diligent a man as ever lived.
> Too hard a task.
> A cousin of the artist, and in his way no less remarkable a man.

The indefinite article is placed after *what, many* and *such* :

> What a shame !   What a confounded shame ! (**28.7₅**).
> Many a poor woman knocked at his door without getting anything.
> Such a short time.

17.5₂. With regard to the place of the indefinite article, it is further noticeable that *quite* and *rather* are often attracted to the verb instead of to a following adjective which they might seem naturally to qualify :

> He is (or seems, became, etc.) quite (or rather) an old man.
> He had rather a startled look.

This leads to the same word-order where there is no attraction to the verb :

> At quite a reasonable price—by the side of *at a quite reasonable price.*
> At rather an early period=at a rather early period.
> With rather a startled look.

17.5₃. The indefinite article is placed between *half* and a substantive :

> George drank half a bottle of wine with each of his meals.
> With half a moon peeping occasionally through the window.
> I have told you that half a dozen times.
> I arrived with the conventional half-crown in my pocket; literally and absolutely half a crown.

There is a tendency to treat such combinations as wholes and thus to keep *a* even when a definite word or another indefinite article precedes :

> For the next half an hour.
> That half a crown will make no great difference.
> I have got another half a crown a week increase.

While this will be regarded as slipshod by many writers, the indefinite article is obligatory when *and a half* is added after another numeral or numerical indication, even if the whole is definite in meaning :

> During the two and a half years of my apprenticeship.
> During the century and a half which followed the Conquest (Macaulay).
> His year and a half of peace had effaced all the ill effects.

An analogous case is seen in

> The hour and a quarter which he could afford to allow himself.

17.5₄. With regard to the repetition of the indefinite article we have similar rules as those found in **16.7₄**. Thus one article suffices if the two items belong naturally together :

> Give me a knife and fork, please. (Cf. my knife and fork.)
> At this moment a gentleman and lady entered together.

But if a contrast is intended, the article is repeated :

> A gentleman and a lady cannot be expected to agree on such questions.

Coleridge's " A sadder and a wiser man " is more emphatic than " a sadder and wiser man."

The Pronoun of Difference

17.6₁. *Other* may be called the pronoun of difference and is thus the direct opposite of *same*.

Used with the definite article it generally has reference to two (*the other hand*; thus also *her other arm* and *every other day*), but this reference is absent in *the other day* (= ' a few days ago ') and when *other* is used with the indefinite article (written as one word : *another*) or without any article :

> Have another cup.
> If you take one glass, you will take another and another.

'Tis one thing to be tempted, Escalus, Another thing to fall (Sh.).
I won't say another word.
Some of his pupils admired him, others detested him.
Some one or other may have seen us.
(Somehow or other they got away.)

17.6₂. The reciprocal use of *each other* and *one another* has been mentioned in **11.6**. These combinations are now felt as units, as is shown by the formation of a genitive and by the placing of a preposition before them :

They know each other's weak points.
We looked at one another (at each other; in the old language one at another, each at other).
Imparadised in one another's arms (Milton).

The Pronoun of Discretion

17.7. *Certain* as a pronoun refers to some one or something that is really definite and might be mentioned, though I do not choose for the moment to say expressly who or what :

A certaine man went down from Hierusalem to Jericho (AV.).
Certain of his friends had already begun to suspect him.

The Pronoun of Unspecified Quantity

17.8₁. *Some* as used with a mass-word indicates an unknown or unspecified quantity, with a plural word an unknown or unspecified number :

He ate some bread and some grapes.
Some children are able to sing before they can talk.
She won't be ready for some time yet.
Sometimes he does not stop working till midnight.
There is something (= some truth) in that.

With a ' countable ' in the singular it has the same meaning of the unknown or unspecified ; it is often strengthened by the addition of *or other* :

Some one (or other) must have touched my papers since I went out.
Some old philosopher once said that you should know something of everything and everything of something.

Before a numeral it means ' approximately ' :

This happened some forty years ago.

17.8$_2$. There is a recent, originally American, use of *some* (stressed) to indicate excellence or high degree :

" Some dress !" she said admiringly.

You certainly are some traveller.

For the difference between *some* and *any*, see **17.**9$_3$.

The Pronouns of Indifference

Any

17.9$_1$. *Any* indicates one or more, no matter which ; therefore *any* is very frequent in sentences implying negation or doubt (question, condition).

He never had any money.

No one said anything for some time.

We had ceased to pay any particular notice to the song.

There is hardly anything left in the bottle.

They sat there without any one to wait on them.

Has anything happened ?   You look scared all of you.

I wonder if there are any walnuts on that tree.   Can you see any ?

Few, if any, will ever praise him.

17.9$_2$. If there is a negative in a sentence containing *any*, the meaning of the whole is generally negative :

I can't do anything = ' I can do nothing.'

But if *anything* is pronounced emphatically and with compound (falling-rising) intonation, the meaning is positive :

I can't do anything = ' there are some things which I can't do.'

17.9$_3$. The difference between *some* and *any* is clearly brought out in examples like the following :

You may come any day, but you must come some day (or other) to see me.

You must find some excuse—oh, any excuse will do.

He would do something for her, though not much.

He would do anything for money.

Any doctor will say something to please his patients.

Some doctors will say anything to please their patients.

Any boy will be able to tell you that (= all).

Some boys will be able to tell you that (not all).

More people go to London than to any other big town.

I like London better than some of the other big towns, for instance New York.

He is older than any of his school-fellows (he is the oldest).

He is older than some of his school-fellows (he is not the youngest).

He did not like some of his wife's friends (=he disliked some of them).

He did not like any of his wife's friends (= he disliked all of them).

Couldn't you play something—anything (= Please, play something, no matter what).

Some of the man's money, if he had any, was due to us.

He had the look of a man who sees a ghost or something worse, if anything can be.

17.9$_4$. From " we may expect her back any minute " we understand the use in

My wife will be back any minute now.

Note also the use in *anything but happy* (= not at all happy).

When a man is willing to pay any price for a thing, he will probably have to pay a very high price ; hence the meaning of *any* in combinations like :

We have had any amount of letters on the subject (*i.e.* many).

We saw any number of mummies at the Museum.

17.9$_5$. The old *aught* meant the same as ' anything ' : it was frequently used in the phrase *for aught I know*. (The corresponding negative is *naught, nought* : *set at nought* ; also used for the cipher O ; hence *naughty*.)

17.9$_6$. The temporal adverb *ever* generally corresponds to *any* (= at any time) :

Are you ever sea-sick ?   No, hardly ever.

Napoleon was a military genius, if ever there was one.

The greatest genius that ever lived.

She is just as beautiful as ever.

After an interrogatory pronoun, and before *so, ever* is often used loosely in colloquial speech :

Who ever told you that story ?

Whatever are we to do ?

We saw ever so many mummies at the Museum.

In some connexions *ever* corresponds to *all* (= always) :

Ever since their marriage.

For ever and ever.

Either

17.9₇. While *any* is the pronoun of complete indifference, *either* indicates indifference with regard to two :

It seemed impossible for either of us to remain (=Neither of us, neither she nor I could remain).

He was more inclined to eating than to sleeping, and more to drinking than to either (Fielding).

Either has a different meaning in :

Father and son were sitting on either side of a big fire (*i.e.* one on one, and the other on the other side).

17.9₈. *Either* is sometimes extended to more than two :

Nor does it appear in any way desirable that either of the three classes should extend itself (Ruskin).

This is at any rate less objectionable when *either* is used as a conjunction :

A narration of events, either past, present, or to come (N.E.D.).

CHAPTER XVIII

PRONOUNS OF TOTALITY

Positive (*all, both, every, each*).—Negative (*no, none, neither*).

Positive

18.1₁. *All* is the typical pronoun of totality. If we say "all boys know that" the boys are lumped together, while in "every boy knows that" the boys are considered separately, though one point is mentioned in which they agree. Finally, we may say "any boy knows that" : no matter what boy you take, he will know it. Here *any* is a synonym of *every*, and the two words may be used together to strengthen the effect : "on every and any occasion." But in other combinations these words are not synonyms : *every* cannot be substituted for *any* in "he may turn up any day"; nor can *every* be used in the sentences given in **17.**9.

All women and *every woman* mean practically the same thing, only looked upon in different ways. Instead of saying "all were happy," or "all happened according to our wish," it is now more usual to say "everybody was happy" and "everything happened according to our wish." Isolated *all*, however, is used in cases like :

Rich and poor, all must die.
All's well that ends well.
All that he could do was to run away.
That is all.

In the saying "All right" *all* originally meant 'everything' as the subject of (*is*) *right*, but now *all* is felt to be a tertiary qualifying *right*, so that we can say :

Everything is all right.

18.1₂. *All* is used with words in the singular, meaning 'the whole of' :

All England is changed or changing.
All the world knows that.
All my money. With all my heart.
We walked all the way to Harrow.

A special case is the combination of *all* with a name denoting a part of time :

> He spent all summer in France.
> The wind was east all yesterday.

Here *all* is, of course, distinct from *every*; the two may be combined :

> The church is open every day and all day.

18.1₃. *All* is very frequent with plural words :

> All his friends.
> All these people.
> All the young men fell in love with her.

But *all* is to some extent ambiguous, as it may mean either ' all taken together ' or ' taken separately '; only in the latter case can we substitute *each* or *every* :

> All the angles of a triangle are 180° (*i.e.* together).
> All the angles of a triangle are less than 180° (better : each of . . . is . . .).
> All the boys of this form are stronger than their teacher (if working together).
> All the boys of this form are able to run faster than their teacher.

Instead of the old *all we, all you* we now say *we all, you all* or *all of us, all of you*; also combined :

> We are all of us most obliged to you.

18.1₄. *All* is used in apposition to the subject :

> He is all skin and bones.
> She was all attention.
> I am all anxiety on his account.
> It is all over.
> It is all one to me.

18.1₅. *All* is found in a great many prepositional phrases :

> Above all. After all. At all. In all.

Note especially *for all* = ' in spite of ' with obliteration of the original meaning of *all* :

> For all his wealth he is not contented.
> I am as well bred as the Earl's granddaughter, for all her fine pedigree.

He may die, for all I care.

A man, handsome still, for all that his hair was thinned by time (='though').

Further: by all means. At all events. At all costs. Beyond all doubt, etc.

18.1₆. The meaning of *all* is weakened in

That makes all the difference (='a great deal of difference').

Both

18.2. *Both* means the same thing as *all*, only applied to two :

He had both hands full.

Both (the) brothers had come.

Both my daughters are married.

They are both of them married.

Both of you=You both.

When used as a conjunction, *both* may be applied to more than two objects :

The God that made both Skie, Air, Earth and Heav'n (Milton).

Both man and bird and beast (Coleridge).

Every

18.3₁. The difference between *all* and *every* has already been discussed in **18.1₁.** *Every* may be used with a possessive pronoun :

I have seen it in your every glance, and heard it in your every word (Dickens).

18.3₂. We must here mention the use to indicate repetition :

He comes here every day, every second day (also, more colloquially, every other day, with *other* in its old meaning of an ordinal).

Every third word a lye (Sh.).

But it is now more usual to employ the cardinal number here :

He brings out a book every three years (where *three years* is taken together, cf. **21.4₇**).

He was stopped every dozen yards by friends who greeted him.

Every year or two.

Every now and then (every now and again, every once in a while).

18.3₃. With the weakened meaning of *all* in *all the difference* should be compared :

There is every prospect of success.
What is the use of keeping it secret? Every use.

Each

18.4₁. While *every*, like *all*, refers to a complete totality, *each* (like the interrogative *which*) refers to a limited number :

Each of his children.
Give these boys a shilling each (**9.6₂**).
We each lit a cigarette.
I paid sixpence each for these cigars.

18.4₂. Note the elliptical expression :

He spoke slowly, pausing between every sentence.
Looking up furtively between each mouthful—

meaning really between every (each) and the next.

Negative

18.5. *No* (*none*) and *neither* are negative pronouns of totality ; *no* corresponding to *all*, *every* and *each*, and *neither* corresponding to *both* (or *either*).

No one spoke for some time (All were silent, everybody was silent).
None of them spoke (They were silent).
Neither spoke for some time (Both were silent).
Shoes there were none.
He had no money.
Everybody's business is nobody's business.
Nothing ever happened.
By no means.
They could none of them move.

The colloquial " I shall be back in no time " may be compared with the exaggeration in the case of *all* and *every* (**18.1₆, 18.3₃**).

Never is the temporal adverb corresponding to *no*.

GENDER

19.1$_1$. In nature we find **sex,** male and female; outside animated beings everything is sexless.

In grammar we speak of **genders.** In Latin, German and other cognate languages each substantive has a definite gender, masculine, feminine or neuter. The distinction has some connexion with the natural distinction between male, female, and sexless, but in a great many cases it seems to be purely arbitrary without any reference to natural conditions. This was the case also in Old English, but in Modern English we have no traces left of this system, though perfect simplicity has not been achieved.

19.1$_2$. In substantives we distinguish :

Words denoting animated beings without regard to sex, e.g. *friend, thief, worm ; nation.*

Words denoting male beings, e.g. *father, bull.*

Words denoting female beings, e.g. *mother, cow.*

Words denoting something inanimate, e.g. *star, storm, idea, kindness.*

19.1$_3$. In pronouns we find :

Words used of animate beings without regard to sex, e.g. *who, somebody.*

Words used of male beings, e.g. *he.*

Words used of female beings, e.g. *she.*

Words used of inanimate ' things,' e.g. *it, what, something.*

Words used of animates as well as of inanimates, e.g. *each, some, they.*

We shall now consider these distinctions more in detail and

shall then find that the logical distinctions just made are not always carried through consistently.

Substantives

19.2. (A) In the names of living beings we sometimes find three separate words, one common to both sexes, one for the male, and one for the female, *e.g.*

parent	father	mother
child	son	daughter
child	boy	girl
monarch	king	queen

Note that the word *child* has two meanings, each with its corresponding one-sex words.

horse	stallion	mare
ox ·	bull	cow
sheep	ram	ewe
swine (hog, pig)	boar	sow
deer	stag, hart	hind
(fowl)	cock	hen

19.3₁. (B) In other cases we have two separate words, one for the male and one for the female, *e.g.*

*man	woman	bachelor	spinster
gentleman	lady	baron	baroness
lord	lady	*Jew	Jewess
master	mistress	abbot	abbess
mister (Mr)	Missis (Mrs) and Miss	monk (friar)	nun
lad	lass	*dog	bitch
brother	sister	*lion	lioness
uncle	aunt	*tiger	tigress
nephew	niece	drake	*duck
bridegroom	bride	gander	*goose
widower	widow	drone	*bee (queen-bee)

Those words in the list (B) which are marked with a star may also be used without any reference to sex ; or rather, we should say inversely that these names, which are properly common-sex words, are also used to denote one particular sex, chiefly the male—the female only in the case of some animals the males of which have comparatively little importance. (Note that in the list (A) *horse*, besides being a common-sex word, may be used in the sense of stallion.)

19.3₂. The word *man* requires special mention on account of its ambiguity. It may mean a human being without regard to sex, as in *every man* and *no man* ; but in most combinations it will be understood of a male human being, as in

> I saw there an old man whom I did not know.
> Two or three young men made a fearful noise, etc.

In **21.5** we shall see various uses of *man* and *men* in a generic sense.   The ambiguity is particularly striking in Miss Hitchener's feminist poem, which amused Shelley :

> All, all are men—women and all!   And in Carlyle's
> Atrabiliar old men, especially old women, hint that they know
>   what they know.

The ambiguity has recently led to a growing use of the substantivized adjective *human* :

> What wretched little mites we humans are !

As the first part of a compound *man* always denotes sex (see below), but as the second part of a compound *man* may be used in either sense :

> Elizabeth was a great statesman.
> Mrs C. was the spokesman of her sisters and chairman of a score
>   of clubs.

But *stateswoman, chairwoman, horsewoman*, etc., are also used, while *kinsman, madman, nobleman* and other similar words are used of males only.   Nationality-names like *Englishman, Irishman, Frenchman* denote male sex, though in the plural they comprise both sexes.   Some compounds, like *footman, alderman*, have no corresponding forms in *-woman*.

19.3₃. It is a natural linguistic consequence of the social preponderance during many centuries of men that when a word for one sex is derived from a word for the other, it is nearly always a male word that is taken as base. The ending most frequently used is *-ess*, e.g. *duke—duchess, emperor—empress, god—goddess, waiter—waitress, launderer—laundress, traitor—traitress*, etc.

A more learned ending is seen in *prosecutor—prosecutrix, testator—testatrix* and a few others.

Compare also : *hero—heroine* ; *czar—czarina*.

The only instances in which the derivation is in the inverse direction are easily accounted for : *widow—widower, bride—bridegroom*.

19.34. Where we have a separate feminine name, it sometimes means ' having such and such a position or function or vocation,' sometimes ' married to a man of such and such a position.' *Queen* has the former meaning in Queen Elizabeth, the latter in the case of the present queen of England ; *ambassadress* similarly may have both meanings. An *emperor's* wife is an *empress*, but a *murderess* does not mean ' a murderer's wife.'

19.41. (C) Finally we have a great many words for animate beings which do not indicate sex :

Cousin, friend, enemy, Christian, fool, criminal, servant, neighbour, foreigner, European, etc.

Animal, cat, rabbit, eagle, sparrow, fish, trout, frog, worm, fly, etc.

Here belong nearly all substantives derived from verbs to denote agents :

Reader, teacher, boarder, intruder, liar, debtor, possessor, drunkard, student, inhabitant, copyist, etc. Similarly such derivatives from substantives as *librarian, musician, violinist, novelist, prisoner*, and words in *-ster*, e.g. *punster, songster, huckster*, with the sole exception of *spinster*, originally ' one (man or woman) who spins,' now ' unmarried woman.'

On account of social conditions many words which properly belong to class (C) have been and are practically always used of men only :

Shoemaker, baker, merchant, lawyer, soldier, etc. Nowadays this is being changed with regard to words like *professor, doctor* and *member of Parliament*.

Another consequence of social condition is that two words are required for *host* and *hostess*, but only one for *guest*.

But *nurse, cook, dressmaker* are nearly always used of women. *Witch* used to be a two-sex word.

While *youth* is now generally used of a man, *a young person* means 'a young woman.'

Fellow is used of the two sexes in compounds like *fellow-sufferer* and *schoolfellow*; but used by itself it is restricted to the male sex.

19.4₂. In the predicative a word which is otherwise generally used of men only, may be used of a woman:

> She was master of the situation.
> Ann was always a lover of beautiful art.

19.5. When a special indication of sex is wanted with one of the two-sex words, this can always be done by the addition of the adjectives *male* and *female*, respectively: *a male reader, a female cousin, a male sparrow, a female frog*, etc. *He* and *she* also may be preposed, especially with names of animals: *a he-rabbit, a she-ape*, etc. Note the American *he-man*.

Sportsmen and lovers of animals in many cases prefer more intimate or picturesque ways of denoting sex than those just mentioned, chiefly by means of combinations with sex-words from other species, sometimes even names which do not exclusively denote one particular sex: *dog-otter* and *bitch-otter, roe-buck* and *roe-doe, buck-rabbit* and *doe-rabbit, peacock* and *peahen, cock-pheasant* and *hen-pheasant*, etc. In some cases human names are used: *jackass* and *jenny-ass, billy-goat* and *nanny-goat, tom-cat* and *tabby-cat, jack-sparrow*.

For human beings the following compounds are used, among others:

Man friend or *gentleman friend, woman friend* or *lady friend, boy friend, girl friend*; *manservant, woman servant, maid-servant, servant-girl*; *woman doctor* or *lady doctor*.

Cf. the old-fashioned " my gentle (or fair) readers."

Pronouns

19.6₁. Those pronouns that are applicable to animates as well as to inanimates offer no difficulty : *some boy, some girl, some cat, some stone,* etc. *These boys . . . they, those books . . . take them,* etc.

It is quite natural that we should have a common-sex interrogative pronoun *who,* as it happens very often that in asking such a question as " Who bought it ? " we do not know whether the buyer was a he or a she. Similarly we have the common-sex words, *somebody, anybody, nobody* (and the corresponding forms with *one*).

19.6₂. In the third person it would have been very convenient to have a common-sex pronoun, but as a matter of fact English has none and therefore must use one of the three makeshift expedients shown in the following sentences :

The reader's heart—if *he or she* have any (Fielding).
He that hath eares to heare, let *him* heare (AV.).
Nobody prevents you, do *they* (Thackeray).
God send every one *their* harts desire (Sh.).
Anybody in *their* senses would have acted in that way.

19.6₃. The use of *he* and *she* in speaking of human beings and animals, whose sex is known to the speaker, and of *it* in speaking of what is inanimate, offers nothing of interest ; but it is interesting to notice that the same three pronouns may also be used outside their proper sphere.

Let us first take *it*. *It* is used very extensively of animals whose sex is either unknown, as generally in speaking of lower animals, or at any rate indifferent to the speaker. On the other hand, a sportsman or the owner of the animal in question will generally prefer saying *he* or *she*, as the case may be. As *it* is impersonal, " objective," one may show one's sympathy with the animal world by using the more subjectively coloured *he* or *she* even when one knows nothing of the sex of the particular animal one is speaking of, *he* perhaps more often than *she*, though one will speak of " the hare in her form " (*i.e.* nest or lair).

It may be used of a human being, especially a baby. In speaking of children in general it is used as a common-sex word, for instance in :

Hushed as a babe upon its mother's breast (Byron),

but *it* may also be said of an individual child, though, of course, the child's parents or nurse will generally say *he* or *she* ; however, Juliet's nurse says :

When it did tast the worme-wood on the nipple of my dugge (Sh.).

Though the ghost of Hamlet's father appears in a masculine form, the pronoun *it* is used :

Looke where it comes againe . . . Speake to it, Horatio (Sh.).

19.6₄. Inversely *he* or *she* may be said of a thing instead of *it* in order to show a certain kind of sympathy with or affection for the thing, which is thereby, as it were, raised above the inanimate sphere. The best-known instance is *she* said of a ship or boat (even if it has a masculine name) ; railway-men will speak of the locomotive or train, and motor-owners of their car, as *she*. Some people will similarly refer to their pipe or watch as *he*. In such cases the speaker does not really attribute sex to the thing in question, and the choice of a sexual pronoun is occasioned only by the fact that there is no non-sexual pronoun available except the inert *it*.

19.6₅. Alongside of this popular use of the sexual pronouns we have another, which is due to a strong literary tradition and in which it is generally the Latin gender that determines the choice of *he* or *she*. Thus the sun is *he*, the moon *she*. When a country is spoken of as a personal agent it is called *she* :

England is justly proud of *her* great poets.

Similarly

Oxford taught me as much Greek and Latin as *she* could (Ruskin).

When *Nature, Fortune*, etc., are personified, *she* is the pronoun used :

Nature had lavished *her* gifts on him.

Similarly *she* is used of such abstract notions as :

Musicke with *her* silver sound (Sh.).
I love *Wisdom* more than *she* loves me (Byron).
Science has failed because *she* has attempted the impossible.

But *love* is often spoken of as *he* (after *Eros, amor*), and so is *time*.

19.7. While the distinction between *who* and *which* as interrogative pronouns has nothing to do with gender, but depends on the difference between an indetermined question and one referring to a definite number (Which of her boys, or Which of these pictures, do you like best?), the relative *who* corresponds to *he* or *she,* and *which* to *it.* Thus :

Her only child, who is now in Africa, often sends her money.
I recommend this book, which is the best he has ever written.

But if we know nothing of the sex we may say :

What became of the child which was born after her husband's
death? (though *that* would here be better).

This distinction between relative *who* and *which* is comparatively recent. Shakespeare and the Bible often have *which* referring to persons :

Our father which art in heaven.

With names of animals and of countries both pronouns may be used. Note the different point of view in :

Norway, which is more mountainous than Sweden.
It is Great Britain rather than America who is likely to suffer
most.

A predicative and a verbal idea are viewed as neutral, hence *which* in sentences like the following :

Authorities that are free to speak, which the King himself is
not.
Dressed like the country gentleman which he was not and never
would be.
I go there whenever I have time, which isn't often.

19.8. While the interrogative genitive *whose* is never used of things, the relative *whose* may be used to avoid the postponed *of which* :

> A hill, whose peak was still buried in the fog (Stevenson).
> Something had happened during his absence, of whose nature he was ignorant.

(Cf. on Genitive **14**.8.)

Where now we have the genitive *its*, the old form (up to the beginning of the seventeenth century) was *his*, thus in Shakespeare :

> The lampe that burnes by night, Dries up his oyle, to lend the world his light.

CHAPTER XX

NUMBER

Numerals. — Ordinals. — Singular and plural. — Substantives. — Irregularities.—Learned plurals.—The unchanged plural.—Compounds.—Pronouns.—The meaning of plural.—Special meaning in plural.—Words used in plural only.

20.1₁. To indicate a definite number we have the so-called **cardinal numerals** : *One, two, three*, etc.

It will be seen that the first numerals up to *twelve* are formed unsystematically, but that there is some system in the words from 13 to 19, which are formed by composition of the numbers *three, four*, etc., with *teen*, a modified form of *ten*—the first part of the compound being also in some cases modified ; another system comprises the 'tens' formed by means of *-ty* : here, too, some of the first parts are modified : *twenty, thirty, forty, fifty*. *A hundred, a thousand, a million, a billion* are again unsystematic ; but otherwise the higher numerals are formed systematically by multiplication and addition, *e.g.* 2569, *two thousand five hundred and sixty-nine*. In additions of tens and ones the old practice as in *five and twenty* has now generally given way to the opposite order without *and* : *twenty-five* ; this is imperative when *hundred* precedes : 325, *three hundred and twenty-five*.

From the numerals in *-teen* is evolved the indefinite numeral *teens* : *she is still in her teens*.

As still more indefinite numerals may be considered *some, many, few* (*a few*), *numerous*, etc. Note also the use of *odd* : *forty odd*.

Instead of saying *one time* and *two times* we say *once, twice*. The third corresponding word *thrice* is obsolete.

One is also used as a pronoun (**17.1**, cf. **8.3₆, 8.4**) ; weakened forms are *an* and *a* (**17.1₂**).

20.1₂. Corresponding to these cardinals we have **ordinals** denoting position in a series. Here, too, we find that the first ones, which are most often used, are unsystematically formed : *first, second, third* (this evidently derived from *three*) ; but from the fourth we have everywhere the same ending -*th* added to the cardinal, though this sometimes undergoes some modification in form : *fifth, twelfth*, while the modification in *eighth* and *ninth* is merely orthographic. Corresponding to -*ty* we have -*tieth*.

The ending -*th* may be applied also to *dozen* and to mathematical symbols like *n* : *the dozenth, the nth*.

Ordinals are used outside their proper sphere to denote fractions : *one-third, three-fourths*, etc. Note the irregular *half*. Other indications of fractions : *quarter* (fourth), *per cent* (hundredth).

Cardinals are used instead of ordinals (through the influence of reading) in cases like *Book three* (Book III), *Chapter IX, in the year* 1914, etc., thus always after *number*, which may be said to be a device to make a cardinal into an ordinal.

Singular and Plural

20.2₁. Outside these numerals we have grammatical expressions of number in most substantives, in some pronouns and in some verbal forms, but neither in adjectives nor in particles. While some languages distinguish a singular (for one), a dual (for two)—sometimes even a trial (for three)—and a plural, English like most of the cognate languages has now only a singular and a plural. The only remainder of a dual is *both* (**18.2**).

Substantives

20.2₂. The regular way of forming the plural is by adding the *s*-ending with its threefold pronunciation (**5.6₃**).

[iz] after sibilants (hissing sounds) [z, s, ʒ, ʃ] : *noses, horses, foxes, bridges, dishes, churches* ;

[z] after voiced non-sibilants : *bees, boys, ladies, flowers, cabs, kings, lambs, doves.*

[s] after voiceless non-sibilants : *caps, links, lamps, hats, cliffs.*

Spelling. A mute *e* is inserted between *o* and *e* in all familiar words : *heroes, potatoes* ; but neither in words felt as foreign : *albinos, ghettos, solos*, nor in curtailed words like *photos, pianos*, nor when there is a vowel before *o* : *folios, cameos.*

After a consonant -*y* is changed into -*ies* : *flies, ladies, babies.* But after a written vowel *y* is retained: *boys, days*; thus also generally in proper names: *Henrys, Pollys*.

After a sibilant *-es* is added in the spelling, except, of course, in such words as *horses, bridges*, where an *-e* is written in the singular.

Corps [kɔ·ə] makes regularly [kɔ·əz], though the spelling is identical in both numbers.

20.2₃. Some words have a voiceless consonant in the singular and the corresponding voiced sound in the plural (5.6), namely:

(1) a dozen words in [f], written *f* or *fe*, plural [vz], written *ves*; thus:

> *thief*, pl. *thieves*
> *wife*, pl. *wives*

In the same way are formed the plurals *calves, halves, knives, leaves, lives, loaves, selves* (*ourselves*, etc.), *sheaves, shelves, wolves*.

Other words in *-f* retain this in the plural, e.g. *cliffs, cuffs, roofs, dwarfs, sheriffs, beliefs, safes*; thus also words originally French like *chiefs, fiefs, griefs*, though *beef* has the archaic *beeves*. The ending is also [fs] in words like *coughs, laughs, troughs*; *paragraphs*, etc.

Vacillation is found in the plural of *scarf* and *wharf*. *Staff* originally made the plural *staves* (note the different vowel sound); but a new singular was developed from this: *stave* in the two senses 'piece of a cask' and 'stanza, piece of music,' while a regular plural has been formed, *staffs*, 'bodies of men'; cf. also *flagstaffs*.

(2) Words with a long vowel or diphthong before [þ] change this into [ð] before [z]; the change is not shown in the spelling: *bath* [ba·þ], *baths* [ba·ðz]; thus also *paths, mouths, oaths, sheaths*, though with some vacillation.

The voiceless sound of *th* is always retained after a short vowel, as in *smiths, myths, deaths*, and after a consonant: *months, healths*; thus also after a written *r*, though this no longer has a consonantal sound: *births, fourths, hearths*. The old regular plural of *cloth* was *clothes* (with regard to the vowel cp. *staff, staves*), but in meaning as well as in sound the two are now so different that *clothes* must be considered a word apart, and a new plural has been formed, *cloths* (table cloths, horse cloths [klɔ·ðz], in the sense 'different kinds of cloth,' also pronounced [klɔþs].

(3) [s] is changed into [z] in one word only: *house* [haus], pl. *houses* [hauziz].

20.2₄. An unvoiced [s], where we should expect the voiced ending, is found in two words :

> *die*, pl. *dice.*
> *penny*, pl. *pence* (cf. **5.6₃**).

From the latter we have the compounds *twopence, threepence* (both with changed vowel sound in the numeral [tʌpəns, þripəns]), *fourpence, fivepence* (older *fippence*), *sixpence.* Note the double plural ending in *sixpences.* On the use of the form *twopenny* as an adjunct see **21.6₂.** When individual coins as such, different from the value, are meant, the regular plural, *pennies*, is used. *Three halfpence* (note the pronunciation [heipəns]) ; when the coins are meant, both *halfpennies* and *halfpence* occur.

20.3₁. There are a few survivals of earlier formations : *oxen, children* ; *men, women, feet, geese, teeth, mice, lice.* It is worth noting that such irregularities are preserved in the most familiar and popular words only, the reason being that the plural forms occur so very often in ordinary speech that children hear them frequently at an early age. Some of the words are used much more frequently in the plural than in the singular ; this is particularly true of the last few of the list given here.

The old form *brethren* is preserved through the influence of the Bible, while the regular new formation, *brothers*, is the only one in ordinary use.

20.3₂. A totally different kind of irregularities is found in many learned words, where scholars have introduced the plural as well as the singular form from foreign languages. As examples may be given :

Singular	Plural
nebula	*nebulæ*
stimulus	*stimuli*
radius	*radii*
desideratum	*desiderata*
phenomenon	*phenomena*
crisis	*crises*
series	*series*
species	*species*

There is, however, a strong natural tendency to inflect such words as are in everyday use in the English way : no one thinks of using a learned ending instead of saying *ideas, circuses, gymnasiums*, etc. *Formulas, dogmas*, and *funguses* are more English than *formulæ, dogmata*, and *fungi*. *Indexes* is used in ordinary language, but *indices* in mathematics ; *geniuses* means ' men of genius,' but *genii* ' spirits.' *Stamina* in Latin is the plural of *stamen*, but in English it is apprehended as an independent singular. Similarly *errata* (the Latin plural of *erratum*) is used as a singular with the meaning ' list of printer's errors.'

The Latin plurals are always preferred where the addition of the English ending *-es* would produce a harsh sequence of three hissing sounds: *bases*, not *basises, analyses, axes, hypotheses, oases*.

A Hebrew plural in *-im* is found in *cherubim, seraphim*, now usually *cherubs, seraphs*.

The Unchanged Plural

20.4₁. Many substantives are unchanged in the plural, either always or in certain employments.

Thus some names of animals : *sheep, deer, swine*. The unchanged plural is further found in many names of animals that are hunted because of their usefulness to man : *snipe, wild duck* (but *tame ducks*), *waterfowl* (but generally *fowls* in a farmyard), *fish* (by the side of *fishes*), *salmon, trout*, etc. Foreign names of animals are often unchanged : *buffalo, giraffe, nilghai*.

> There are as good fish in the sea as ever came out of it.
> Fishes are cast away that are cast into dry ponds.

Next we have the unchanged plural in some words indicating number : six *brace* of pheasants, four *dozen*, three *score* years and ten, two *hundred* times, five *thousand* a year, three *million* people. When these words are not preceded by a numeral, they take *s* : *dozens* of times, *hundreds* of people, etc.

Pairs and *couples* are now more usual than the unchanged plurals *pair* and *couple*.

The unchanged plural of measures of length (*foot, fathom, mile*) is now generally given up, except *foot* in an indication of a person's height : *five foot ten*.

Stone (the measure of weight) has the unchanged plural, but *pound* instead of *pounds* is antiquated. (On *five pound note*, see **21.6₂**.)

Note, further, six thousand *horse* (= horse soldiers) and ten thousand *foot*, five *cannon*, many small *craft*, two hundred *sail* (= ships), five thousand *head* of cattle.

20.4₂. In the familiar *these kind of tools, those sort of speeches*, we may look upon *kind* and *sort* as unchanged plurals; but there is a tendency to treat *kind of* and *sort of* as inseparable units; cp. the vulgar *kind of* before a verb : "I kind of admire her." In literary style *books of that kind* is preferred to *those kind of books*.

In *that kind of thing* we have a survival of the old unchanged plural, *thing*.

Plural of Compounds

20.5₁. In most compounds (whether written as one or as two words) only the final element takes the plural inflexion : *postmen, gentlemen, silver spoons, fountain pens, boy messengers, woman-haters, breakwaters, afternoons*, etc.

It is often difficult to decide whether we have one or two words; hence in some cases both ways of spelling are allowed. The first part of a compound may often be considered an adjunct to the second (**8.5**, **21.6**), and adjuncts are not inflected in the plural; *family names* and *Christian names* are treated grammatically in the same way, though *family* is a substantive and *Christian* an adjective.

In *postmen, gentlemen*, etc., the vowel of *men* is obscured, but in *gentle men*, which is no compound, it retains its full sound.

20.5₂. When *man* or *woman* is the first element and serves to denote the sex of the whole, both elements take the plural form : *men-servants, women writers* (cp. *maid-servants, lady guests, girl friends*, with the first element unchanged).

20.5₃. Combinations like *the Johnson children, the Dodson sisters, the Smith brothers* are treated as compounds, but this is not the case when we say *the sisters Dodson, the brothers Smith*, etc.

20.5₄. With compound titles there is sometimes hesitation, *e.g.*

between *Lord Chancellors* and *Lords Chancellor*. A title before a name is generally unchanged : *two Mr Bertrams*.

Gonerils, Regans, and *Lady Macbeths* (Ruskin).

The Miss Browns is a more natural plural form than *the Misses Brown*.

20.5₅. *Handful* is treated as one word (note the spelling with one *l*) and has the plural *handfuls* ; this is quite natural because a person may have three handfuls of peas, though he has only two hands ; similarly *spoonfuls, basketfuls, mouthfuls* ; but with less familiar compounds one may inflect the first part of the compound : *bucketsfull* of tea.

Two *donkeysful* of children (Thackeray).

With other compounds containing an adjective as the last member there is sometimes hesitation : *knights-errant* and *knight-errants, postmasters-general* and *postmaster-generals, courts-martial* and *court-martials*.

20.5₆. Compounds containing a preposition or adverb inflect the first element : *sons-in-law, lookers-on, goings-on*. But if the first part is the base of a verb, the word is generally inflected as a whole : *drawbacks, go-betweens*. *Lock-outs* is more usual than *locks-out*.

The plural of *good-for-nothing* is *good-for-nothings* ; the reason for this exception to the general rule is obvious : *good* is an adjective, and *goods-for-nothing* would suggest a wrong idea.

Pronouns

20.6₁. While some pronouns are the same in singular and plural, e.g. *who, what, the, no, all*, and while others are used only in the singular, e.g. *each, an (a)*, or only in the plural, as *both*, there are some with separate forms for the two numbers :

I	we
he, she, it	they
myself	ourselves
yourself	yourselves
himself, herself, itself	themselves
this	these
that	those

20.6₂. In the earlier language *thou* (*thee*) was used in addressing one person, and *ye* (*you*) in addressing more than one. But, as already remarked (**14.**5), politeness has led to the dropping of the forms *thou*, *thee*, and *ye* from ordinary colloquial use, though they have been retained in more solemn language. Thus *you* only survived, and the old distinction between the two numbers is lost (except in *yourself, yourselves*), but a new way of expressing the plural has developed in those cases in which the use of the form *you* by itself might be mistaken : *you people, you girls, you gentlemen*, etc. Cp. dialectal *yous*; in the southern part of the United States *you-all* (with stress on *you*) is used as a plural of *you*.

The Meaning of Plural

20.7₁. The meaning of the plural number is obvious in most cases; *horses* means (one) horse + (a second) horse + (a third) horse, and so on. It is perhaps less obvious that *we* is not the plural of *I* in the same way as *horses* is the plural of *horse*, for it means *I* + some one else or some other people (**15.**2); *you* in the plural may sometimes mean several people addressed at the same time, but it may also mean *you* (the one person addressed) + one or several persons to whom one is not speaking just now. In about the same way, when we speak of *the sixties*, we mean the years 60 + 61 + 62 . . .

20.7₂. The use of the plural is perfectly logical in combinations like *the eighteenth and nineteenth centuries, the English and French nations, in the third and fourth chapters*. But sometimes the singular is preferable in analogous combinations, because the use of the plural might lead to misunderstanding, thus Macaulay writes : " In this, and in the next *chapter*, I have seldom thought it necessary to cite authorities," and Thackeray, " The elder and younger *son* of the house of Crawley were never at home together," where the plural form of the verb shows the plural idea, while *son* is in the singular, because the form *sons* might suggest the existence of more than two.

In speaking of a married couple we say : " Their married *life* was a singularly happy one," but in speaking of two brothers : " Their married *lives* were led under totally different circumstances."

In some set phrases the singular is used even with reference to a plural subject :

> Women have a better ear for music than most men.
> We were afraid that we might catch our death of cold.
> They lost heart—but in a different sense : they lost their hearts
> to two sisters.

There is nothing strange in saying *the Carlyles*, when Mr and Mrs Carlyle are meant, but it is rather strange that it should be possible to say *the John Philipses* to denote Mr John Philips with his wife and children, even though none but the father be called John Philips.

20.7₃. Some plurals have acquired meanings which are not found in the corresponding singulars, *e.g.*

> *air* (of the atmosphere), *airs* : give yourself airs.
> *bearing* (various meanings), *bearings* : take one's bearings.
> *colour, colours* (flag).
> *custom, customs* (duties).
> *honour, honours* (at cards, and at a University).
> *letter, letters* (learning, literature).
> *manner, manners* (behaviour).
> *order, orders* (take orders, as a clergyman).
> *pain, pains* (take pains).
> *quarter, quarters* (lodgings ; headquarters).
> *spirit, spirits* (in two senses, as in " the custom of keeping
> up spirits by pouring down spirits ").
> *writing* (handwriting), *writings* (written works).

20.7₄. Some words are hardly ever used except in the plural, *e.g.* such names of composite objects as *trousers, spectacles, bowels, whiskers* ; the names of some games : *billiards, draughts, theatricals*. Note here the use of *pair*, as in *a pair of trousers, of scissors, of spectacles*. In some words belonging to this category there is a tendency to use the plural form as a new singular : *a scissors, a barracks, a golf links, a chemical works*. Cp. also *a long innings*.

CHAPTER XXI

NUMBER—*concluded*

Thing-words (countables) and mass-words (uncountables).—
Same word used in both ways.—Plural mass-words.—Vacilla-
tion.—Individualization.—Collectives.—Special complications.—
Higher units.—The generic number.—Number in secondary words.
—First part of compounds.—Verbs.

Mass-Words

21.1₁. The categories of singular and plural naturally apply to
everything that can be counted; such ' **countables** ' are either
material beings and things, like *girls, horses, houses, flowers,* etc.,
or immaterial things of various orders, like *days, hours, miles,
words, sonatas, events, crimes, mistakes, ideas, plans,* etc.

Let us use the term ' **thing-words** ' for all such words, using
the word *thing* in its widest application. But a great many
words do not in that way call up the idea of something possessing
a certain shape or precise limits. These words are called ' **mass-
words** ': they stand for something that cannot be counted;
such ' **uncountables** ' are either material and denote some
substance in itself independent of form, for instance *silver,
quicksilver, water, butter, tea* (both the leaves and the fluid), *air*
—or else immaterial, for instance, *leisure, music, traffic, success,
commonsense, knowledge,* and especially many ' nexus-words '
formed from verbs, e.g. *admiration, satisfaction, refinement,* or
from adjectives, e.g. *safety, constancy, blindness, idleness.*

On the meaning of the term ' nexus-word,' see **9.**7 and xxx.

While countables may be ' quantified ' by means of such
words as *one, two, many* (*a great many*), *few* (*a few*), mass-words
cannot take such adjuncts, but may be quantified by means of
much and *little.* Cp. also *a great many horses—a great deal
of money.* But there are some quantifiers which may be used
with both classes: *some bird, some birds ; some silver ; plenty
of birds ; plenty of leisure.*

21.1₂. The distinction between thing-words (countables) and

mass-words (uncountables) is easy enough if we look at the idea
that is expressed in each single instance. But in practical
language the distinction is not carried through in such a way
that one and the same word stands always for one and the same
idea. On the contrary, a great many words may in one connexion stand for something countable and in another for
something uncountable, see, for instance :

a cake, many cakes	much cake
two big cheeses	a little more cheese
a tall oak	a table made of oak
have an ice	there is no ice on the pond
to-day's paper	a parcel in brown paper
various noises	a good deal of noise
confidential talks	much talk
different feelings	he did not show much feeling
many experiences	much experience

Time is countable in two distinct significations (we had a
delightful time | I have been there four or five times), but it is
a mass-word when we say :

I have no time for such nonsense.

Lamb is a thing-word when meaning the live animal (two
young lambs), but a mass-word when used of meat (lamb or
pork, sir ?). *Fish* is used in the same two ways, and that may
be one of the reasons why *fish* has come to be used as an unchanged plural by the side of the form *fishes* (**20.4**). Compare
also : *many fruits* and *much fruit* ; *a few Japanese coins* and
pay him back in his own coin.

His *hair* is sprinkled with grey = he has some grey *hairs*.
Shee hath more *hair* then wit, and more faults then *haires* (Sh.).
Is your house built of *stone* or *brick* ?
Many *stones* (*bricks*) have gone to the building of that house.

Besides meaning a kind of wood as material *oak* may be used
as a mass-word to denote a mass of live trees ; correspondingly
with other plant-names :

Oak and *beech* began to take the place of *willow and elm* (Stevenson).
A bed of *mignonette*.

Bread is a mass-word (and *a loaf* may be considered the corresponding thing-word) ; yet we may say " I've had two *breads*," meaning ' two portions of bread ' ; cp. two *whiskies*.

Verse is a thing-word when we say " some of his verses are not harmonious," but may also be used as a mass-word : " a book of German verse " (in contrast to *prose*). Cf. " a continual flow of *jest* and *anecdote*."

21.2₁. From a purely logical point of view we may say that as mass-words denote what cannot be counted, the ideas of singular and plural are not applicable to them ; strictly speaking, therefore, they should not have the form of either of these numbers. But as a matter of fact, most languages are bound to choose between the two numbers, and mass-words therefore may be divided into the two classes of singular mass-words and plural mass-words. To the former class belong all the examples hitherto given ; examples of the second class, mass-words which are plural from a formal point of view, are : *sweetmeats, weeds* (in a garden), *embers, dregs, sweepings ; sweets, goods ; ashes* (cf., however, *cigar-ash*). Some names of diseases are also plural mass-words : *measles, hysterics, rickets*—though we may say " measles is very infectious."

On the plural mass-word *clothes* and its relation to *cloth*, which may be both a mass-word and a thing-word, see **20.2₃**.

21.2₂. In some cases there is vacillation between a singular and a plural form : *victuals* is more common than *victual, oats* than *oat*.

His *wages* were not high | how *much wages* does he get ? | a fair *wage*.

Brain and *brains* : he has no brains or little brains.

You cannot take too much *pains* (**20.7₃**).

There is an old singular *mean*, which is used by Shakespeare in the sense of *means*, but the original plural *means* is now used also as a singular : *every other means*.

21.2₃. The words in *-ics*, denoting sciences and occupations, are plurals, but are not infrequently treated as singulars : *mathematics, statistics, politics* and others : " Politics doesn't (or don't) interest me."

Individualization

21.3₁. We have seen that some mass-words may also be used as thing-words, but this is not always possible, and as it is often desirable to single out things consisting of some mass, this must then be done by means of such expressions as *a lump of sugar, a piece of wood.*

Furniture is a mass-word, but as there is no corresponding thing-word, we say, for instance, " not a single piece of furniture " | " two clumsy articles of furniture."

Corresponding expressions are used with immaterial mass-words to denote individual outcomes of some quality or manner of action :

> We must prevent this piece of folly.
> An insufferable piece of injustice.
> Two pieces of bad news.
> Another piece of scandal.
> The most interesting bits of information.
> A last word (or piece) of advice.
> An extraordinary stroke of good luck.
> An act of perfidy.
> A matter of common knowledge.

Wordsworth speaks of " That best part of a good man's life. His little, nameless, unremembered *acts Of kindness and of love,*" but we may also use the word *kindness* of an individual act showing that quality :

> I thanked her for this mark of affection, and for all her other *kindnesses* towards me (Dickens).

21.3₂. *Business* is generally a mass-word, as when we say " business is slack " | " he does a good deal of business with them " | " a still better stroke of business." But it is a thing-word when it means a particular occupation, or place of business (shop), as in " his happy ideas would stock twenty ordinary businesses." It should be mentioned that the word is now dissociated from the adjective *busy* and is pronounced in two syllables, while the new word *busyness* (three syllables) is always a mass-word with the meaning ' the quality of being busy.'

Collectives

21.4$_1$. If we look at the meaning of such a word as *nation*, we see that it denotes a collection of individuals which are viewed as a unit. The same is true of *family, clergy, party*, etc. Such words are termed collectives. As they denote at the same time a plurality and a unit, they may be said to be doubly countables and thus from a logical point of view form the exact contrast to mass-words : they are at the same time singular and plural, while mass-words are logically neither.

Many words which do not themselves denote a plurality of individuals acquire the meaning of a collective in certain contexts, as when we use the *Bench* of a body of judges, or speak of a *town* or *village* and mean its inhabitants.

21.4$_2$. The double-sidedness of collectives is shown linguistically in various ways : by the number of the verb and by the pronoun referring to it, as will be seen in the following examples.

Collectives treated as singulars :

> Mine is an old family.
> Is it better to have a clergy that marries than one that does not marry ?
> Each nation must be able to judge for itself.
> No party which respects itself can be in favour of that measure.

Collectives treated as plurals :

> All my family are early risers.
> The clergy were all of them opposed to his proposal.
> A nation, who lick, yet loathe the hand that waves the sword (Byron).
> The police themselves would not credit it.
> Half the hotel were scandalized at her.
> Your sex are not thinkers (George Eliot).
> The Government congratulated themselves on the result of the election.

Sometimes even good writers treat a collective in the same sentence as a singular and as a plural :

> The Garth family, which was rather a large one, for Mary had four brothers and one sister, were very fond of their old house (George Eliot).

Nodding their heads before her goes the merry minstrelsy (Coleridge).

The note that catches a public who think with their boots and read with their elbows (Kipling).

21.4₃. While *nation* is always treated like an ordinary collective, its synonym *people*, though still used in the same way (a people who hate us | two different peoples), has come to be also used in a somewhat different way as a kind of plural of *person* : people say | one or two people might drop in | many people.

21.4₄. This way of counting the individuals that go to make the collective is found occasionally with other collectives, though the usage is not established in the same way as with *people* :

Twenty police.

The church with its twenty-eight thousand clergy.

A fly can give birth to a million offspring.

A few cattle.

As *troop* means ' a body of soldiers,' it may be used in the plural with a numeral in the same signification, but it may also be used with higher numerals counting the individuals composing the troops. Macaulay thus writes " He scattered two troops of rebel horse," but in a subsequent passage, " The King's forces consisted of about two thousand five hundred regular troops."

21.4₅. Some words present special complications. Thus *youth* may mean (1) young age : in his youth he was a teetotaller ; (2) young people collectively, with plural or singular construction : such privilege has youth, that cannot take long leave of pleasant thoughts (Wordsw.) | among the British youth his contemporaries ; (3) a young man ; twenty youths.

Similarly *acquaintance* : (1) I hope to make his acquaintance ; (2) his acquaintance give him a very different character (Goldsm., now rare) ; (3) one of my friends or acquaintances.

Though *an enemy* always refers to a single hostile being, *the enemy* may be used with a plural verb in the sense ' the hostile forces ' :

The enemy were retiring.

21.4₆. English has a faculty unparalleled in other languages of turning numerals, either by themselves or in conjunction with primary words, into a new kind of collectives by creating **higher units,** which are treated as substantives in the singular. Thus we speak of a cricket *eleven* and of another college *eight*. Such words, of course, may be put in the plural :

> Two cricket elevens.
> For many tens of thousands of years.
> They came by twos and threes.
> Three nines make twenty-seven.

In cases like these a Chinese grammarian says that " English commonsense has triumphed over grammatical nonsense."

21.4₇. In the same way a whole group of words containing a numeral may be treated as a singular meaning a unity of a higher order. The unification may be shown grammatically either by the form of the verb or by an adjunct in the singular, or by both in the same sentence :

Examples :

> *Forty yards is* a good distance.
> *Is twenty hundred kisses* such a trouble ? (Sh.).
> I want a receipt for *that two hundred pounds.*
> I stayed there for *one short seven days.*
> *The second six months* seemed to him much longer than the first.
> *No two natures* were ever more unlike than those of Dryden and Pope.
> *Every five minutes* (**18.3₂**).

A special case of unification is seen in compounds with *pence* : *a sixpence*, with its plural *sixpences*. We must also mention *a fortnight*, from *fourteen night*, and *a twelvemonth* : *night* and *month* are old unchanged plurals.

The Generic Number

21.5. An assertion about a whole species or class—equally applicable to each member of the class—can, of course, be made by means of *every* (every man, every cat), *any* (any man, any cat), or *all* with the plural (all men, all cats). Very often, however, the generic character is not thus expressly indicated, but implied, and curiously enough language for that purpose uses now the singular, now the plural, now a definite and now an indefinite form, as will be seen in the following synopsis :

(1) the singular without any article : *man* is mortal ;

(2) the singular with the indefinite article : *a cat* has nine lives ;

(3) the singular with the definite article : *the dog* is vigilant ;

(4) the plural without any article : *dogs* are vigilant ;

(5) the plural with the definite article : *the English* are fond of out-door sports.

21.5₁. The singular without any article is used with mass-words—material and immaterial, see :

> Lead is heavier than iron.
> Blood is thicker than water.
> Time and tide wait for no man.
> Art is long, life is short.
> History is often stranger than fiction.
> True Love in this differs from gold and clay.
> That to divide is not to take away (Shelley).

But with names of living beings this way of implying the generic character is found with two words only, *man* and *woman*.

Man used generically may refer to all mankind without any regard to sex :

> The proper study of mankind is Man (Pope).
> God made the country, and man made the town (Cowper).
> His arms were long, like prehistoric man's.

But *man* may also be used in contrast to *woman* generically :

> Man delights not me ; no, nor woman neither (Sh.).
> Man is the head, but woman turns it.
> Woman is best when she is at rest (or, more colloquially, A woman . . .).

21.5₂. When the indefinite article is used generically with a substantive in the singular, it may be considered a weaker *any* :

> *An owl* cannot see well in the daytime.
> *An oak* is hardier than *a beech*.

21.5₃. When the definite article is used with a singular in this generic signification, it may be said to denote the typical representative of the class :

> *The owl* cannot see well in the daytime.
> *The early bird* catches *the worm.*
> *The Child* is father of *the Man* (Wordsworth).

This form is very frequent, though it may in many cases be ambiguous, for " the origin of *the ballad* " may refer either to ballads in general or to the special ballad we are just discussing.

The definite article is found in this way before adjectives, especially in philosophic parlance, when *the Beautiful* means everything that is beautiful.   Other examples in **8.3**.

21.5₄. Generic plural without an article is very frequent :

> Owls cannot see well in the daytime.
> Be yee therefore wise as serpents and harmeless as doves (AV.).

But it should be noted that *men* used in this way nearly always refers to males (as *man* in the second employment mentioned above, **21.5₁**) :

> *Men* were deceivers ever (Sh.).
> I am studying *men*, she said.   In our day this is the proper study of womankind.

21.5₅. The plural with the definite article in the generic sense is nowadays used chiefly with adjectives : " *the old* are apt to catch cold " (=old people are . . .).   See **8.3₂**.

Substantives in the plural with the definite article are used in scientific or quasi-scientific descriptions to indicate more definitely than the forms mentioned above that the whole species is meant :

> The owls have large eyes and soft plumage.

21.5₆. Note also the use of both numbers in relative clauses to denote a whole class : *he that touches pitch* (or *they that*, or *those who, touch pitch* ; or, *whoever touches pitch*) will be defiled.

Number in Secondary Words

21.6₁. The notions of singularity and plurality properly belong to primaries only, but not to secondaries.   But many languages make their adjuncts agree in number with the

primaries. In English this is the case with *this* and *that* only :
these boys ; *those boys* (cf. also the quantifiers : he has *much
money* and *many friends*. She had *a little coffee* and *a few
biscuits*). In the great majority of cases adjuncts have the
same form, whether they belong to a singular or to a plural
primary ; see, for instance :

My black coat. My black trousers.
The other beautiful poem. The other beautiful poems.
A little child. Little children.
What a fool ! What fools !

Hence it is possible in English (but not in those languages
which require agreement in such combinations) to apply one
and the same adjunct to two words of different number :

My wife and children (French : ma femme et mes enfants).
He wore the same coat and trousers as last year.

21.6₂. In the first part of compounds the general rule is to use
the singular form, even if the conception is naturally plural.
(It should be remembered that the first part of a compound is
really a kind of adjunct). Thus we have *six shilling books* | *a
five pound note* | *a seventy-mile drive* | *sixpenny magazines*, etc.,
and similarly from words not used in the singular form when
standing by themselves : *oatmeal, a billiard table.*

This rule, however, is not absolute. There are exceptions,
chiefly in modern compounds, and especially if there is no
singular in use or if the plural form is scarcely felt as such :
trousers-pocket is found alongside with *trouser-pocket* ; *pains-
taking* ; *a clothes brush* ; *a customs officer* ; *a two-thirds majority* ;
a savings-bank ; *the Parcels Delivery Company.*

In some cases the reason for the use of the form in *s* is obviously
the desire to avoid misunderstanding ; thus in *a goods-train* ; *a
Greats tutor* (Greats, an Oxford examination) ; *the seconds-hand
of a watch.*

21.6₃. Note the old compounds *two pennyworth, six pennyworth* (often pronounced [penəþ]), in which *pennyworth* may be
considered an invariable substantive. But *twopenceworth* may
also be found. *An engine of fifty horse power* is originally to be

analysed as a compound of *fifty-horse* and *power*, but now it is practically *fifty* + an invariable compound *horsepower*.

21.6₄. With genitival compounds there is some difficulty in the spelling ; the general rule is to spell *a bird's nest* (although it may, and usually does, contain more than one bird), but in the plural *birds' nests* ; similarly, *his tailor's bill*, but *their tailors' bills*, *a printer's error*, but *many printers' errors*; *ladies'* (or *lady's*) *maids*. In such cases the sound is the same, and the differentiation in spelling is artificial. But where there is a difference in pronunciation, we may find such anomalies as " he is always communicative in *a man's party* " (Thackeray), where the singular *party* induces the singular form in *man*, and inversely " in her *men's clothes* she looked tall." *A woman's college*.

Verbs

21.7₁. No distinction is made in verbs between the two numbers except in the present tense, and there it is found in the third person only, which in the singular ends generally in *s* ; for details see **23.1₄**.

In the preterit we have the solitary example *was*, plural *were* ; in all other verbs the plural is like the singular : I *went*, we *went*.

21.7₂. It should be noted that singular and plural in verbs has nothing at all to do with the verbal idea : when we say " birds sing " with the plural form of *sing* (cp. the singular : a bird *sings*) this does not denote several acts of singing, but is only a meaningless grammatical contrivance showing the dependence of the verb on its subject. It is therefore really superfluous to have separate forms in the verb for the two numbers, and English has lost nothing in clearness, but has gained in ease, through the dropping of nearly all the forms that in former stages of the language distinguished the two numbers in verbs.

21.7₃. As for the use of the plural form where it is distinct from the singular, no difficulty is felt in most of the cases in

which the subject is itself in the plural or consists of two or
more words joined by means of *and*, e.g.

> There *are* more things in heauen and earth, Horatio,
> Then *are* dream'd of in your philosophy (Sh.).
> Time and tide *wait* for no man.

21.7₄. But when the two joined words form one conception,
the verb is put in the singular, as in

> Accuracy and precision *is* a more important quality of language
> than abundance (N.B. one quality, not two).
> The sapper and miner was at work (one person; Dickens).

Here we may quote also :

> Father and mother *is* man and wife; man and wife *is* one flesh
> (Sh.).

Sometimes, when the singular is used, the reason is that only
one of the ideas was present in the speaker's or writer's mind
at the time, as in

> *Is* Bushy, Green and the Earl of Wiltshire dead? (Sh.).

21.7₅. As subordination expressed by *with* means practically
the same thing as co-ordination with *and*, writers sometimes use
the plural in sentences like the following :

> Don Alphonso, With other gentlemen of good esteeme *Are*
> journying (Sh.).

This, of course, is blamed by grammarians, but in the predicative the plural is established in " He is great friends with
Henry," etc.

21.7₆. When two words in the singular are connected by
means of *or* (*nor*) grammarians prefer the verb in the singular :

> Neither Coleridge nor Southey *is* a good reader of verse (De
> Quincey).

But as the idea is often addition rather than separation, there
is good excuse for those writers who use the plural, *e.g.*

> Snuff or the fan *supply* each pause of chat (Pope).
> Without that labour, neither reason, art, nor peace, *are* possible
> to man (Ruskin).

Cf. **21.4₂** on the plural after collectives.

21.7₇. Usage wavers in arithmetical formulas : What *are* (or *is*) twice three ? Six and six *is* (or *are*) twelve.

There is also a natural hesitation when *is* or *are* is to be placed between two words of different number :

Fools are my theme (Byron ; =My theme is fools).
Manners is a fine thing (Swift).
The stars were our only guide.
Our only guide was the stars.

CHAPTER XXII

DEGREE

Positive, comparative and superlative.—Regular forms.—Irregularities.—*More* and *most*.—Meaning.—Superiority, equality and inferiority.—Seeming comparatives.—Gradual increase.—Parallel increase.—Weakened comparatives.—Higher degree than the positive.—*Too.*—*Prefer.*—Superlative.—Superlative in speaking of two.—Limited superlative.—*Most.*—Latin comparatives.

Forms

22.1₁. From a formal point of view we have two degrees of comparison in adjectives and adverbs, namely, **Comparative** and **Superlative.** The regular way of forming them is by adding the endings -*er* and -*est* to the ground-form, which is called **Positive,** *e.g.*

Positive	*Comparative*	*Superlative*
small	smaller	smallest
soon	sooner	soonest

Merely orthographic peculiarities are seen when *y* after a consonant is changed into *i*, when a consonant is doubled after a short vowel, and when a mute *e* disappears, *e.g.*

dry	drier	driest
happy	happier	happiest
thin	thinner	thinnest
big	bigger	biggest
free	freer	freest
polite	politer	politest

The following phonetic modifications should be noted :
An *r* regains its consonantal value before the endings :

dear	dearer	dearest
poor	poorer	poorest

Syllabic [l] becomes non-syllabic :

simple	simpler	simplest

The sound of [g] appears after [ŋ], written *ng* :

strong	stronger	strongest

This change is found in *strong, long* and *young,* the only adjectives of that form, whose degrees of comparison are really living ; in occasional new-formations like *cunninger, cunningest,* [ŋ] only is sounded.

22.1₂. In the following words we have survivals of earlier phonetic modifications :

old	elder	eldest
late	latter	last
nigh	near	next

But on account of the irregularities of these forms the connexion between them has been loosened, and various new forms have come into existence.

Elder and *eldest* have been largely supplanted by *older* and *oldest,* and are now chiefly used preceded by some determining word (genitive, possessive pronoun or article) ; they generally refer to persons connected by relationship ; note, however, the substantive *elder* with the plural *elders.* *Older* must be used when followed by *than* or when *than* can easily be supplied (in these cases Elizabethans still could use *elder*) :

> My eldest son is called John, after my eldest brother.
> Pliny the elder.
> The elder brother, who was much older than Frank.
> Ann is old, but her sister is older still.

22.1₃. As a real comparative and superlative corresponding to *late, later* and *latest* are now always used. *Latter* is used in contrast to *former* and, further, in such connexions as *these latter days, latter-day saints, the latter part* (or *half*) *of the century.* *Last* is the opposite of *first* (these two mark the beginning and end of a series), or it may be used of the period immediately preceding the one in which we are now or of which we are now speaking (*Last Wednesday* ; for *the last few years* : here opposed to *next*). *Latest* has not the same element of finality as *last* ; it is opposed to all the earlier :

> Mr G.'s latest book, which we hope will not be his last.
> The old Archbishop breathed his last yesterday morning.
> At last he went away.

You must be there at the latest at five (=not later than five).
(But : Have you heard Mr N.'s last ? =his latest joke.)

22.1₄. *Nigh* is now obsolete (together with the analogical formations *nigher* and *nighest*).   *Near* has ceased to be a comparative, and from such applications as *Come near !* has come to mean the same thing as the old *nigh*, so that even a new comparative and superlative have been formed : *nearer* and *nearest*. *Next* is now completely isolated and means immediately following or close to :

I shall start next Friday (next year, etc.).
What next ?
He lives next door.
It is next to impossible.   (On *next best*, see **22.7₅**.)

22.2₁. In the following irregular cases we have really no positive corresponding to the comparative and superlative, which are formed from independent roots :

(good, well)	better	best
(bad, evil, ill)	worse	worst
(little)	less	least
(much, many)	more	most
(far)	farther, further	farthest, furthest

Worse may occasionally be the comparative of such adjectives as *dreadful, vile, wretched, wrong*, etc.—the essential thing is that it is the opposite of *better*.

22.2₂. *Worse* and *less* are the only comparatives in the language that do not end in *-r* ; therefore the popular instinct seized on them and added the usual ending *-er*.   But while *worser*, which was formerly frequent (for instance in Sh.), has gone out of polite use, *lesser* still lives, and a differentiation has taken place, so that *less* generally refers to quantity and is opposite to *more*, while *lesser* refers to size and especially to value or importance ; *lesser* is more literary than *less*.

The later you come, the less time will there be for discussion.
More glory will be wonn, or less be lost (Milton).
The Lesser Bear.   The Lesser Prophets.
Cowley was one of the lesser poets of the period.

Woman is the lesser man, and all thy passions matched with mine,
Are as moonlight unto sunlight, and as water unto wine
  (Tennyson).
I have not the least inclination to yield to him.
Not the least of his merits was his work in the slums.

Before *than*, and adverbially, *lesser* is never used :

In less than half an hour.
The last comer, who turned out to be no less a person than the
  Prime Minister.
Less acute men would have noticed nothing.

Littler and *littlest* may occasionally be found :

Where love is great, the littlest doubts are fear (Sh.).

Note the combination : the least little drop.

22.2₃. Both *farther, farthest* and *further, furthest* may be used
of distance in space and time ; but in the derived sense, ' in
addition, besides, to a greater extent,' the form with *u* is
preferred :

We may go further and say . . .
On further inquiry we found out the entire truth.

Cf. *furthermore.*

22.3₁. Comparatives in *-er* and superlatives in *-est* are formed
freely from monosyllables and from words of two syllables
ending in a vocalic sound (e.g. *pretty, narrow, clever*) or in syllabic
l (**22.1**), or else having the stress on the last syllable (*polite,
severe*). They are also formed from such frequently used adjectives as *handsome, quiet, pleasant*. But with all longer words,
especially if ending in a hard group of consonants, these endings
are avoided, and comparison is effected by means of preposed
more and *most* ; this is even the case with some short words.
Thus we have :

ridiculous	more ridiculous	most ridiculous
difficult	more difficult	most difficult
real	more real	most real
right	more right	most right

Similarly with words like *elementary, peculiar*, etc.
Sometimes the superlative in *-est* is in frequent use (*correctest,*

solidest, stupidest), while the comparative in *-er* is rarer. With many words the preference for one or the other way of forming the degrees of comparison depends on individual taste.

Words indicating nationality never take the endings *-er* and *-est*; always *more* (*most*) *French*, etc.; similarly *Roman*.

22.3₂. With regard to compounds, we form such comparatives and superlatives as:

well-known	better-known	best-known
hard-working	harder-working	hardest-working

and similarly *a better-hearted fellow* and *the dullest-witted boy*, but in other cases *more* or *most* is preferred, e.g. *more old-fashioned, the most good-natured*.

The most far-fetched arguments for the most short-sighted policy.

22.3₃. There is a decided tendency to use *more* if the comparison is not between two persons or things, but between the same person or thing at two different times:

Every month I become a year more old (Kipling).
Her voice grew more gentle, more low.

The *-er* form will, however, be used in such familiar cases as:

The patient feels better, though the temperature is higher [than yesterday].

22.3₄. When two qualities of the same person or thing are compared, the rule is to use *more*:

His mother was more kind than intelligent.

But in speaking of two dimensions, we may say, *e.g.*

The windows were much wider than they were high.

22.4. With regard to adverbs, the same rules for the use of the endings *-er* and *-est* or *more* or *most* prevail as for adjectives, *e.g.*

soon   sooner   soonest

She works harder than her husband.
The man who stayed longest and spoke loudest.

beautifully   more beautifully   most beautifully

By the side of *more easily* the shorter form *easier* may be used, especially in the familiar phrase :

This is easier said than done.

On the other hand, some writers are fond of such adverbs as *kindlier, clearlier, plainlier*, etc.

Meaning

22.5₁. After these considerations (mostly of a formal character) we shall now look into the meaning of these degrees of comparison.

If we compare two persons or things in regard to some quality, we find three possibilities :

    1. Superiority : more dangerous (better) than.
    2. Equality : as dangerous (as good) as.
    3. Inferiority : less dangerous (less good) than.

Obviously 1 and 3 are closely connected as indicating inequality and requiring *than*, while 2 requires *as*, before the second member of comparison.

Comparisons with *less* are not very frequent ; instead of *less dangerous than*, we often say *not so dangerous as*, and whenever there are two adjectives of opposite meaning, we say, for instance, *weaker than* rather than *less strong than*.

22.5₂. Some adjectives and adverbs are on account of their meaning incapable of comparison, e.g. *several, half, daily, own, future*. Others, which strictly speaking should seem incapable of being put in the comparative or superlative, are used thus in a slightly modified meaning : *more perfect* and *most perfect* really mean 'nearer and nearest to perfection.' Similarly *fuller, fullest*.

22.5₃. Some adjectives are seemingly comparatives, being formed in *-er* from particles (which cannot be used as adjectives) : *inner, outer, upper*. That these are not real comparatives is seen by the impossibility of using *than* with them. But real superlatives are formed from them : *inmost, outmost, upmost*; with these should be classed some superlatives in *-most* from substantives : *topmost, headmost* (rare), *backmost, eastmost* (more usual *easternmost*), and others. There are also some super-latives in *-ermost* from the above-mentioned forms : *innermost, uppermost,* etc., cp. *bettermost.*

Utter is an old formation from *out* (with the vowel shortened as in *latter*) ; it has lost its local meaning and now denotes degree : *utter darkness, an utter scoundrel. Utmost* has kept more of its local meaning (*the utmost edge,* etc.), but is also chiefly used of degree : *with the utmost care,* etc.

22.6₁. To indicate a gradual increase we use two comparatives connected with *and* :

Conditions are getting worse and worse every day.
He became more and more eloquent towards the end of his speech.

Poets will vary this figure :

The piper loud and louder blew,
The dancers quick and quicker flew (Burns).
I grow bolder and still more bold (Shelley).

22.6₂. To indicate a parallel increase in two mutually de-pendent cases *the . . . the* is used ; *the* is an old instrumental of *that,* meaning ' by so much.' Generally the determinant is placed before the determined :

The more he reads, the less he understands.
The longer he stayed, the more sullen he became.
The noisier they were, the better was their mother pleased.

Sometimes *that* is inserted in the determinant clause :

The more that was known about the incident, the more indignant people became.

The determinant clause may be·put last :

They liked the book better the more it made them cry (Goldsmith).

We have a corresponding use of *the* before a comparative in cases like

I like him all the better on account of his shyness.
" He won't come." " So much the better. The more fool he."
The young people were plainly the worse for drink.

22.6₃. A comparative may sometimes be used though the idea of comparison is not very prominent : *the younger generation* ;

the higher criticism, etc. " You had better stay "=" it will be good for you to stay." The idea of comparison is often particularly weak in *rather* : " It's rather warm today."

22.6₄. It is very important to keep in mind that the comparative does not mean a higher degree of the quality in. question than the positive does in itself : " Peter is older than John " does not imply that Peter is old, and the comparative may therefore really indicate a lesser degree than the positive would in " Peter is old." Nor does it, of course, say anything about John's being old—if this is meant, we say " Peter is still older than John."

22.6₅. On the other hand, such a combination as *more than kind* means that *kind* is an inadequate expression and thus criticizes the use of the simple term *kind* :

> She was more than old-fashioned, she was antediluvian.
> You're worse than unfair. You're ungenerous—you're mean.

Compare also : They are all *kinder than kind.*
A similar use is found with *more than* before a verb :

> The boy more than justified the favourable opinion they had formed of him.
> It was a moonless night, but the brilliancy of the stars more than made up for the want of moonshine.

22.6₆. We have what might be termed a latent comparative in the word *too,* which means " in a higher degree than enough or than is allowable or advisable " :

> I am afraid we shall be too late for dinner.
> This is too good to be true.
> Too much and too little of a good thing spoils it.

The comparative meaning is weakened in the colloquial :

> I am only too glad (too delighted) to do this for you.

22.6₇. Another latent comparative is contained in the verb *prefer* (='like better '). This is normally followed by *to* (as the Latin comparatives, see **22.₉**) :

> I prefer claret to sherry.

But occasionally the character of a comparative may induce the use of *than* after *prefer*, thus to avoid clashing with another *to* in :

> And you preferred to go to a moneylender than to come to me?
> (Galsworthy).

22.7₁. The superlative does not indicate a higher degree than the comparative, but really states the same degree, only looked at from a different point of view. If we compare the ages of four boys, A, B, C, and D, we may state the same fact in two different ways :

> A is older than the other boys, or
> A is the oldest boy.

In both cases A is compared with B, C, and D ; but the result is in the former case given with regard to these three (the other boys), in the latter with regard to all the boys, A included. The comparative must thus be supplemented by a member expressed by means of *than* or understood. The superlative, on the other hand, is often followed by *of* or *among all*. But as both forms really express the same idea, we should not be surprised to find a confusion (pretty frequent in older writers), resulting in such blendings as

> A king, whose memory of all others we most adore (Bacon).
> Parents are the last of all others to be trusted with the education of their own children (Swift).

22.7₂. Another blending occurs when the singular is used where we should expect the plural after *of* : as *the best temper* and *the best of tempers* mean the same thing, many people will say and write :

> He was evidently not in the best of temper (or health).
> People taking the gentlest of exercise.

This is particularly frequent with words that are seldom or never used in the plural number.

22.7₃. When there is no direct comparison (with *than*), some grammarians—in accordance with Latin syntax—insist on the use of the comparative if two, and the superlative if more than two are referred to :

The better part of valour is discretion (Sh.).
Rome of Cæsar, Rome of Peter, which was crueller? which was
    worse (Tennyson).

But apart from such set phrases as *the lower lip, the upper end,
the lower classes,* the natural tendency in English is to use the
superlative in speaking of two :

Put your best leg foremost.
Whose God is strongest, thine or mine ? (Milton).
We'll see who is strongest, you or I (Goldsmith).

22.7₄. It is a natural consequence of the nature of the superlative that it is most often used preceded by a defining word :

The richest man in the town.
My youngest boy.
Thackeray's best novel.
That best part of a good man's life,
His little, nameless, unremembered acts
Of kindness and of love (Wordsworth).
There you may see England at its best—and in its best.

Still, a superlative may be used after *any* or *no* :

On any smallest occasion (=any, even the smallest).
Football, or any other roughest sport.
Rightly viewed no meanest object is insignificant (Carlyle).

22.7₅. The superlative may be limited by some addition like :

The next best (=better than all the others with the exception of
    one).
St Paul's is the third longest cathedral in Christendom.
The largest but one (but two, three, etc.).

22.8₁. In consequence of the almost universal tendency to
exaggerate, people will often use the superlative where they
mean only a very high degree, as in

I should do it with the greatest pleasure.

22.8₂. This leads to the use of *most* as a strengthened *very* before
an adjective. Here *most* is no longer a real superlative and is
distinguished from real superlatives by being used (1) with the
indefinite article, and (2) in the predicative without an article :

The Bishop is a most learned gentleman.
This procedure is most dangerous.

Compare also the colloquial :

This is most awfully kind of you.

More may mean ' a greater number of (people),' and *most* ' the greatest number of (people),' *e.g.* :

More people go to London than to any other place in Europe.
Most young Englishmen are fond of outdoor sports.

Note, in consequence of what has been said above, the following expressions :

(1) I got to know most respectable people in the town (=the greatest number of respectable people).

(2) I got to know the most respectable people in the town (superlative of *respectable*).

(3) I got to know some most respectable people in the town (=some highly respectable).

With a shorter adjective this would correspond to

(1) I got to know most (of the) kind people in the town.

(2) I got to know the kindest people in the town.

(3) I got to know some most kind people in the town.

22.8₃. In the idiomatic :

He was not best pleased to see us—

we have another example of a superlative, which has come to mean only a very high degree.

22.9. Some adjectives are taken from Latin comparatives : *anterior, interior, inferior, superior, major, minor.* When they are used with the force of comparatives, they do not take *than*, but *to* : *prior to the war, inferior to other brands*, etc. When used as substantives, they are combined with the genitive : *John's superiors* =' those that are higher (in office) than John.' But very often they have nothing left of the comparative meaning : *These cigars are very inferior indeed.*

From Latin superlatives we have, e.g. *extreme, supreme.* But they are not superlatives in English, and nothing hinders us from forming a superlative and saying : *with the extremest care.*

TENSE

23.1₁. It is important to keep the two concepts **time** and **tense** strictly apart. The former is common to all mankind and is independent of language; the latter varies from language to language and is the linguistic expression of time-relations, so far as these are indicated in verb forms. In English, however, as well as in many other languages, such forms serve not only for time-relations, but also for other purposes; they are also often inextricably confused with marks for person and mood.

Time is universally conceived as something having one dimension only, thus capable of being represented by one straight line. We may arrange the main divisions in the following way :

$$\text{---------------------} \times \text{---------------------} \rightarrow$$

A : past　　　B : present　　　C : future

Or, rather, we may say that time is divided into two parts, the past and the future, the point of division being the present moment, which, like a mathematical point, has no dimension, but is continually fleeting (moving to the right in our figure).

23.1₂. Under each of the two divisions of infinite time we may refer to some point as lying either before or after the main point

of which we are actually speaking. In this way we get the
following seven points :

The subordinate " times " are thus orientated with regard to
some point in the past (Ab) and in the future (Cb) exactly as
the main times (A and C) are orientated with regard to the
present moment (B).

After-future may be left out of account as having practically
no grammatical expression.

23.1₃. We shall now consider the tenses actually found in
English verbs. It would be conducive to clearness to have two
sets of terms, one for notional time, and the other for grammatical tense. This, however, is not easily accomplished except
for section A, where we can use the term **past** for the time
division, and **preterit** for the tense found, *e.g.* in *was, drank,
called* ; for the other sections we have no simple terms and must
therefore say ' **present time** ' and ' **present tense,** ' ' **future
time** ' (or ' **futurity** ') and ' **future tense,** ' whenever there is
any fear of misunderstanding.

The English verb has only two tenses proper, the Present and
the Preterit.

23.1₄. The **Present tense** is identical with the base of the
verb **(7.6)**. To this is added, on the one hand, -(*e*)*st* in the
obsolete *thou*-form of the second person singular (*thou goest,
doest* or *dost, wishest, drinkst* or *drinkest* ; irregular : *art, hast,
shalt, wilt*)—on the other hand, the *s*-ending with its three
phonetic forms **(4.6, 5.6₃,** cf. **14.6₂)** in the third person singular :

[iz] after hissing sounds : *kisses, praises, wishes, judges.*
[z] after voiced sounds : *goes, sends, begs, ploughs, lives.*
[s] after voiceless sounds : *beats, takes, coughs.*

Irregular : *says* [sez] from *say* [sei].
              does [dʌz] from *do* [du·].
              has [hæz] from *have* [hæv].
              is [iz] from *be* [bi·], I *am* [æm].

The old ending was *-th* : *kisseth, saith, doth* or *doeth, hath.*

Some verbs form a class apart as auxiliaries; they have neither infinitive nor participles and add no *s* in the third person singular of the present tense : *can, may, must, will, shall*; *need* and *dare*, which sometimes, but not always, add *s*, are related to this class (32.1$_5$). On *ought* see 24.3$_3$.

23.2. The **Preterit** is formed in various ways; as its form is in most verbs either identical with, or closely similar to the second participle, it will be convenient here to treat the two together.

In all regular verbs—a great many old ones, and all recently formed or recently borrowed from other languages—the Preterit and the (second) Participle are formed by the addition of the ' weak ' ending, which has three phonetic forms according to the final sound of the base (4.6) :

[id] after [d] and [t] : *ended, rested*;
[d] after voiced sounds other than [d] : *gathered* [gæðəd], *called, screwed, managed*;
[t] after voiceless sounds other than [t] : *locked* [lɔkt], *hopped, kissed, coughed, wished.*

The chief irregularities may be classed as follows :

(1) *d* is added, but the vowel of the base is changed :
    say [sei]—*said* [sed].
    flee—fled.
    hear [hiə]—*heard* [hə·d].
    sell—sold; thus also *tell—told.*

(2) *d* is added, and the consonant of the base is omitted :

have—had.

make—made.

can—could ; *will—would* ; *shall—should* ; these three verbs have no participle.

(3) *t* is added in some verbs

after *n* : *burn—burnt, learn—learnt, pen—pent.*

after *l* : *dwell—dwelt, smell—smelt, spell—spelt, spill—spilt, spoil—spoilt.*

Spoil in the sense of ' plunder ' is a different verb, which is regular.

(4) *t* is added, but *d* disappears before it :

bend—bent, lend—lent, rend—rent, send—sent, spend—spent, build—built, gird—girt.

Gilt is an adjective, while the preterit and participle of *gild* are regular : *gilded.*

(5) *t* is added, the vowel of the base is changed :

deal [di·l]—*dealt* [delt], *dream—dreamt, feel—felt, kneel—knelt, lean—leant, mean—meant.*

creep—crept, keep—kept, leap—leapt, sleep—slept.

Before this *t*, a *v* is naturally changed into *f* : *leave—left, bereave—bereft* (or *bereaved*), *cleave—cleft* (or *cleaved,* ' split ').

lose—lost.

(6) *t* is added after further change of the base :

bring—brought, think—thought.

seek—sought, beseech—besought, teach—taught.

catch—caught, buy—bought.

may—might ; this verb has no participle.

dare—durst ; this form is obsolete, and *dared* has taken its place ; cf. **32.1**$_5$.

(7) Some bases ending in *d* or *t* are unchanged in the Preterit and Participle.

rid, shed, spread.

> burst, cast, cost, cut, hit, hurt, let, put, set, shut, slit, split, sweat, thrust.
>
> must; this verb has no participle; on the preterit, see **24.6₇**.

Sweat is often regular, thus always in the sense of paying workers very badly. Americans say *quit* for British *quitted*. Both *broadcast* and *broadcasted* are used in the Preterit, in the Participle generally only *broadcast*. Similarly, *forecasted* is found by the side of *forecast*.

(8) In other verbs ending in *d* and *t* the vowel is changed :

> bleed [bliˑd]—*bled* [bled], breed—bred, feed—fed, lead—led, read—read, speed—sped.
> meet—met.
> light—lit (also lighted).
> shoot—shot.
> fight—fought.
> sit—sat, spit—spat.
> bind—bound, find—found, grind—ground, wind—wound.
> hold—held.
> stand—stood.
> get—got.

Get formerly had the participle *gotten*, which is retained in *forgotten*; Scotch people and Americans generally make a distinction : *I have gotten* = ' I have acquired,' *I have got* = ' I possess, have ' (**23.5₅**).

(9) In the following verbs, too, we have vowel change without any addition; the same vowel is found in Preterit and Participle.

> spin—spun, win—won.
> cling—clung, fling—flung, sling—slung, sting—stung, string—strung, swing—swung, wring—wrung.
> slink—slunk.
> hang—hung; in the special sense ' hang a criminal ' *hang* is often regular.
> dig—dug, stick—stuck.

strike—struck.

shine—shone; when *shine* means ' make shine ' (boots, etc.), ' polish,' it is regular.

(10) Different vowels in Preterit and Participle ; no addition :

swim—swam—swum.

begin—began—begun.

ring—rang—rung ; thus also *sing* and *spring.*

drink—drank—drunk ; thus also *shrink, sink* and *stink.*

run—ran—run.

come—came—come.

(11) The Participle ends in *n* :

blow—blew—blown ; thus also *grow, know* and *throw.*

draw—drew—drawn.

fly—flew —flown.

slay—slew—slain.

lie—lay—lain.

see—saw—seen.

do—did—done.

bear—bore—born(e).

The spelling *borne* is used in all senses except that of birth, but in that sense, too, *borne* is written in the active (she has borne five children) and if *by* follows (borne in a stable by the Virgin Mary) ; but : " he was born blind ; born in a stable ; all the children born to them ; the first-born son ; he was born in 1899."   Of course, this distinction is purely artificial.

swear—swore—sworn ; thus also *tear* and *wear.*

fall—fell—fallen.

steal—stole—stolen.

rise—rose—risen.

freeze—froze—frozen.

choose—chose—chosen.

give—gave—given.

strive—strove—striven ; thus also *thrive.*

weave—wove--woven.

bid—bad(e)—bidden or *bid.*

forbid—forbad(e)—forbidden.

> *ride—rode—ridden*; thus also *stride*.
> *hide—hid—hidden* or *hid*; thus also *chide*.
> *tread—trod—trodden*.
> *smite—smote—smitten*; thus also *write*.
> *bite—bit—bitten*.
> *beat—beat—beaten*.
> *eat—ate* (rarely *eat*)—*eaten*.
> *forget—forgot—forgotten*.
> *break—broke—broken*.
> *speak—spoke—spoken*.
> *take—took—taken*; thus also *forsake* and *shake*.
> *wake* besides *woke—woken* has also *waked* and in the Participle *woke*; *awake* makes *awoke* or *awaked*, but has no Participle in *n*. There is also a regular verb *waken*.

In the old language there was a good deal of uncertainty with regard to the keeping or dropping of the final *-en*; cp., *e.g.* Milton's New Presbyter is but old Priest *writ* large. Shakespeare has *chose, broke, spoke* by the side of *chosen, broken, spoken*, etc.

A remainder óf this vacillation is still seen in *broke* (' ruined,' financially) by the side of *broken*.

There is a tendency to use forms in *-en* preferably before a substantive : " He is drunk—a drunken plebeian " (Dickens).

(12) The Participle has two forms, in *-d* and in *-n*.

> *hew—hewed—hewed, hewn*; thus also *strew*.
> *saw—sawed—sawed, sawn*.
> *mow—mowed—mowed, mown*; thus also *show* and *sow*; *sew*, pronounced [sou] in spite of the spelling.
> *shear—sheared—shorn*, rarely *sheared*.

Some verbs by the side of the regular forms in *-d* have participles in *-n*, which are specially used as adjuncts before substantives : *carven* images, a *well-shaven* chin, *swollen* glands.

(13) Two verbs form their Preterits from a different root altogether :

> *be, am, is, are—was, were—been*.
> *go—went—gone*.

Tense-Phrases

23.3₁. Besides the two uncompounded tenses, Present and Preterit, we must recognize two tense-phrases, namely, the **Perfect,** formed by means of the present tense of the auxiliary *have* + the second participle : *I have written, he has written,* etc., and the **Pluperfect,** formed by the preterit of the same auxiliary and the second participle : *I had written, he had written,* etc.

These tense-phrases go back to very old times. Originally *have* here had its full meaning ' possess, hold ' : *I have caught the fish* = ' I hold (have) the fish as caught ' (cp. the modern " There, I have you beaten "). Afterwards this meaning was lost sight of, and *have* came to be a mere grammatical instrument (auxiliary) to mark time-relation ; thus it became possible to use it with all kinds of verbs, even those in which *have* as originally used would give no sense : *I have lost* (*thrown away, forgotten, seen*) *the key.* With intransitive verbs, too, *have* is now the usual auxiliary, but formerly *I am come, I am become,* etc., was used very extensively (**23.**5).

23.3₂. By the side of these tenses and tense-phrases we have **expanded** forms :

the Expanded Present : *am writing,*
the Expanded Preterit : *was writing,*
the Expanded Perfect : *have been writing,*
the Expanded Pluperfect : *had been writing.*

On the use of the expanded forms, see **24.**7.
On the use of *will* and *shall* to denote future time, see ch. xxv.

Use of the Present Tense

23.4₁. The Present Tense is first used about the present time. In the strict sense as a point without any dimension the present has little practical value, and in the practice of all languages " now " means a time with appreciable duration, the length of which varies greatly according to circumstances, the only thing required being that the theoretical zero-point falls within the period alluded to.   This applies to cases like :

He is hungry | he is ill | he is dead.
It rains.

She plays wonderfully well (cp. She is playing wonderfully well, **24.**7).

Our children eat very little meat.

We call him the Nabob. He earns five thousand a year.

Some people prefer music-halls to the opera.

Twice two is four. Gold is heavier than silver.

Twelve pence go to a shilling, and twenty shillings go to a pound, but where all the pounds go to, I have never been able to discover.

The evill that men do, lives after them; The good is oft enterred with their bones (Sh.).

All men are lyers (AV.).

None but the brave deserves the fair (Dryden).

These examples show a gradual transition from what is more or less momentary to " eternal truths " or what are supposed to be such. If the present tense is used, it is because the sentences are valid now; the linguistic tense-expression says nothing about the length of duration before or after the present moment. The definition given above covers the whole range of sentences adduced, as well as expressions of intermittent occurrences like :

I get up every morning at seven (even if spoken in the evening).

The steamer leaves every Tuesday in winter, but in summer both on Tuesdays and Fridays (the present moment falls within the limits of what is spoken about, for the saying concerns the present arrangement).

A peculiar use of the Present Tense is found in statements of what may be found at all times by readers :

It says in the Bible, " Thou shalt not steal."

Milton defends the liberty of the press in his *Areopagitica.*

A related usage is found in " *I hear* (*I am told, I see in the papers*) that the King is ill."

The proper meaning of *I forget* is ' I cease to remember, it drops out of my memory,' but it is frequently used as a kind of negative to *I remember*, thus it is really identical with ' I have forgotten ' : I forget how old he is.

23.4₂. Next, the Present tense is used in speaking of the past. This is the so-called ' historic Present ' (a better name would be the ' dramatic Present '), which is pretty frequent in connected narrative : the speaker, as it were, forgets all about time and recalls what he is recounting as vividly as if it were now present before his eyes.   Very often, this Present alternates with the Preterit.   Examples :

> He tooke me by the wrist, and held me hard; then goes he to the length of all his arme; And with his other hand thus o'er his brow, He fals to such perusall of my face, As he would draw it.   Long staid he so (Sh.).

> I stepped up to the copper.   "If you please, sir," says I, "can you direct me to Carrickmines Square?"   "I never heard of any such Square in these parts," he says.   "Then," says I, "what a very silly little officer you must be!"; and I gave his helmet a chuck that knocked it over his eyes, and did a bunk (Shaw).

23.4₃.   Third, the Present tense may be used in speaking of some future time, chiefly when something is settled as part of a programme or agreement; the sentence generally contains an indication of time :

> I start for Italy on Monday next.
> We dine to-morrow with the Cannings.
> "Have you been long in England?"   "Only a couple of days."
> "How long do you stay?"

Note the alternation with *will* and *shall* :

> To-morrow I leave England.   You will never see me again.   This is the last time I shall ever look on you.

In clauses after conjunctions of time this use of the Present tense is the rule, because futurity is sufficiently indicated in the main verb :

> Shall there be gallowes standing in England when thou art king? (Sh.).
> When at last the end comes, it will come quietly and fitly.

Note the difference between the two clauses in :

> We do not know when he will come, but when he comes he will not find us ungrateful.

We have the same use of the Present tense in conditional clauses :

> Will you come for a walk in the afternoon if it does not rain?   I don't know if it will rain, but if it does, I shall stay at home.

When and *if* in those of the clauses here mentioned which contain *will* are interrogative conjunctions, not conjunctions of time and condition as they are in those in which *will* is not used.

23.4₄. In clauses beginning with *after* and *as soon as* the Present tense frequently stands for what at the future moment referred to in the main clause will be past (the before-future, Ca in 23.1₂) :

> We'll sign the document the day after I come back (=pedantic : after I shall have come back).
> I shall let you know as soon as I hear from him.

Correspondingly with *before* and *till* :

> I pardon thee thy life before thou ask it (Sh.).
> Wait till the train stops.

Auxiliaries of the Perfect and Pluperfect

23.5₁. As already stated, the Perfect and Pluperfect are now regularly formed by means of the Present and Preterit of *have* with the second participle. But formerly the auxiliary *be* was extensively used with verbs of movement, *e.g.*

> A foolish thing is just come into my head (Swift, now *has*).
> He was now got to a little copse (Scott, now *had*).
> Mr Harley was gone out (Swift, now *had*).
> The ladies are not here, they are walked down the garden (Defoe, now *have*).
> Silence is become his mother-tongue (Goldsmith, now *has*).

Nowadays, a distinction is made, so that the combination with *has* is a real perfect, but that with *is* is a pure present. *He is come* means ' he has come and is now here.' While *he has gone* calls up the idea of movement, *he is gone* emphasizes the idea of a state (condition) and is the equivalent of ' he is absent, he is not here (there).' Hence the use, *e.g.* in

> I shall be gone before you wake in the morning—

and especially with the indication of the length of absence :

> He was gone but a little time.
> Don't be gone too long !
> The moon is risen = " the moon has risen and is now in the sky."

He is enlisted = ' he has enlisted and is now serving.'

The snow has melted very fast (the happening). The snow is quite melted (the resulting state).

I am determined = ' I have determined and am firm in that resolution.'

The army had advanced far into France (a real pluperfect).

The season is far advanced (*advanced* is an adjective rather than a participle).

23.5₂. The imperative *be gone !* means the same thing as *go* (at once) !, and the same meaning is found in the infinitive after *let, must* and some other phrases which have reference to the future :

Let us be gone. We must be gone.
Shall we be gone?
They were impatient to be gone.

23.5₃. By the side of *he has done* we have *he is done*, e.g.

I am only too glad to be done with all responsibility.

Done may here be considered an adjective ; cp. also :

It was rather hard to be finished with life at twenty.

Inclusive Time

23.5₄. The Perfect is used with an indication of some length of time to denote what has lasted so long and is still :

He hath beene dead foure dayes (AV.).
How long have you lived here?

This may be called the inclusive present ; correspondingly we have an inclusive past and future ; if we imagine a man who was married in 1910, speaking in the year 1930, he will say : (1) I have been married twenty years ; (2) In 1920 I had been married ten years ; (3) In 1940 I shall have been married thirty years.

I have got

23.5₅. In colloquial English *I have got* (*I've got*) has to a great extent lost the meaning of a perfect and has become a present with the same meaning as *I have* (have in my possession) ; and in the same way *I had got* (*I'd got*) has come to be a notional preterit. The reason obviously is that on account of its frequent use as an auxiliary, *have* was not felt to be strong enough to carry the meaning of ' possess ' and therefore had to be reinforced. The phrase with *got* is now used not only with objects denoting things (*I have got a knife*), but also with immaterial objects (*I've got no time*) and before an infinitive with *to*.

Somehow the combination with *got* seems more required in questions than in positive statements. " Have you it here ? " is much more unnatural than " I have it here." The reason is that in such a sentence as " Has he got a pen ? " we have the same word-order as in the ordinary type of question : " Does he want a pen ? " | " Can I have a pen ? " etc., with a weak auxiliary at the beginning of the sentence (v—S—V—O, **10.**4). On the other hand, if there is no object, *have you* cannot be expanded into *have you got* :

> If only it were quite certain you had got any opinions to represent. But have you ? (Ruskin).

There are some restrictions to the use of *have got*. Though the infinitive *to have got* may be used (He seems to have got plenty of time), the infinitive without *to* never adds *got* after *can*, *may* and the other auxiliaries ; hence the different expression for the three times in " You never did have any sense, you haven't got any sense now, and you never will have any sense."

Nor is *got* inserted in the imperative, in the perfect and the pluperfect :

> Don't have anything to do with him.
> I've had no time.
> I'd had no time.

Further, *have* is always used without *got* when it forms one semantic whole with its object, as in *have a look, a smoke, a bath* (**7.**8₂).

> Did you have a good passage ?
> I had five dances with her.

Thus also when *have* means ' partake of ' (eat, drink) :

> He had a steak and a glass of beer.

Before an infinitive with *to* the phrase with *got* is extremely frequent (*This is all you have got to do*), even when the subject is not a person (*something has got to be done*). A distinction may be made between " We don't have to change at Crewe " (the ordinary rule, we never have to) and " We haven't got to change at Crewe " (this time). While sentences like " We had to leave him there " are extremely frequent (*had to*= a notional preterit of *must*), the combination " We had got to leave " is rare, and in a question " Had you got to leave him ? " is never said instead of " Did you have to leave him ? " or " Had you to leave him ? "

On American *have gotten*, see **23.**2(8).

Use of the Preterit and Perfect

23.6₁. The difference between the Preterit and the Perfect is in English observed more strictly than in the other languages possessing corresponding tenses. The Preterit refers to some time in the past without telling anything about the connexion with the present moment, while the Perfect is a retrospective present, which connects a past occurrence with the present time, either as continued up to the present moment (inclusive time, **23.**5₄) or as having results or consequences bearing on the present moment.

The question " Did you finish? " thus refers to some definite portion of the past, while " Have you finished? " is a question about the present status and equals " Are you through? " Note also the difference in a dependent clause : " He resolved that he would smoke no more," but " He has resolved that he will smoke no more."

23.6₂. The Preterit is therefore the proper tense whenever the sentence contains such time indications as *yesterday, the other day, in 1901*, etc., or is a question about the time : " When did you see him? "

23.6₃. On the other hand, when the time indicated is not yet completed (*today, this year, not yet*), the Perfect is naturally used :

I have worked hard today.

He has been a conscientious worker so far.

This rule, however, requires some qualification, for sentences containing such time indications as the last mentioned ones may refer to some definite part of the period, either expressly mentioned or implied. Thus you may ask a friend who generally meets a young lady on his way to the office : " Did you see her today ? "

> When I came here today, I thought everything was all right.
> I saw him today engaged in an animated contest (=when I saw him, he was engaged).
> A friend who called today told me that Nevinson was dead.

This morning, when said in the morning itself, requires the Perfect :

> I have not looked at the paper this morning.

But when said later it takes the Preterit :

> I did not look at the paper this morning (which may be followed by " but only read it after lunch").

Once has two meanings : in the strictly numerical sense of ' one time, but not twice or frequently ' it may be combined with both tenses :

> I have seen him once only (in the whole of my life).
> I saw him once only (while he was here).

But in the weakened sense ' once upon a time ' it requires the Preterit (and is generally placed before the verb) :

> I once thought he would marry her.

23.6₄. *Always, ever* and *never* may be combined with both tenses, but the Preterit is more idiomatic, and the reference to ' now ' which is implied in the Perfect will often be felt to be unnatural or unnecessary. It will, however, be necessary in such a sentence as this :

> She spoke, as indeed she has always spoken, simply, clearly, and vividly (this emphasizes her practice at all times, while *she always spoke* might mean ' in those days only').

It is worth observing that " Have you ever heard of such a thing ? " is a real question, asking for information, while

" Did you ever hear of such a thing? " generally is, what the
abbreviated " Did you ever? " always is, merely an emotional
exclamation.

23.6₅. Very often a sentence contains no express indication of
time, and yet the Preterit may be required, because a special
point of time is implied by the context or by the whole situation.
Thus when you ask, " Did you sleep well? " the implication is
' in the night just passed.'   Or when a person on arriving,
instead of saying " I have come," says, " I came back to ask
you something," implying something like " when I decided to
return, my reason was that I wanted to . . ."

23.6₆. We now see the reason why in speaking of dead people
the Preterit is used, except when the reference is to the result
as affecting the present day.

> Newton believed in an omnipotent God.
> Newton has explained the movements of the moon (*i.e.* in a way
>   that is still thought to be correct; if we said, " Newton
>   explained the movements of the moon from the attraction
>   of the earth," the implication would be that the explana-
>   tion has since been given up).
> Although Milton had no predecessors, he has had several imitators.

23.6₇. The Preterit may be used without any exact indication
of time, expressed or implied, when a comparison is drawn
between present and past conditions :

> England is not what it was.
> Cp. also : Lady Murray, Miss Thomson that was.

Otherwise such vague implications of the past are not expressed by the simple Preterit, but by means of the phrase
used to.   This denotes not only habitual or repeated action (as
in *I used to call on him every Sunday*), but also a permanent state
in the past.   The relation between this expression and the
simple Preterit will be clear from the following sentences :

> I used to live at Chelsea (no time indicated).
> In 1914 I lived at Chelsea.
> I lived there about ten years; cp. also " I have lived about ten
>   years at Chelsea " (and I still live there).

I was living there when my father died.
I used to know her mother pretty well.
I knew him immediately he entered (=recognized).
He does not stammer half so badly as he used to.

The pronunciation is [ju·st(t)u] with assimilation of the voiced sounds [zd] to the following [t] (5.6$_5$).

23.6$_8$. In such proverbial sentences as

Men were deceivers ever (Sh.),
Faint heart never won fair lady—

we have a stylistic trick to make the hearer himself draw the conclusion that what has hitherto been true is so still and will remain so to the end of time.

23.6$_9$. The simple Preterit is often used for the before-past time in clauses beginning with the conjunction *after* (cp. the corresponding use of the present tense, **23.4$_4$**) :

For years after it occurred I dreamt of it often.
He stood motionless after she disappeared (=had disappeared).

In temporal and conditional clauses the Perfect may be used for the before-future time ; this corresponds exactly to the use of the present tense for future time dealt with in **23.4$_3$**, and like this is an example of economy of speech :

When you have signed the cheque, I will hand you the letter.
We shall start at five if it has stopped raining by that time.

The Pluperfect

23.7$_1$. If we have two successive happenings in the past,

—————————X—————————Y—————————(now)

e.g. First I saw him, and then he saw me,—

the pluperfect serves to connect them grammatically :

I had seen him before he saw me.
I saw him before he had seen me.
He saw me after I had seen him.
He did not see me till I had seen him.

In clauses beginning with *after* we have already seen (**23.6$_9$**) that the simple preterit often means the same thing as the pluperfect. The latter must, however, be considered the normal tense :

After we had had tea, the discussion began.

In cases like the following both tenses may be used :

As soon as he (had) discovered the police, he ran away.

With *when* it is sometimes, but not always, possible to use the preterit for a before-past :

When he came back from India, he was made a member of Parliament.

But : When he had finished his book he took a long rest.

The pluperfect is used in a peculiarly vivid way for simple past time in

I had soon told my story [=I told my story, and that did not take long].

23.7₂. The pluperfect *had hoped* is often equivalent to *hoped*, only it implies that the (past) hope was not fulfilled :

We had hoped he would recover.

I had hoped to have seen you (for the infinitive, see **24.5**).

Similarly : I hadn't expected that.

Tenses of the Infinitive

23.8₁. In the infinitive we have only two tenses, the present infinitive, *(to) take*, and the perfect infinitive, *(to) have taken*. The former refers not only to the present time, but generally to the same time as is indicated by the main verb, thus :

It does him good
It did him good
It has done him good
It had done him good
It will do him good
It will have done him good

} to take long walks.

23.8₂. With verbs and other expressions which naturally have reference to futurity the present infinitive may be said to take the place of the missing future infinitive :

He hopes (expects, intends, means, wants) to go there.

In order to get there in time we must start now.

He is sure to get there in time, etc.

The same element of futurity may, of course, be referred to something in the past :

> He expected to get away after a short time.
> In 1903 he went to America never to return.

May with the present infinitive often serves to denote possibility or permission in the present time :

> He may be rich for all I know.
> You may smoke here if you like.

But often the combination serves to denote futurity, though of a vaguer and more uncertain kind than *will* or *shall* :

> He may turn up yet.
> You may find the door closed when you get there.
> Wee know what we are, but not what we may be (Sh.).

In clauses like the following *may* is chiefly used in slightly formal language :

> I hope (pray) that you may arrive safely.

The familiar sentence,

> I shall hope to see you when we return to town,

really means a present hope of a future visit ; *shall* is shifted on to *hope*, because it is impossible to say " I hope to shall see."

23.8$_3$. The perfect infinitive besides its ordinary temporal function, as in

> 'Tis better to have loved and lost Than never to have loved at all
> This day week I hope to have finished my work

(in the latter example it is notionally a before-future $=$ I hope I shall have finished)—has an important function as ' imaginative infinitive,' see **24.5**.

Imperative

23.8$_4$. As the meaning of the imperative is a request, and as a request has always reference to the future, we should expect the imperative to be always in the same tense : we need not specify *Come here !* or *Take that !* as either present or future imperative. But as a matter of fact we find the perfect imperative *Have done !* which in spite of its form has reference to the future and means

the same thing as ' Stop that at once ! ' or ' Don't go on ! ' : the
urgency of the demand is emphasized through the form, which
implies that the person addressed should already before this have
ceased the offensive action ; cf. *be gone*, **23.**5₂.

Participles

23.9₁. As we shall presently see, the time relations of the two
English participles are not so simple as might be inferred from
their usual names, present participle and past participle.   They
will therefore here be called the first participle (always ending in
-*ing*) and the second participle (sometimes ending in -*d*, -*t* or -*n*,
sometimes with no particular ending, **23.**2).

The First Participle

When the first participle is used as an adjective, as in *a charming
lady* or *she is very charming,* it has no more reference to any
particular time than adjectives like *beautiful.*

When its use is of a purely verbal character, as shown, for
instance, by its having an object, the same is generally true.
In all cases like

He came,
He comes,   } carrying a heavy burden on his back—
He will come,

we have a vague simultaneity with something else, rather than
any definite reference to one particular time.   Similarly in

He is President, for the time being.
The war made us all into barbarians, for the time being.

If *the coming war* means ' the future war,' this is because the
verb *come* so often refers to the future (**24.**8₃, **32.**2₂).

The Second Participle

23.9₂. Here we must distinguish two classes of verbs.

(1) Conclusive verbs.   The action is either confined to one
single moment, e.g. *catch, surprise, awake, leave, end, kill,* or
implies a final aim, e.g. *make, bring about, adorn, construct, beat.*
If the second participle of such a verb is used as an adjunct, **we**

see plainly that it is a perfect participle, it denotes the result of an action in the past : a caught fish | a killed bird | left property | a paid bill | a lost battle | his collected works | armed men | married people | a reserved seat | trained nurses.

(2) Non-conclusive verbs. Here we find verbs denoting feelings, states of mind, etc. : the activity, if any such is implied, is not begun in order to be finished. Examples : *love, hate, praise, blame, see, hear.* If the participle is used as an adjunct, it says nothing about time : an honoured colleague | an admired friend | a reserved expression on his face. Placed in a sentence denoting some time in the past, the participle indicates merely contemporaneousness : he was a well-known barrister, etc.

The distinction will be seen to be important when we come to speak of tenses in the passive, **24.1.**

Perfect Participle

23.9₃. A perfect participle (active) consists of *having*+ the second participle.

> Having arranged everything to his own satisfaction, he went home by the 10.30 train.

In the passive correspondingly :

> All this having been settled, he went home, etc.

Tenses of the Gerund

23.9₄. Substantives do not ordinarily admit of any indication of time : *his movement* may correspond in meaning to ' he moves (is moving),' ' he movèd (was moving) ' or ' he will move (be moving).' Similarly the Gerund in *-ing* had originally, and to a great extent still has, no reference to time : *on account of his coming* may be equal to ' because he comes ' or ' because he came ' or ' he will come,' according to circumstances. *I intend seeing the king* refers to the future, *I remember seeing the king* to the past.

But side by side with this timeless form we have a perfect : *having* with the second participle :

> He hated himself for having ever married her.

With *after* both the simple form and the perfect may be used ; the former is an example of the same kind of economy as we saw in **23.**4$_4$, **23.**6$_9$:

After having rung the bell } he retired into the shade.
After ringing

After *on* in the same sense the simple form is preferred :

On ringing the bell, etc.

A perfect in the passive is seen, for instance, in

His arm was not in a sling, and showed no symptom of having been damaged.

CHAPTER XXIV

TENSE—*continued*

Tenses in the Passive

24.1₁. The use of the tenses in the passive is not exactly
parallel to that in the active, chiefly because the passive is
formed by means of the second participle, which, as we have
seen in **23.9₂**, frequently has no reference to time, though it is
often a perfect participle.

With non-conclusive verbs there can be no doubt : the passive
is in the same tense as the auxiliary : *he is admired* is a present
tense, because *is* is present and *admired* is no tense in particular ;
was admired is a preterit. Similarly with *it is (was, has been)
generally believed*, etc. In all such cases the participle is a
predicative of being (**13.1** ; 5), and we may therefore speak of
a passive of being.

24.1₂. With conclusive verbs the time-relation is not so
simple : sometimes the participle is a predicative of being,
sometimes one of becoming. We have the former in " He is
buried at Croydon " (=lies buried), the latter in " When is he
to be buried?—Oh, don't you know ? He has been buried
already ; he was buried yesterday."

" His bills are paid " may mean two things, either the present
action as in " His bills are paid regularly every month " =' he
pays,' or the (present) result of a past action as in " His bills
are paid, so he owes nothing now " = ' he has paid.' There is,
however, a strong tendency to get rid of the ambiguity caused
in this way, and we may say that where the Elizabethans had

practically only one form, *is taken,* the language of our own days has at its disposal four expressions :

> (1) is taken,
> (2) is being taken (**24.9₁**),
> (3) has been taken,
> (4) gets taken.

24.1₃. As will be readily understood, the pure meaning of a present tense is chiefly found when habitual actions are spoken of, *e.g.*

> You can't do that sort of thing. It isn't done.
> He is easily taken in.
> Foreign names are easily forgotten.
> I am called every morning at six.

In the second sense, where the participle really implies some action in the past, the combination of the present *is* + the participle is still freely used in all those cases in which we think more of the resulting state than of the action, *e.g.*

> The battle (the key) is lost.
> She is dressed.
> His signature is attached to the document.
> He is tired.
> The gun is loaded.
> The door is shut.
> His leg is broken.

When the action itself is more prominent in the mind than the result, the perfect (*has been taken,* etc.) is now generally preferred where in former times the present was used, *e.g.* in the following quotations from *Macbeth* :

> Is execution done on Cawdor?
> Let that bee, Which the eye feares, when it is done, to see.
> Your castle is surpriz'd : your wife and babes Savagely slaughter'd.

But *is done* is still frequent in the sense ' has been done ' ; cp.

> If it were done, when 'tis done, then 'twere well, It were done quickly (also from *Macbeth*).
> The gods themselves cannot annihilate the action that is done (Carlyle).

24.1₄. In the preterit, *was* is also used in two senses, (1) the state, (2) the transition to the state, *e.g.*

(1) The house was surrounded by firs and birches.
(2) Here, in 1823, the Indians were surrounded by the English.
(1) He was dressed in the latest fashion.
(2) The children were dressed every morning by their mother.
(1) At that time they were not yet married.
(2) They were married last year.

24.1₅. Similar examples of the perfect, pluperfect, and infinitive :

(1) We have only been married a week.
(2) The murderer has already been executed.
(1) In seventeen years she had been engaged eleven times.
(2) We saw the church where they had been married.
(1) They may not be married (=perhaps they are not a married couple).
(2) I am afraid we may never be married.

Other Auxiliaries in the Passive

24.1₆. *Get* and *become* are now increasingly common as auxiliaries for the passive of becoming ; with some verbs the distinction between them and *be* is particularly useful :

At that time he was not yet married.   He got (became) married in 1920.
He took it into his head rather late in life that he must get married.
I have been acquainted with Morris for quite a long time ; in fact, I don't know when and how I got acquainted with him.
The galleries became filled with people from the surrounding districts.

Stand is often used in judicial expressions like *stand condemned* and *stand rebuked*.

IMAGINATIVE USE OF TENSES
The Preterit of Imagination

24.2₁. This term is here used for the preterit found in sentences like :

I wish I had money enough.
If I had money enough, I should pay you.
You speak as if I had money enough.

In all such cases we deny the reality or possibility of certain suppositions; the implication is " I have not money enough." In the main sentence of the second example we state what would be likely under the imagined condition that I had money enough, or what may be considered the logical consequence of its truth or realization.

Correspondingly we have a pluperfect of imagination (I wish I had had money enough, etc.), see **24.4**.

24.2₂. Originally this use was restricted to a separate mood-form of the preterit, the preterit subjunctive, and the unreality was denoted by the mood rather than by the tense.   But in course of time the distinction between the forms of the subjunctive and those of the indicative came to be blotted out, and now in 99 per cent. of cases it is impossible from the form to tell which of the two moods is used, thus, e.g. *if he came, drank, held, sent, ended,* etc.   The only forms in which the distinction survives are *was (indicative)* and *were (subjunctive)*, and even here it should be noted that the plural form *were* belongs to both moods.   It is no wonder, therefore, that here, too, the indicative should come to be used instead of the subjunctive, and since the seventeenth century we see an increasing tendency to say *I wish he was . . ., if he was . . ., as if he was . . .* instead of the earlier *were*, a tendency which has to some extent been counteracted by the teaching of grammarians that *were* was the correct form, at any rate in serious literature.   As, however, no inconvenience has ever been felt by the fact that there is no corresponding difference in other verbs (*if I had, did*, etc.), it seems doubtful whether the theoretic opposition to *if he was*, etc., will be strong enough to prevail against the natural evolution of language.

24.2₃. Wishes (unrealizable or hardly realizable) may be introduced in various ways :

I wish I had a cause to seeke him there (Sh.).
I would to heaven I had your potencie (Sh.).
Would I could doubt it !
If one had but two heads and neither required sleep ! (Huxley).

24.2₄. Conditions are introduced not only by *if* and *unless*, but also in other ways :

> Suppose you tried your luck !
> Fancy your wife attached to a mother who dropped her h's ! (Thackeray).
> A nation which stopped working would be dead in a fortnight.

24.2₅. With regard to *was* and *were* (sg.) it has already been mentioned that *were* is chiefly a literary survival, which does not belong to natural spoken English except in such fixed phrases as *if I were you* and *as it were*.   Cf. **24.2₆** on *if he were to* with an infinitive.

When a condition is expressed without any conjunction by the word-order of a question, *were* is the rule :

> Were it not for him, I should speak up.

It may be a consequence of the more colloquial tone of *was* that it is decidedly better adapted for emphatic use than *were*, and is therefore preferred in negative statements.

> The captain says he wishes I were black ; I wish I was (Marryat).
> I wish it wasn't Sunday to-day.
> You speak as if there wasn't enough for all of us.

Macaulay, who generally uses the form *were*, writes with stress on *was* :

> It was not impossible that there might be a counterrevolution, and it was certain that, if there *was* a counterrevolution, those who had lent money to William would lose both interest and principal.

24.2₆. A distinction is often made between *if he was to* (with an infinitive) and *if he were to*.   The former retains the meaning of obligation or arrangement that is found in " he is to return at six," while the latter has lost that meaning and indicates merely a vague possibility in the future, nearly the same thing as *if he should* . . .

> If I was to be shot for it I wouldn't tell.
> If he were to call, tell him to wait.

24.2₇. In the typical examples of the preterit of imagination the reference is to the present or future time, or rather to no

time at all, as the reality of the supposition is denied.   But sometimes the unreality may refer to some time in the past, and
then *was* is preferred to *were* : she spoke as if she was ashamed
(not *were*)—but : she speaks as if she were (or *was*) ashamed.

> Frederic would, he said, stand by her . . . as if he was not
> already bound to stand by her (Macaulay).

In clauses of condition which have regard to some time in the
past, but do not deny the reality or possibility, *was*, not *were*,
is the rule, even in old authors :

> It was never acted ; or if it was, not above once (Sh.).

Very often no real condition but only a contrast is meant :

> If I was a bad carpenter, I was a worse tailor (Defoe ; =I was
> really bad as a carpenter and worse as a tailor).

24.3₁. In the main sentence of rejected condition (expressed
or implied) *would* and *should* is now the rule (Chap. XXVI),
but formerly the simple preterit was usual, and *were* is still
found in this way in literary language :

> She were an excellent wife for Benedick (Sh.).
> That were a pity ! (=would be).

Another survival is *had better* and analogous phrases :

> You had better go at once.   I had rather stay.

24.3₂. *Could* is also used in main sentences of rejected condition instead of the clumsy and over-emphatic *should* (*would*)
be able to :

> Lord, I could not endure a husband with a beard on his face (Sh.).
> I had an early breakfast ; now I could eat a little more.

When no conditional clause is found, this *could* is often hardly
more than a weaker or diffident variety of the present tense
can, thus especially in questions :

> You won't be angry, will you ?   How could I ?
> Could you tell me the right time ?

Similarly, *might* is frequent in such sentences with reference
to the present time :

> You might do me a great favour (if you would . . .).
> Are you going already ?   You might stay a little longer.

24.3₃. It is through an analogous employment that the preterits *ought* (*to*) and *should* have come to be a stronger and a weaker expression of present duty : *ought* is historically the preterit of *owe* and thus meant ' had to ' (would have to), but the conditional meaning is no longer felt.

You ought to (you should) enlist at once.

24.3₄. After *it is* (*high*) *time* we have an interesting use of the imaginative preterit in speaking really of the future. Originally this, too, was in the subjunctive, as in

'tis hie (high) time that I were hence (Sh.),

but as in the majority of cases there is no formal distinction between the subjunctive and the indicative, *e.g.*

It's time we sent the children to bed—

it has become usual here also to use the indicative *was* :

It is time this was put an end to.

The Pluperfect of Imagination

24.4. In the first place this refers to some time in the past :

I wish he had not seen us (implying that he has seen, or saw, us).
If I had only known ! (but I did not know).
If it had not been for Jack, I should have died there and then.
Any ordinary person who had ventured to insult me in that way, would have been killed on the spot.
He flung himself into the chair as if nothing uncommon had occurred.

In the second place the pluperfect of imagination refers to the present time to emphasize the impossibility or improbability :

I wish I had been rich enough to give you the money (but I am not).
If I had had the money (at the present moment) I should have paid you.

Perfect Infinitive of Imagination

24.5₁. The perfect infinitive is often used with an imaginative value, but in many cases it is possible to substitute the simple

infinitive, which is therefore preferred by many purists.
Examples :

> It would have been wiser to have left it unsaid (=if you had left
> it unsaid)—or, to leave it unsaid.
>
> In other circumstances the two ladies might have found it im-
> possible to have lived together so long.

We say " you ought to follow her example " if the fulfilment
is still possible, but " you ought to have followed her example "
if this is no longer possible.   Similarly, the perfect infinitive is
often used after a verb meaning intention, hope or expectation
in the past to denote that the intention was not carried into
effect :

> I thought thy bridebed to have deckt, sweet maid (Sh.).
>
> I hoped to have asked you some day to rejoin us here.
>
> He was once inclined to have presented his poem in person, but
> his resolution deserted him (S. Johnson).
>
> It was on the tip of my tongue to have given him a sharp answer.
>
> I had intended to have sent it a month ago, but did not.

A plan that was not carried out, is also expressed in the
frequent phrase *was to have* (*done*, etc.) :

> George was to have been of the party; but he did not appear.

24.5₂. The following three synonymous expressions may be
found exemplified in good authors :

> I should have liked to see her.
>
> I should like to have seen her.
>
> I should have liked to have seen her.

The imaginative perfect infinitive is frequent after *had better* :

> You had better have stayed with us.

24.5₃. An imaginative perfect infinitive is also seen in sentences
like :

> A Jew would have wept to have seene our parting (Sh. =if he had
> seen).
>
> The colonies, so united, would have been sufficiently strong to
> have defended themselves.
>
> I had found timber enough to have built a good boat, if I had
> known how.

Indirect Speech

24.6₁. When one wishes to report what someone else says or has said (thinks or has thought)—or what one said or thought on a previous occasion oneself—two ways are open to one, either to give the exact words : direct speech, or to adapt the words according to the circumstances in which they are now quoted : indirect speech. In the latter not only the persons are often shifted (**15.**3), but also the tenses are often changed if the main sentence is (or would be if it were expressed) in the past. Typical examples are :

Direct Speech	Indirect Speech
	He said (thought) that :
" I am glad to see you "	(1) he was glad to see me
" I saw her on Tuesday "	(2) he had seen her on Tuesday
" I have not seen her yet "	(3) he had not seen her yet

Let us call these uses of the tenses :

(1) back-shifted present
(2) back-shifted preterit
(3) back-shifted perfect

The pluperfect cannot be further shifted : " I had already seen her before she bowed " becomes " he said that he had already seen her before she bowed." The indirect " had seen " thus corresponds to three direct tenses, *saw*, *has seen* and *had seen*.

The shifting of the tenses is often quite natural and, in fact, inevitable, when the fact reported belongs definitely to the past, as in " he told me that she was ill, but now (he tells me that) she is all right again."

24.6₂. Very frequently, however, the shifting is not required logically, but is due simply to mental inertia : the speaker's mind is moving in the past, and he does not stop to consider whether each dependent statement refers to one or the other time, but simply goes on speaking in the tense adapted to the

main idea. A typical example is found when the speaker dis-
covers the presence of someone and exclaims :

> Oh, Mr Summer, I didn't know you were here (you are here, but
> I didn't know).

Thus also :

> I tried to forget who I was.
> Who told thee, that thou wast naked? (AV.).
> What did you say was your friend's name?

24.6₃. *If I am* is shifted into *if I was* :

> I told him that I would never send him away, if he was willing to
> stay with me.
> He said that if England was to be saved, it must be by the younger
> generation.

Note that this *was to* is different from *were to*, which is not
shifted :

> He said that if any visitor were to ask, no information should be
> given.

There is a curious use of the preterit dependent on a not
expressed main verb in cases like this : Someone has told me
" I am going to Bristol on Thursday." A little later I remember
that he is going, but forget the date, and ask : " What day were
you going to B. ? " or " Was it on Thursday or Friday you were
going to B. ? " (=What day did you say you were . . .).

24.6₄. A present that expresses an " eternal truth " or something similar may be shifted :

> My father convinced me that nothing was useful which was not
> honest.
> It was a saying of his, that no man was sure of his supper till he
> had eaten it.

But on the other hand, when the idea of a universal truth is
quite obvious, the tense may be unshifted :

> We learnt at school that 2 and 2 is 4.
> " In such a sentence as *the ancients did not know that Africa . . .
> an island*, we hesitate whether to use *was* or *is* " (Sweet).

24.6₅. When Falstaff reappears (in Sh., *Henry IV*, First Part, V. 4), John of Lancaster exclaims : " But soft, who have we here ? Did you not tell me this fat man was dead ? " Here the use of the preterit somehow expresses that the saying was untruthful ; similarly in

> I thought you were a gentleman (=now I see you are not).
> The ancients thought that the sun moved round the earth.

The wrongness of a supposition may even lead to a further shifting into the pluperfect, though the real time-relation is the same as if the simple preterit had been used :

> I thought you had been a gentleman.
> Why, I imagined those fellows had been asleep.

24.6₆. Back-shifting takes place not only after expressions of a real past, but also after the imaginative preterit :

> If we went, people would think we were mad.
> " I suppose you are glad." " I should think I was."
> It would have been well for me if I had never known what love was.

24.6₇. *Must* is not often used in speaking of a real past (here we generally say *had to* : " I had to go to town yesterday morning "), but is very frequent as a shifted present :

> She said she must be back by seven.
> He knew suddenly who the woman must be.

24.6₈. There is no shifting in cases like the following, because *may be* and *thank Heaven* are to be considered fossilized expressions (used as tertiaries ; cp. dial. *mebbe* =perhaps) :

> I thought may be you could help me.
> Mrs Crupp said, thank Heaven she had now found summun she cared for ! (Dickens).

24.6₉. There is generally no shifting in verbal reports of proposals or motions in the subjunctive (imperative) :

> Eleven members voted against the motion that the bill be read a second time.
> He suggested that Lyman be put forward as the candidate.

Where there is no verbal report, it is more natural to insert *should,* though this is often left out, especially by American writers :

She insisted that he (should) knock before entering.

Similarly *should* is often omitted by Americans after *lest* :

They were in a panic, lest they be overtaken by the police.

The Expanded Tenses

24.7₁. By the side of the simple tenses we have in English expanded tenses, *e.g.* :

Simple	*Expanded*
he works	he is working
he worked	he was working
he has worked	he has been working, etc.

These expanded tenses are now used much more extensively than formerly. Where Polonius asks " What do you read my Lord ? I meane the matter that you reade my Lord," he would now rather say " What are you reading ? " In the Gospel of St Mark the Authorized Version has only twenty-nine expanded tenses, but has seventy-eight simple tenses where now expanded tenses would be naturally used.

The chief use of the expanded tenses is to serve as a frame round something else, which may or may not be expressly indicated. This is easily understood if we start from the old phrase *he was on hunting,* which meant ' he was in the course of hunting, engaged in hunting, busy with hunting ' ; he was, as it were, in the middle of something, some protracted action or state, denoted by the substantive *hunting.* Here *on* became phonetically *a,* as in other cases, and *a* was eventually dropped, exactly as in other phrases : *burst out on laughing, a-laughing, laughing; fall on thinking, a-thinking, thinking; set the clock on going, a-going, going,* etc. If we say *he was (on) hunting,* we mean that the hunting (which may be completed now) had begun, but was not completed at the time mentioned or implied in the sentence ; this element of relative incompletion is very important if we want to understand the expanded tenses, even if it is not equally manifest in all cases.

24.7₂. If, then, the action or state denoted by the expanded tense is thought of as a temporal frame encompassing something else which as often as not is to be understood from the whole situation, we may represent the two sentences *he is writing* (now) and *he was writing* (when I entered) in the following diagrams :

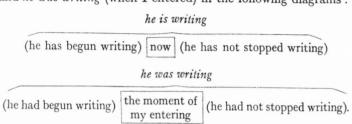

he is writing

(he has begun writing) | now | (he has not stopped writing)

he was writing

(he had begun writing) | the moment of my entering | (he had not stopped writing).

In a connected narrative, therefore, the expanded tenses often occur in a description of the general situation, which serves as setting to what happened, which is expressed by means of simple tenses :

> One morning the three sisters were together in the drawing-room; Mary was sewing, Lucy was playing on the piano, and Jane was doing nothing; then suddenly the door opened and John burst into the room, exclaiming . . .

Note also the frequent phrase " as I was saying " (namely, when we were interrupted), and the way in which the frame is implied in the word *know* :

> Boswell asks: "Does not Rousseau talk nonsense?" and Dr Johnson answers: "True, Sir, but Rousseau knows he is talking nonsense. A man who talks nonsense so well must know he is talking nonsense."
> Browning knew what he was talking about when he talked of poetry.

The contrast between the two tenses is seen clearly in instances like the following :

> Mrs Gregg looked at Mary very carefully and then smiled. Mary was also smiling.
> Lucy wanted to turn her head, but she dared not; she was blushing. She blushed because of the dreams she had once had concerning him.

24.7₃. Often a contrast between habitual and actual doing at the one moment spoken of may be brought out by means of the two kinds of tenses :

He is a night watchman and sleeps of mornings. He is sleeping now.

The girls and teachers, gathered round the other table, were talking pretty freely : they always talked at meals.

It was freezing as it only freezes in March.

24.7₄. In his *Book of Snobs* Thackeray writes, " If I should go to one of the tea-parties in a dressing-gown and slippers, I should be insulting society, and eating peas with my knife " : the expanded form implies identity of the two acts (" going to . . . would be insulting society ") ; if he had said " I should insult society " the insult would be something independent of the unfashionable dress.

We may have two expanded tenses to express the fact that two things always happen at the same time :

Every morning when he was having his breakfast his dog was staring at him.

But if one of the two facts is looked upon as the frame of the other, only one verb is expanded :

Every morning when he was having his breakfast his wife asked him for money.

He looked at her repeatedly when she was not looking.

Whenever I looked up he was looking.

24.7₅. In clauses beginning with *while (whilst)* or *as*, expanded tenses are naturally frequent :

As we were going along, she asked me what my father had said.

But the simple tenses may also be used because the ' frame ' is already sufficiently indicated by the conjunction :

He was considering; but while he considered, his companion stepped ashore.

If we say " You can tell me the story while we eat," both the telling and the eating are to take place in the future ; " while we are eating " would imply the present, the eating having already begun at the time of speaking.

24.7₆. *Always* and synonyms with the expanded tenses often indicate all the times we are just now concerned with, not all times in the history of the world (as in " the sun always rises in the east ") ; the expressions often have an emotional colouring :

You are always finding fault with me.

We say :

Smokers always drink (= all smokers are drinkers).
When he is in Paris, he always reads *Le Temps* (= the paper he constantly reads is *Le Temps*).

If we were here to substitute *are always drinking, is always reading Le Temps*, it would imply that they did nothing else but drinking and reading *Le Temps*, respectively.

24.8₁. *He has collected much evidence against her* means that he has finished his work of collecting, but nothing is said about the time when he did it ; in *he has been collecting much evidence against her*, on the other hand, we understand that the collecting began some time before, and may be continued some time after, the present moment. It thus contains the twofold implication that it is recently that this collection has taken place, and that it may not yet be completed.

The first implication (recent happening) is also found in the following instances :

I am afraid he has been drinking.
I heard it at Mr Palmer's, where I have been dining (*i.e.* today).
All during this wonderful May that we have been having, I used to run down and see her (may be said towards the end of May, or in the beginning of June).

The second implication of the expanded perfect, namely, incompleted or even ineffectual action, is seen, for instance, in :

I have been reading Shakespeare lately; I have read all the comedies and some of the histories.
Our friend lands at Southampton tonight. He has always been coming; this time he has come.

24.8₂. The expanded infinitive often serves to emphasize the present moment, as in *What can he be doing?* as against the more general *What can he do?*

But in many connexions *be -ing* becomes a sign of the immediate future, as in *We'd better be dressing for dinner*, while *We'd better dress for dinner* may be said early in the morning and refers only to the kind of garment, not to the time. Similarly after *must* and after words like *wish, want to*, etc.

> I am afraid I must be going.
> I will not interrupt you any longer.   You want to be reading.
> He was impatient to be doing something.

After *will* and *shall* the expanded infinitive may be used exactly in the same ways as the expanded present, only transferred to the future :

> I shall be having breakfast in a minute [shall have begun breakfast].
> Stop him.   He'll be doing something desperate.

The expanded infinitive gives the possibility of a nuance : *people will come* speaks only vaguely of the future ; *people are coming* speaks of the immediate future ; *people will be coming* refers to the coming as near, though not exactly immediate :

> My children are at school, and they'll be coming home.
> I shall be seeing you before long.
> My wife will soon be inquiring after me.

Special Cases

24.8₃. Verbs of movement when used in the expanded tenses generally express a near future ; cp. the phrases at auctions :

> Going ; going ; gone !—

and, further :

> Christmas is coming, the geese are getting fat (here the former verb refers to the future, the latter to the present time).
> He is going to Spain this spring.
> John is leaving at the end of the term.

24.8₄. This leads to the use of *is going to* with an infinitive as what may be called a prospective present, and *was going to* as a prospective past.   Here *going* has become a mere grammatical implement and no longer implies any movement, as is most clearly seen in combinations like " he is going to go," or " to come," as in Dickens's description of Pecksniff's horse :

> He was full of promise, but of no performance.   He was always, in a manner, going to go, and never going.

Also :

> He is going to be married this spring.
> Are they going to be gone long?
> He was going to answer back, but was stopped by his mother.

24.8₅. As *die* means ' cease to exist ' or ' leave this world,' the expanded form is frequently used to express the future :

> Her mother was dying, or perhaps already dead.

Hence also the transferred meaning :

> He is dying to make your acquaintance (= longing for it).

A futuric use of the expanded tense is also seen in

> We are dining out today.

24.8₆. There are some verbs that are not very frequently used in the expanded tenses, *e.g.* those expressing psychological states such as *know, like, love, hate, hope*—though *I'm liking*, etc., are in recent times used more often than formerly—*see, hear*, when denoting simple acts of perception—but *he is seeing the sights of the town* and *he's hearing lectures* are, of course, all right.

24.8₇. The expanded tenses cannot be used with those verbs that do not take *do* in interrogative and negative sentences; indeed, most of them (*may, must*, etc.) have no form in *-ing*. *Is having* is, however, pretty frequent, especially when *have* means ' enjoy, partake of, cause to,' etc., *e.g.* :

> Thanks, we've been having a few glasses already.
> We're having a dinner-party tonight.
> I'm having the manuscript copied for you.

With *be* (" he is not being very polite," etc.) the form is comparatively recent, in fact younger than the corresponding passive *is being built*, which we shall now deal with.

Passive

24.9₁. In the passive the old construction was *the house is* (*was, has been,* etc.) *building,* which is easily accounted for if we start from *is on* (*a*) *building,* which meant ' is in (under) construction,' *e.g.* in

> Let us seem humbler after it is done Then when it was a dooing (Sh.).

Examples without *a* :

> Whil'st this play is playing (Sh.).
> While these measures were taking (Scott).
> While the parcels were bringing down and displaying on the counter (Jane Austen).
> The hay was making under the trees (Shelley).
> Everybody here is talking of a steam-ship which is building at Leghorn (*Id.*).
> While innocent blood was shedding (Macaulay).

A phrase still in use is *there is nothing doing.* Cp. also *something is missing* and *something is wanting* (while in the active sense *in* is added : *he is wanting in tact*).

24.9₂. The construction *is building* in a passive sense was liable to misunderstanding in some combinations and could not be applied to all verbs. Hence it was natural that a new construction, clearer, but clumsier, *is being built,* should come into existence, as in

> Somebody is always being murdered (Dickens).
> The horses were being led out to watering (G. Eliot).
> Dick felt that he was being hardly used (Kipling), etc.

Even a long time after the new construction had come into use (some of the earliest printed examples are found in Southey, Coleridge, Lamb, Keats), people objected very strongly to it as " clumsy and unidiomatic " or " an outrage upon English idiom, to be detested, abhorred, execrated," etc. But in spite of all opposition on the part of grammarians and others it must now be considered a fixed element of the English language.

Conclusion

24.9₃. We may sum up by saying that through the enormous extension during the last few centuries of the expanded tenses the language has been enriched with means of expression that allow nice logical distinctions and at the same time in many cases have emotional value. In comparison with the uncompounded verbal tenses these forms with *be* + participle serve to actualize and vivify, one effect of which is the curious approximation in time to the present moment seen both when *he has been drinking* expresses the recent past, and when *we must be dressing* denotes the immediate future, while *he has drunk* and *we must dress* say nothing about the distance in time from the present moment. But it is here as with other happenings in linguistic history, which though on the whole progressive and beneficial, are not so in every respect : this development, too, has its disadvantages, for the expanded forms are undoubtedly heavy (and hence not often used in poetry), and the clumsiness is especially felt in the passive constructions, whence we see that combinations like *he has been being* (*introduced*) are practically impossible. Nor is it always possible to carry through a sharp logical line of division between the simple and expanded forms, consequently the choice of one or the other form is in some cases of very little importance for the meaning of the sentence.

CHAPTER XXV

WILL AND SHALL

Full verb *will.*—Auxiliary *will.*—Volition.—Habit.—Volition-coloured future.—First person.—Second person.—Condition.—Pure future.—*I will.*—Before-future.—Supposition.—*Shall.*—Obligation.—Command.—Promise or threat.—Questions.—Pure future.—First person.—Before-future.—Questions.—Summary.

Will

25.1₁. We must distinguish two verbs *will* : the full verb and the auxiliary. The former (which is purely literary) is fully inflected (he *wills, willed,* inf. (*to*) *will, willing*), and can take an ordinary object :

Hamlet wishes to will, but never wills anything.
Whatever God wills is holy, just and good.

25.1₂. The auxiliary lacks infinitive and participles, it has no *s* in the third person singular. Its forms are

present *will,* weak *'ll,* negative *won't,*
preterit *would,* weak *'d,* negative *wouldn't.*

Archaic forms of the second person : *wilt,* weak *'lt* ; *wouldst,* weak *'dst.*

This auxiliary is combined with an infinitive without *to* ; but the infinitive is often supplied from the context.

25.2₁. The verb *will* primarily denotes will, volition. As will is popularly ascribed to lifeless things as well as to living beings, we have, *e.g.*

Murder will out.
Seeing that death, a necessary end, Will come when it will come (Sh.).

Applied to lifeless things *will* often denotes power, capacity, etc. :

The hall will seat five hundred.
That will do.

25.2₂. What one does willingly, one is apt to do frequently; hence *will* often denotes habit :

> He will sit for hours without saying a word.
> Many will swoon when they do look on bloud (Sh.).
> Accidents will occur in the best-regulated families.

25.2₃. To denote actual will (volition) with regard to the present time *will* is chiefly used in connexion with *have* or in negative sentences :

> Who will have some lemonade?
> I won't stand any nonsense.
> I will not be intimidated or talked back to.

25.3₁. It is a natural consequence of the notion of volition that it generally has reference to what is to happen in the future ; hence the auxiliary *will* comes to be used extensively to express first a volition-coloured future and finally a future time without such colouring. In course of time the meaning of the verb has become weakened, and to express real volition we must now generally use other verbs : *mean, intend, want, choose.* Where the Authorized Version has :

> Get thee out, and depart hence ; for Herode will kill thee—

most people will nowadays misunderstand it as a prediction, but the meaning is " means to kill."

25.3₂. A volition-coloured future is frequent in the first person, where *I will do that* means ' I am willing (determined) to do that, and I shall do it.' Besides volition it thus generally indicates certainty of fulfilment, and often implies promise or threat, which in the other persons is denoted by *shall* :

> I'll tell you some other day. I won't forget it.
> I'll take care that it shall be all right.
> I will never again taste a drop of spirit.
> I will call him to account. He shall pay dearly for this affront.

Note the two expressions of volition in :

> I will come a short time before dinner, as I want to have a private talk with you.

25.3₃. As one has rarely occasion to ask someone else about one's own will, *will I* (*will we*) is only used in cases like the following :

"Will you come with me ? " "Will I ? " (meaning : ' How can you doubt it ? Of course I will ').
Will I open my heart to that scoundrel ? Of course not.
We won't quarrel the first day Harry is here, will we ? (=' I hope you won't quarrel with me ').

In Irish and American *will I ?* is often used for *shall I ?*

25.3₄. For obvious reasons *you will* is rarely used as a real statement about the will of the person addressed ; but it often means a request or order :

You will pack at once and leave this house.

On the other hand, questions about the will of the second person are perfectly natural, especially in requests or invitations :

Will you let me have a look at that letter ?
Will you come for a walk this afternoon ?
Will you pass the mustard, please ?

Thus frequently after an imperative :

Stop that noise, will you ?

25.3₅. In conditional clauses *will* is used to express volition in the future, as the simple present tense is generally sufficient to denote the future (**23.**4₃) :

If you will say so, you shall have a kis (Sh.).
I shan't be happy unless he'll come.

If a determination or intention is meant, *want* must be used in a conditional clause :

If you want to smoke, you must go into another carriage.

Pure Future

25.4₁. We next come to those cases in which *will* has lost the meaning of volition, and has come to denote nothing but futurity. This is extremely frequent in the second and third persons :

Look out, or you will be run over.
I am afraid you will have to submit.

You (he, she) will come of age next year.
You (he, she) will be forgotten long before the end of the century.
The next war will be more cruel than can be imagined.
The patient will probably die before evening.
You (he, she) will get wet through if the rain does not stop soon.

Though the meaning of *will* is thus weakened, it may be stressed to denote certainty of a future event :

Death may come any day, but it *will* come some day.

In questions in the second person *will you* is now increasingly frequent instead of *shall you* :

When will you be off ?

In most cases, however, there is at any rate some remnant of the meaning of volition.

25.4₂. In questions in the third person *will* generally means nothing but the future :

Will the moon rise soon ?
Will he be able to go to Switzerland this summer, do you think ?
What will happen if you refuse ?

Impatience may be shown by stressing *will* :

When *will* the strike be over ?

25.4₃. In the first person *will* does not lend itself so well as in the others to the expression of mere futurity, as *I will* and *we will* are so extensively and so naturally put in requisition to express volition, and as the other auxiliary, *shall*, has come to be much used with *I* and *we* to express mere futurity. Still *I* (*we*) *will* is gaining ground in this function where strict grammarians prefer *shall*, and this cannot be thought unnatural, seeing that there are many border cases in which it is difficult to know whether volition or pure future is meant, and that the abbreviated form *'ll* is so handy.

There is a special inducement to use *will* when *I* is combined with *you* or some word in the third person ; we say " We shall get there first " ; but

I expect you and I will get there before the others.
Sir Thomas and I will be delighted if you will join our party.

25.4₄. The Scotch and Irish, hence also the Scotch-Irish parts of America, use constantly *I (we) will* :

We'll have rain before the week is out.

I am not going to live to be an old man.   I will not get old.

They even use *will* in questions like :

O, when will I forget that ? (Scott).

What time'll I come for you ? ('am I to ').

What will I say when they ask me ?

25.4₅. *Will* with the perfect infinitive expresses the before-future :

He'll have forgotten by the end of the term.

25.4₆. Besides the uses of *will* so far mentioned it is often used to indicate a mere supposition :

This, I think, will be the key.

He is waiting for us downstairs; he will be wondering where we are.

In the same way with the perfect infinitive :

You will have heard the rumour ('I suppose you have heard ').

She won't have seen you come.

Shall

25.5₁. The forms of this verb are :

Present *shall* [ʃæl], weak [ʃ(ə)l], negative *shan't*.

Preterit *should* [ʃud], weak [ʃəd], negative *shouldn't*.

Archaic forms with *thou* : *shalt, shouldst*.

Shall is used with an infinitive (which may often be understood from the context).   Its original meaning of obligation, compulsion, necessity or constraint, physical or moral, is still visible in certain combinations, though in others it has lost its old force, so that *shall*, like *will*, is often nothing but an empty auxiliary, a grammatical implement without any real meaning of its own.

In the rest of this chapter the word ' obligation ' will be used as a general term for various kinds of constraint, etc.

25.5₂. In the first place *shall* may express fatal obligation or necessity, independent of human will; it thus approaches the meaning of *must*, but is now generally supplanted by *is sure to, is certain to* :

> Death is certaine to all, all shall dye (Sh.).
> Who wins his Love shall lose her,
> Who loses her shall gain (Andrew Lang).

25.5₃. More often the obligation is due to human will, either explicit or implicit. While the reference in the preceding paragraph was to no definite time, here it is to some time in the future :

> I am determined she shall have no cause to complain.
> The very first condition of legal justice is that it shall be no respecter of persons.
> Thou shalt love thy neighbour as thy selfe (AV.).

Here we see *shall* used in a command ; in a negative command, *i.e.* a prohibition, *shall* is no longer used as it was in the Bible : " Thou shalt not kill " would now be more idiomatically " You must not kill." In later use *you shan't* means an assurance that, so far as it depends on the speaker, the other person will not succeed in doing this or that :

> Positively, you shan't escape.

25.6₁. *You shall* or *he shall* comes to mean a promise, *i.e.* it implies an obligation on the part of the speaker :

> You shall have the money as soon as I can get it.
> You shall not find me ungrateful for what you have done.
> Aske, and it shal be given you (AV.).
> ' I wish to have it done at once.'   ' It shall be done immediately, sir.'
> I have it from an old gentleman who shall be nameless.

Or it may be a threat :

> Not one halfpenny shall you ever have of mine.
> There is many a soule Shall pay full dearly for this encounter (Sh.).

Note the alternation in the same promise between *will* in the first person and *shall* in the others :

> For whither thou goest, I will goe; and where thou lodgest, I will lodge : thy people shall be my people, and thy God my God (AV.).

I will be silent; you shall never see me.
Marry me, and I will save your life. All shall be well. I will
    begin again.

25.6₂. In questions *shall* in the third person asks about the
will of the person addressed :

What shall it be? [=What kind of drink do you want?]
When shall the wedding be?

This is asked of the person who is to decide; " When will the
wedding be? " is asked of someone else; in both cases " When is
the wedding to be? " is now more frequent.

25.6₃. In a corresponding way *shall I (we) ?* is a question about
the will or advice of the person addressed :

Now, shall I take your hand?
Shall I help you to some cheese? or will you carve for yourself?
What shall I do? Which way shall I turn? [Often: am I
    to . . .]

For another meaning of *shall I (we)*, see **25.7₅.**

Pure Future

25.7₁. We next come to the use of *shall* without the tinge of
obligation, though we might often say that the underlying idea
is that of fatal necessity or the will of God as determining the
future.

It is probably under the influence of the Bible that *shall* is used
in literary style in solemn predictions :

Nation shall rise against nation, and kingdome against kingdome,
    and there shall be famines, and pestilence (AV.).
Oh, East is East, and West is West, and never the twain shall
    meet (Kipling).

25.7₂. In relative and temporal clauses (often implying a
condition) *shall* is frequently used in literary style, where the
simple present tense is now more idiomatic :

But whatsoever els shall hap to night, Give it an understanding,
    but no tongue (Sh.).
Whosoever shall deny me before men, him will I also deny before
    my father (AV.).

He that shall walk with vigour three hours a day, will pass in
seven years a space equal to the circumference of the earth
(S. Johnson).

When this shall fall into your hands, I shall have disappeared.

He will hold thee, when his passion shall have spent its novel
force (Tennyson; =prose *has spent*).

25.7₃. *I (we) shall* comes to be the natural auxiliary of the
future, because *I (we) will* is so frequently needed to express
volition, and because in most cases when one has to speak of
the future with regard to oneself, the implication is of some
more or less fatal necessity :

I shall come of age next year.

We shall be forgotten before the end of the century.

We shall get wet through if the rain does not stop soon.

Shall may be emphasized :

I don't know when I shall die, but I know that I *shall* die some
day.

When a future state of one's own feelings is to be mentioned
I shall is the natural expression, because one does not like to
imply that they depend on one's will :

I shall feel sorry when he dies.

I shall always remember your kindness.

I shall is required in cases like the following, because the
speaker feels that the future event depends on other things than
(or besides) his own present will :

Perhaps I shall go abroad next summer.

I hope I shall go abroad next summer.

I am afraid I shall be arrested.

Note the contrast between the two auxiliaries :

I do not like him, and I will never marry him.

I love him, but I am afraid I shall never marry him.

I will never see him again if that's what you wish, but I shall always
love him.

25.7₄. *I (we) shall* with the perfect infinitive serves to express
the before-future (cf. **25.4₅,** *will*) :

When you open this, I shall have been long dead.

In temporal clauses the same expression is found in literary style, but it is more natural to leave out the formal indication of the future and use the simple perfect :

> He will leave to-morrow morning before I shall have (before I have) finished breakfast.

25.7₅. *Shall I ?* (besides the use mentioned in **25.6₃**) may ask about some future event :

> As a people shall we ever really like the French ? Will they ever really like us ?
> Shall I (we) get there in time if I (we) take the 3.20 train ?

25.7₆. *Shall you?* from asking about an obligation has come to be a question about the pure future, distinct from *will you ?*, which is principally a question about the other person's will or willingness : *Shall you ?* is, perhaps, most natural where the future is independent of the will of the person addressed :

> Shall you get there in time if you take the 3.20 train ?
> Shall you see John today ? (=Will John come to your place ?)

But *shall you?* is also often used when the future may be (wholly or partially) dependent on the will of the person addressed, if it is the future and not the will the speaker wants to make certain about, thus very often where *will you ?* might be understood as a request :

> Shall you be in if I call in the afternoon ?
> Shall you dine with us on Tuesday ? (I have invited you already, but have forgotten your reply).
> When shall you be back, do you think ?

There is, however, a great tendency to use *will you?* even where there is no question about will (**25.4**).

Summary

25.8₁. We have come to the end of this survey of the various functions of the two verbs *will* and *shall*, in which we have seen that they still to some extent preserve the old meanings of volition and obligation, but often combine these with the idea of futurity, and finally very often denote futurity pure and simple without any visible trace of the original meanings. Matters are thus far from simple, chiefly because the English language to express the three distinct ideas of volition, obligation and futurity possesses only two auxiliaries; but also because there is always some inherent difficulty in speaking with certainty of what is yet to come, more particularly so if it is to be viewed as independent of human will. And where a future event is thought of as dependent on human will, the question arises, Whose will? A distinction must be made between the will of the speaker and that of the subject of the sentence : these are identical in the case of the first person, but not in the second and third persons. Hence we have in various sections found different rules according to the grammatical person of the subject.

Further, it must be recognized that the ideas of volition (determination, desire, willingness) and of obligation (necessity, restraint, duty, etc.) are in themselves often vague and indefinite. Emotions such as diffidence, modesty, etc., and further, the difference between statements and questions, also exert their influence on the choice of the auxiliary.

It is no wonder, therefore, that different rules should have prevailed with regard to these verbs at different periods and still prevail in different parts of the English-speaking world.

25.8₂. In the development two powerful linguistic agencies have been at work, the desire for ease and the desire for clearness.

Linguistic ease may be phonetic or syntactic. Phonetic ease is furthered when inconspicuous and easily pronounced forms are used as grammatical ' empty ' words; but this is better fulfilled with *will* than with *shall* : for while we have no examples of the dropping of the sound [ʃ], the sound [w] often disappears in weak positions, cf. such words as *answer, Southwark, hap'orth, Greenwich*, thus *I will, he will, we will, he would*, etc., naturally become *I'll, he'll, we'll, he'd*, etc. This ease has contributed largely to the prevalence of *will* over *shall* as auxiliary of the future. Syntactical ease points the same way, for it is easier always to use the same means to express the same notion than to have to stop to consider whether one or the other auxiliary is to be used. (Syntactical ease also leads to the extensive use of the present tense in speaking of the future.)

But the tendency to use *will* everywhere is to some extent counteracted by the desire for clearness, which requires the notions of volition and of future time to be kept distinct in all those cases in which actual misunderstandings of importance might arise. This leads, on the one hand, to a frequent use of stronger expressions like *want, intend, mean, choose* instead of *will*, and on the other hand, to the preference for *shall* in combinations where one particularly often has occasion to speak of someone's will, namely in the first person, in questions in the second person, and finally in conditional and relative clauses : in these cases it is desirable to have a neutral auxiliary which does not imply volition. The desire for clearness is also responsible for the growing use of the unmistakable expression for future time *is going to*, and similarly for the frequency of *has to* and *is to* where formerly *shall* was used to express obligation.

The present rule may be stated, very roughly, thus : to indicate futurity *will* is used as an auxiliary everywhere, except in those cases in which it might be misunderstood as implying actual will.

CHAPTER XXVI

WOULD AND SHOULD

Would.—Real past.—Habit.—Imaginative.—*I would.*—*Would you.*—Wishes.—Conditioned sentences.—First person.—*Should.* —Real past.—Imaginative.—Obligation.—Advice.—Obligation effaced.—Conditional clauses.—Emotional *should.*—*Will, shall, would, should* in indirect speech.—Notional survey of time-expressions.

Would

26.1₁. *Would,* the preterit of *will,* is comparatively seldom used as a real past to express volition; outside negative sentences such as :

> He knocked at the door, but she would not let him in—

it is chiefly found in clauses of indifference like :

> Doors were shut upon him, go where he would,

and in combination with *have* :

> As luck would have it he did not turn up.
> She would have her will in every way.

26.1₂. *Would* often implies habit in the past :

> He would sit for hours without saying a word.
> She would hang on him, As if encrease of appetite had growne By what it fed on (Sh.).

Finally, *would* is a real past in sentences like the following, where it expresses power, capacity, etc. :

> The hall would sit 1000 people.
> He tried vegetarianism, but that wouldn't do for him.

26.2₁. The chief employment of *would* is imaginative. In the first place it indicates volition under a hypothetical condition :

> I wouldn't be Lady Mickleham's butler if you made me a duke.

In strict (Southern English) language a distinction is made between *I should* and *I would,* the former eliminating and the

latter emphasizing the idea of will.   See the following extract
from Dr Johnson's *Rasselas* :

> If I had the choice of life, I should be able to fill every day
> with pleasure.   I would injure no man, and should provoke
> no resentment; I would relieve every distress, and should
> enjoy the benedictions of gratitude.   I would choose my
> friends among the wise, and my wife among the virtuous;
> and therefore should be in no danger from treachery or un-
> kindness.   My children should, by my care, be learned and
> pious, and would repay to my age what their childhood had
> received.   What would dare to molest him who might call
> on every side to thousands enriched by his bounty, or assisted
> by his power?   And why should not life glide quietly away
> in the soft reciprocation of protection and reverence?

26.2₂. When no condition is expressed, *I would* becomes a
weaker or more modest expression of present will or desire ; in
modern colloquial language the same idea is generally rendered
by *I should like to* :

> I would detain you here some month or two (Sh.).
> And I would be the girdle About her dainty dainty waist
>   (Tennyson).

26.2₃. When *would* is used in the second or third person, the
idea of volition is generally eliminated (**26.**3).   It is, however,
present in the polite request *Would you?* and in conditional
clauses :

> Would you (kindly) tell me the way to Charing Cross?
> If you would sit thus by me every night, I should work better
>   (Browning).
> If you (one, we) would understand a nation, you (one, we) must
>   know its language.
> He neither would have told it if he could, nor could he if he
>   would (Here the meaning of volition is much more salient
>   in the second than in the first *would*).

26.2₄. *Would* is further used in wishes, not only when the
fulfilment depends on the will of the subject, but also in other
cases :

> I wish he would stop that noise.
> I wish you wouldn't repeat what you have heard.

I wish he would die soon.

If only the rain would stop soon!

O wad some Power the giftie gie us To see oursels as ithers see us! (Burns).

26.3₁. Imaginative *would* without any trace left of volition is the regular auxiliary in main sentences of ' condition contrary to fact ' ; cf. **26.**6 :

You (any one) would die if you (he) took a strong dose of strychnine.

It would be a pity if he did not see her alive.

Suppose he came back, what would happen?

Every caress you gave his wife would be sin.

In the last example the condition is implied in the relative clause ; sometimes it is not expressed at all, and may not be easy to supply :

Who would have thought that of him?

If the reference is to a past time, the perfect infinitive is used :

He would have died if he had taken that strong dose of strychnine.

It would have been a pity, had he not seen her.

26.3₂. In strict Southern English usage this *would* in main hypothetical sentences is found in the second and third person only ; but in Scotch, Irish and American *I (we) would* is used very extensively without any idea of volition, and this is now also finding its way to British speakers and writers :

If I had Byron's genius and health and liberty, I would make the next three centuries recollect me (Carlyle).

I know you'll be interested.—Honestly I don't think I would be.

To reach it I would have to pass in front of the window (Galsworthy).

I would like is increasingly frequent, where strict grammarians prefer *I should like* ; hesitation is seen, *e.g.*, in

I would like to have Clive married to her . . . I should like to see Clive happy (Thackeray).

26.4. The hypothetical character is often obscured, and then *would* comes to indicate probability or what one might expect :

That would be in the year 1878.
That's what most men would say.
They were very polite.—They would be.
I don't see that at all.—No, you wouldn't.

It would seem or *one would think* is a more polite or guarded way of saying ' it seems.'

Should

26.5₁. The use of *should* as a real past is even more restricted than the corresponding use of *would* ; but we may see it in the familiar expression to denote surprise at some past occurrence :

When I crossed the street, who(m) should I see but my old friend Tom ?

—if this is interpreted as ' it was then my destiny to see.'

26.5₂. In all other applications *should* is a preterit of imagination, in the first place to express obligation or duty under hypothetical conditions :

If I could work my will every idiot should be boiled with his own pudding (Dickens).

Generally no condition is expressed, and *should* thus indicates present obligation, duty or propriety in general :

A friend should beare his friends infirmities (Sh.).
Maids should be seen, and not heard (Swift).
The sound should be an echo to the sense (Pope).
This is really splendid, though I say it that should not.

Such a sentence as

He is everything he shouldn't be

refers to the present time (or to all times) ; it is unchanged in the past :

He was everything he shouldn't be.

If, however, the idea of duty unfulfilled in the past is to be emphasized, the perfect infinitive is used :

He was everything he shouldn't have been.

26.5₃. In clauses after expressions of determination, desire, command, etc., in the present tense *should* is very frequent :

> It is necessary that the servants should know nothing about this.
>
> He is particularly anxious that his children should have good table-manners.
>
> All expect that you should rowse yourselfe (Sh.).
>
> The doctors wish that she should be kept as quiet as possible.

26.5₄. The meaning of obligation is often weakened ; in this way *should* becomes a usual expression of advice or vague admonition :

> You should see her dance ; it is well worth seeing.
>
> What should I do ? [=What do you advise me to do ?]

Should is thus weaker than the *shall* of threats and promises mentioned in **25.6**.

With the perfect infinitive about something that was not done :

> You should have seen him dance : that would have made you laugh.

Should implies what is almost certain :

> I should know that voice.
>
> He hasn't come yet ; but he should be in directly.
>
> His thoughts should be worth knowing.

26.6₁. We finally come to those cases in which every trace of the meaning of constraint has disappeared. In main sentences of rejecting condition the normal distribution of the two auxiliaries, at any rate in England, corresponds to that used in expressions of the future, thus :

> If he said that, { I should believe him.
> you would believe him.
> shouldn't you believe him ?
> everybody would believe him.

> If he had said that, { I should have believed him.
> you would have believed him.
> shouldn't you have believed him ?
> everybody would have believed him.

But, as already remarked, *would* is becoming frequent instead
of *should*.

When we read the sentence :

I should not have yielded—

we understand it as meaning ' it was wrong of me to yield,'
but if the sentence had been followed by " if you had been
present," the idea of duty immediately disappears, and the only
thing remaining is the colourless *should* corresponding to *would*
in the other persons.

Very often the idea of condition is not only left unexpressed,
but is so vague that it is hardly present in the mind of the
speaker. *I should say* becomes a modest or diffident way of
saying ' I say ' or ' I dare say ' : I should say he was over
fifty. But *I should think* (with stress on *think*) generally implies
scornful assertion :

Is he over fifty ?—Oh yes, I should think so [=Rather !].

26.6₂. We next come to the use in conditional clauses. *If he
called, if he should call*, and *if he were to call* are nearly synonymous expressions of uncertainty with regard to the future, and are
distinct from *if he would call*, which implies volition :

Papa will recover ; and if he should, I will let you know.
How terrible it would be if a time should come when I could not
love you.
Suppose some of the boys had seen me and should find me out.

The condition may be implied in a relative clause :

What would be thought of a painter who should mix August and
January in one picture ?
He would be a rash man who should venture to forecast the remote
results of the war.

26.7₁. We may use the term **emotional should** for the use
of *should* in passing a judgment of an emotional character
(agreeable or disagreeable surprise, indignation, joy) on some
occurrence which may, or may not, be a fact.

A sentence like " Why was the date omitted ? " is a mere
factual question, but " Why should the date of this document

be omitted ? " implies wonder and, possibly, some suspicion of the purity of the motives.   Compare further :

> Where the divell should he learne our language ? (Sh.).
> Why should they try to influence him ? [=I see no reason.]
> Someone asking for you.—Who should ask for me ?

26.7₂. Similarly in clauses :

> It is not good that the man should be alone (AV.).
> It was quite natural that the Russians should hate their oppressors.
> Why she should have done so, I can hardly tell.

" It is strange that she married (or has married) such an old man " merely states the fact ; " It is strange that she should have married such an old man " lays more stress on the strangeness by using the imaginative *should* in the clause.

The judgment itself (*e.g.* What a pity) may be omitted, so that the clause stands by itself as an exclamation :

> That it should come to this ! (Sh.).
> Ah that such sweet things should be fleet, Such fleet things sweet !
>   (Swinburne).

26.7₃. *Should* is also frequent in clauses after expressions of fear :

> Let us leave the house this instant, for fear he should ask further
>   questions.
> I tremble lest some mischance should befall him.
> Speaking in a low voice, lest anyone should hear.

Will, Shall, Would, Should in Indirect Speech

26.8₁. In indirect speech the general tendency is to use the same auxiliary as would have been used in direct speech ; but sometimes the verb is made to conform to the person into which the original subject has been shifted.

First we shall give some examples in which the auxiliary of direct speech has been retained ; in parenthesis we add the form belonging to direct speech :

> When I said I would die a batcheler, I did not think I should
>   live till I were married (Sh.; I will . . . I shall).
> She said that we would go together to the war, that I should be

her knight and she my lady and that we would care for the
wounds of the whole world (we will . . . you shall . . .).

He told me not to make myself uneasy; he would take care it
should be all right (I will . . . it shall . . .).

They told me he would soon be back. Would I wait (he will . . .
Will you . . .).

He asked Rose if she should be sorry (Shall you . . .).

I wanted to know if he would suffer much (Will he . . .).

I took care that there should be no repetition of these atrocities
(There shall . . .).

She thought he would pay if he could (He will if he can, or : He
would if he could).

26.8$_2$. In this way the auxiliary changes according to the
meaning of the pronoun :

He thinks himself that he shall recover, but the doctor says that
he will die soon.

He thought himself that he should recover, but the doctor said
that he would die soon.

An example of *she would* where direct speech would have had
I shall :

Eustacia's dream had always been that, once married to Clyne,
she would have the power of inducing him to return to
Paris (Hardy).

You (he) will (future) becomes *I shall* or *I should* because *I
will* or *I would* would call up too strongly the idea of volition :

Do you think I shall recover soon ?

She said I should please her much more if I would only press her
hand and go away.

They thought I should die.

Notional Survey of Time-Expressions

26.9$_1$. We have finished our examination of the tenses of the
English verb and those auxiliaries which correspond more or
less to the tenses of other languages (Chaps. XXIII-XXVI).
It will now be expedient to look at the same subject-matter from
the other side, starting from the notions of time that are universal,
independent of any special linguistic features, and then asking

ourselves in what different ways they find expression in the English verb.

26.9₂. Principal Divisions of Time.

These may be represented in the following diagram (23.1).

————————————————— × —————————————————

A	B	C
Past	Present	Future

The simple past time (A) is expressed in the following ways :

> He left on Monday.
> Everybody admired her.
> She was admired by everybody.
> I was born here.
> England is not what it was.
> He was dining when I came.
> The house was being rebuilt at the time.
> Well, says he . . .
> I had got no time.
> I used to know him pretty well.
> He would sit quietly for hours (Habit).
> He might be very rich, but he was no gentleman (Possibility).
> Tea would be waiting (Supposition as to fact).
> If I had had the money I should have paid you (Supposition contrary to fact).

26.9₃. The simple present time (B) is expressed by the following means :

> He lives at No. 27.
> He is staying at the Savoy.
> Everybody admires her.
> She is admired by everybody.
> This isn't done.
> The house is being rebuilt.
> I've got no time.
> He will sit quietly for hours (Habit).
> He may be very rich, but he is no gentleman (Possibility).
> Tea will be ready by now (Supposition).
> If I had the money I should pay you (Supposition contrary to fact).

26.9₄. Expressions of the simple future time (C) :

> He leaves on Monday (note that *on Monday* means a different
>   day from that in **26.**9₂).
> I am dining with him on Monday.
> If it rains to-morrow, what then?
> He is sure to turn up one of these days.
> He will turn up one of these days.
> I shall call on them one of these days.
> Everybody will admire her.
> She will be admired by everybody.
> The house will be rebuilt next year.
> He is going to get married.
> The weary ages that have been and are yet to come.
> Come again next week.
> It is time he left.
> He may leave on Monday (Possibility).
> If I had the money on Monday, I should pay you (Improbability).

26.9₅. Subordinate Divisions of Time.

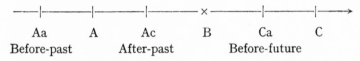

Aa	A	Ac	B	Ca	C
Before-past		After-past		Before-future	

Before-past (Aa, before ' then ') :

> He had left before I arrived.
> When he had gone out of the room, she burst out sobbing.
> After he left England, a son was born to him.

26.9₆. After-past (Ac, between ' then ' and now) :

> She had some foreboding of what was to happen.
> This I was only to find out afterwards.
> Nothing in the early history of Britain indicated the greatness
>   which she was destined to attain (Macaulay).

26.9₇. Before-future (Ca, between now and a specified time in
the future) :

> He will have forgotten before the end of the term.
> Sit down; I'll have done in a minute.
> I shall let you know as soon as I shall have heard from them
>   (stiff; more natural : as soon as I have heard).

He will let you know as soon as he will have heard from them
(more natural : he has heard).
Wait till the rain stops.
We shall start at 5 p.m., if the rain has stopped by that time.

In this survey we have mentioned those time-indications only
which fall within the straight time-line, and have thus found no
place for the retrospective present (*i.e.* perfect, **23.**6) or for
inclusive time (**23.**5₄).

MOOD

Forms.—Indicative.—Subjunctive.—Main sentences.—Clauses.—
Imperative.—*Let*.

27.1. The English verb has three moods, **Indicative, Subjunctive,** and **Imperative**—the Infinitive and the Participles, which are often reckoned among the moods, stand apart and form categories of their own. But the three moods above mentioned are not kept distinct in English in the same clear way as in many other languages. The imperative, like the infinitive, has the same form as the base of the verb **(7.6)**, and the same is true of the present indicative (except the third person singular) and of the whole of the present subjunctive. These may therefore be considered various functions of the same form. In the preterit only one verb has a subjunctive form that is distinct from the indicative, and that only in the singular : *were* (indicative *was*), and as already remarked **(24.2$_5$)**, this form is to a great extent being displaced by *was*, so that the tendency is to get rid of the preterit subjunctive form in all cases.

27.2. The **indicative** is used in all ordinary statements and questions. From simple matter-of-fact sentences it has been extended to many sentences in which formerly the subjunctive was used, so that now it is the normal mood of English verbs. No examples are needed.

27.3$_1$. The **subjunctive** is used in main sentences to express a (realizable) wish, chiefly in set phrases like :

God bless you ! God save the King !
Heaven preserve us !
The Lord have mercy upon us !
Long live the King ! (On the word-orders see **10.4$_5$**.)
Money be hanged !
Other forms for wishes, see **10.4$_6$**, **24.2$_3$**, **26.2$_4$**.

Other related uses of the subjunctive are seen in
Far be it from me to depreciate such pleasures.
Home is home, be it ever so homely.

Suffice it to say that . . .

Know all men by these presents . . . (in juridical parlance).

The archaic conjunction *albeit* ' though ' is made up of *all* (as in *although*) + *be* + *it*.

27.3₂. In the old language the subjunctive served in clauses to express various subjective moods, uncertainty, hesitation, diffidence, etc. But these meanings are no longer felt with the same force as formerly, and as the subjunctive is hardly ever used colloquially, it may now, to a great extent, be considered a literary trick to remove the style from everyday associations. The following sentences will serve to show it in various kinds of clauses :

I move that Mr N. be expelled from this club.

I do not know if (whether) this rumour be true or not.

I did not know if (whether) this rumour were true or not.

If this rumour be true, everything is possible.

Whether this rumour be true or not, we cannot remain here.

He will work if need be (here the indicative cannot be used).

This night before the cocke crow, thou shalt denie me thrise (AV.).

The rustic sits waiting till the river run dry (Carlyle).

As long as there is a man among the company, be he old or young, she monopolizes him completely.

In the first of these sentences *be*=*shall be* ; in most of the others a single indicative would be used in colloquial language, but instead of the subjunctive in the last sentence one would say, *let him be old or young.*

The imaginative use of preterits, and especially of *could, might, ought, would, should* was originally proper to the preterit subjunctive (**24.2, 26.2, 26.5**).

27.4₁. The **imperative** is used in requests, which according to circumstances may range from brusque commands to humble entreaties, the tone generally serving as a key to the exact meaning ; " please " is often added for the same purpose.

Get out of that, quick.

Come in !

Shut that door, please.

The subject of the imperative may or may not be expressly indicated (**10.5, 15.4₂**) ; on the perfect imperative, see **23.8₄**.

The frequent addition of *will you* (or *won't you*) goes to show that the imperative is really felt to be merely a separate use of the infinitive.

27.4₂. We must specially mention the imperative *let*, which is extensively used in desires and exhortations; it serves to bring about the word-order v—S—V—(O), cf. **10.**4 :

> Let us go! (=earlier Go we!).
> Let us have wine and women, mirth and laughter (Byron).
> Let me tell you one thing.
> Let John take the chair.
> Let it be distinctly understood that I will stand no nonsense.
> Let there be light.

On the tendency to use the nominative after *let*, see **14.**3.

Note the distinction : if *let us* is an exhortation, so that the second person is included, the vowel is often dropped : " Let's go." But this is not the case if *let* has its original meaning and *us* is used in contrast to the person(s) addressed : " Let us go " (= set us free), " Let us know the time of your arrival."

27.4₃. Imperatives are often used in such a way that no real request is meant : the hearer or reader is only asked to imagine some condition, and then the consequence is stated :

> Use everie man after his desart, and who should scape whipping ? (Sh.).
> See deep enough, and you see musically (Carlyle).
> Let women into your plans, and you never know where it'll end.

Let alone is often used in such a way that the original meaning is lost sight of, and the whole phrase comes to mean ' not to mention, still less ' :

> I couldn't have stood this for two days, let alone two months.

CHAPTER XXVIII

AFFIRMATION, NEGATION, QUESTION

28.1₁. A sentence may be either affirmative (positive) or negative, or else express a doubt on the part of the speaker, which the hearer is asked to resolve, *i.e.* it may contain a question.

Affirmation

28.1₂. In the first class of sentences we must here especially mention those containing an emphatic assertion. There are in English two means by which the reality or strength of an assertion is emphasized, namely, in the case of auxiliary verbs by using the stressed form with a full vowel (**4.**9), and in the case of all other verbs by a combination with *do* :

> He *was* angry, and no mistake.
> But I *have* told you everything already.
> You *must* go, there is no help for it.
> Death may come any day, but it *will* come some day (**25.**4; cf. **25.**7₃, *shall*).
> I do wish you wouldn't drive so fast.
> A whisky and soda? Yes, I do want a drink.
> Such mistakes may, and sometimes do occur, even in the best books.
> He rarely speaks at our meetings, but when he does speak it is always to the point.
> He was really afraid of looking, but look he did, nevertheless.
> Well, I say, you *are* a swimmer!
> Well, I say, you do swim!

When *have* is not an auxiliary, it may take *do* :

We did have a good time.

With an imperative *do* serves to express a strong entreaty, and is here exceptionally used with the auxiliary *be* :

Do come, there's a good boy !
Do be quiet!

Negation

28.2₁. In English as in other languages we have two tendencies which in some cases may conflict with one another. One is to put the negative word or element as early as possible, so as to leave no doubt in the mind of the hearer as to the purport of what is said ; the other is to attract the negative to the verb of the sentence.

The former tendency is seen in the frequency of negative prefixes, *e.g.*

*n*ever, *n*owhere.
*un*happy.
*in*human, *im*possible, *ig*noble, *il*literate, *ir*religious (various forms of the same prefix in accordance with Latin phonology).
*dis*order,—

and in the place of *not* in

not happy ; not he.
not to mince matters.
not having heard, etc.

Whenever it might seem possible to attract the negative element to either of two words, it is almost invariably put with the first. Thus we may say, either

No one ever saw him smile, or
Never did any one see him smile,

but not the other way round, beginning with *ever* or *any one*.

The second tendency is seen when *not,* or the contracted form *n't*, is placed after the verb, as in *is not, isn't, cannot, can't.* On the contracted forms, see **4.9₃.**

28.2₂. But it is important to note that in English, especially as it has developed in the modern period with its increasing use of auxiliaries, the two tendencies may be reconciled, in so far as the negative, though placed after a verb, comes to stand before the verb which is really significant, as the first verb is only auxiliary :

> He is not looking.
> He will not look.
> I shall not look.
> He does not look.
> He did not look.
> He has not looked.

28.2₃. This, then, is what is at the bottom of the comparatively recent use of *do* in negative sentences, through which *I do not know* and *I did not know* have been substituted for the earlier *I know not* and *I knew not*. This should be compared with the use of the same auxiliary in questions, see **28.6₂**.

In this way *do* is required with all full verbs, but not with auxiliaries. When *have* is not an auxiliary, it may take *do* :

> We didn't have much of a breakfast.
> He doesn't have to go to chapel.
> He did not have the picture framed (different from : he had not framed the picture).

Be in the imperative is now always used with *do* :

> Don't be afraid !

On the use of *do* with *dare* and *need*, see **32.1₅**.

28.2₄. Sometimes it makes a difference whether the negative belongs to one special word or is placed with the verb as belonging to the sentence as a whole, *e.g.*

> Many of us did not want the war, but many others did.
> Not many of us wanted the war (*not many* = ' few ').

28.2₅. In the case of an infinitive the use or non-use of *do* with the main verb serves to make a useful distinction, *e.g.*

> Tommy deserved not to be hated.
> Tommy did not deserve to be loved.
> She did not wish to reflect ; she strongly wished not to reflect.
> The more he endeavoured not to think, the more he thought.

Note also the way in which *not* can be made to stand as the representative of a whole sentence or dependent clause :

"Will he come? " " I hope not."

Thus also " I am afraid not," which is different from " I am not afraid."

But *not* is often placed with the verb even if a more correct analysis would have referred it elsewhere. By the side of the logically impeccable

I came not to send peace, but a sword (Matt. x. 34)

we frequently find sentences like

I do not admire her face, but her voice (what I admire is her voice, not her face).

We aren't here to talk nonsense, but to act (an isolated " we aren't here " would be a contradiction in terms).

Compare the two sentences :

(1) I didn't call because I wanted to see her (but I called for some other reason), and

(2) I didn't call because I wanted to avoid her.

But it should be noted that the spoken language makes here a distinction, as *call* has a rising tone in (1) and a falling tone in (2).

28.2₆. We must here specially mention the use of *not* with *may* and *must*. As a prohibition is the opposite of a permission, a natural way of expressing it is by means of *may not*.

You may not take that (you are not allowed to take that).

As, however, the same combination is often used in a different sense, with *not* belonging logically to the infinitive :

He may not be rich, but he is a gentleman (It is possible that he is not rich)—

may not in the sense of ' is not allowed to ' is comparatively rare, except in questions implying a positive answer (*mayn't I take that* =' I suppose I may ') and in close connexion with a positive *may*, e.g. in answers (" May I take that? " " No, you may not "). Therefore *must not* has become the usual way of expressing a prohibition. But though logically *not* belongs here to the following infinitive (*you must not take that* = ' it is necessary that you do not take '), the usual attraction of the negative to the verb leads to the colloquial form *you mustn't take that*.

28.2₇. On the other hand the negative is often attracted to any word that can easily be made negative. This is found with particular frequency in the literary language, which prefers

This will be no easy matter,
We met nobody,

while in ordinary conversational language we say

This won't be an easy matter,
We didn't meet anybody.

Cf. further

We need detain you no longer.
He was in no case to answer.
He was no ordinary boy (instead of the unidiomatic "a not ordinary boy ").
He, too, [the throstle] is no mean preacher (Wordsworth).

The Meaning of Negation

28.3₁. Though the terms *positive* and *negative* are used both in mathematics and in grammar, their meaning is not the same : in mathematics − 4 means a point as much below O as +4 is above O. In language, on the other hand, a negative changes a term into the contradictory term : *smokers* and *non-smokers* together comprise everybody ; *he will come* and *he will not come* exhaust all possibilities, and *not-happy* means ' anything but happy.'

28.3₂. This general rule, however, requires some very important qualifications. With quantitative terms *not* nearly always means ' less than ' :

Not much = ' little ' ; not many = ' few.'
Not lukewarm = ' between lukewarm and cold,' but not ' boiling hot.'

He does not read three books in a year.
His income is not £200 a year.
He does not see her once in a week.
The bottle is not half full.

Therefore *not one* comes to be a natural expression for
' none.'

But exceptionally these combinations may convey another
meaning; this is the case if we stress the word following *not*
and give it the peculiar intonation indicative of contradiction,
and especially, if the negation is followed by a more exact
indication :

Not *luke*warm, but really hot.
His income is not *two* hundred a year, but at least three
  hundred.
Not *once,* but two or three times, etc.

Not once or twice always means ' several times,' as in
Tennyson's

Not once or twice in our fair island-story
The path of duty was the way to glory.

28.3₃. A distinction is made between *not* and *no* before a
comparative : *no more than three* =' three only,' *not more than
three* =' three at most.' *He paid no less than twenty pounds*
implies astonishment at the greatness of the amount, which
was exactly £20. *He paid not less than twenty pounds* implies
uncertainty with regard to the exact amount, which at the very
least was £20.

28.3₄. If *not* is placed before a word like *all, always,* etc., the
resultant meaning is ' some, sometimes,' etc. :

They are not all of them fools.
He is not always so sad.
This is not found everywhere.

Note the difference between " not at all happy " and " not
altogether happy."

Exceptionally *not* is placed after *all* :

All that glisters is not gold (Sh.).
All is not lost.

But we have a different meaning in

Not all the water in the rough rude sea
Can wash the balme from an anoynted king (Sh.),

where *not* belongs logically to the verb.

Double Negation

28.4₁. If two negatives are applied to *the same idea or word*, as in *not uncommon, not infrequent, not without some fear*, the result is always positive, though the two negatives do not exactly cancel each other : the expression with two negatives is comparatively weak and implies some hesitation on the part of the speaker, which is absent from the blunt shorter expressions *common, frequent, with some fear*.

Cf. also *not for nothing* in sentences like

He was not the eldest son of his father for nothing.

In some cases, however, two, three, or even more negatives in the same sentence are not mutually destructive because applied to different ideas. This was a common grammatical feature in OE. and ME. ; a well-known example is Chaucer's

He *n*euere yet *n*o vileynye *n*e seyde
In al his lyf unto *n*o maner wight.

In ModE. this heaping of negatives is avoided in educated speech, but found in vulgar speech, *e.g.*

*N*obody *n*ever went and hinted *n*o such thing, said Peggotty.

Such repeated negatives are usual in a great many languages in which the negative element is comparatively small in phonetic bulk and is easily attracted to various words. If the negation were expressed once only, it might easily be overlooked ; hence the speaker, who wants the negative sense to be fully apprehended, attaches it not only to the verb, but also to other parts of the sentence : he spreads, as it were, a thin layer of negative colouring over the whole of the sentence instead of confining it to one single place. This may be called pleonastic, but is certainly not really illogical.

28.4₂. A seemingly superfluous negative is frequently found with *neither* or *nor*, as in

> Man delights not me; no, nor woman neither (Sh.).
> I hope things are not so very bad with you neither (Jane Austen).

This, too, is now avoided in literary English.

A different variant of double negation is found colloquially when, in a kind of afterthought, an absolute negative is softened down into a weaker expression, as in

> I've never hardly known him to miss church before (G. Eliot).
> He wasn't changed at all hardly (Kipling).

Weakened and Implied Negation

28.4₃. A negative expression is often used idiomatically in such a way that the negative idea is weakened or even disappears totally, thus in exclamations:

> How often have I not watched him.

Cf. below on negative questions. *Ever so* and *never so* mean virtually the same thing:

> Forgive her all her sins, be they (n)ever so many.
> Please write me a kind letter, let it be (n)ever so short.

An exaggerated negative is seen in the familiar

> I shall be back in no time.

28.4₄. Inversely a negation is often implied in a context that is not negative in form, thus in hypothetical clauses and frequently in questions:

> If I had money enough, I should pay you (see Imaginative use of tenses, **24.₂**).
> Am I the guardian of my brother?
> Shall I ever forget her?
> Who knows?

Thus also in various elliptical and ironical idioms:

> If ever I heard the like!
> See if I do!
> Catch me doing it.
> Much I care.

The devil and other swear-words are often used idiomatically to express negatives indirectly :

> When the devil was ill, the devil a monk would be :
> When the devil got well, the devil a monk was he.

> I am damned (dashed, blessed, hanged) if I know.

Questions

28.5₁. There are two kinds of questions : " Did he say that? " is an example of the one kind, and " What did he say? " and " Who said that? " are examples of the other.

In the former kind—**nexus-questions**—we call in question the combination (nexus) of a subject and a predicate. We may therefore continue with the negative counterpart : " Did he say that, or did he not (say that) ? " and thus make it into a disjunctive or alternative question. The answer to a simple nexus-question is *yes* or *no* ; the answer to a disjunctive question like " Is it black or white? " or " Did he drink sherry or port? " is one of the two alternatives (or else " neither ").

In a simple nexus-question it is therefore of little importance whether the verb is given in a positive or negative form. In offering a glass of beer we may say either " Will you have a glass of beer? " or " Won't you have a glass of beer? "

This, however, is true of unemotional questions only ; a marked tone of surprise will make the two sentences into distinct contrasts : for then " Will you (really) have a glass of beer? " comes to mean " I am surprised at your wanting a glass of beer," and " Won't you have a glass of beer? " the reverse. " Won't you pass me the salt? " may thus imply unwillingness in the person addressed and therefore is more rude than, " Will you pass me the salt? " Very often one of the two forms is chosen to suggest a particular answer, thus *isn't that nice?* comes to mean ' That is very nice.'

Note especially tag-questions in colloquial speech, like :

> He was angry, wasn't he?
> He wasn't angry, was he?
> You feel cold here, don't you?
> He didn't take long to decide that, did he?

28.5₂. In questions of the second kind we have an unknown quantity x, exactly as in an algebraic equation ; we may therefore use the term **x-questions.** The linguistic expression for this x is an interrogative pronoun or pronominal adverb. The pronouns are seen in these examples :

Who said that?
Which of the boys said that?
Which boy do you mean?
Which do you like best, tea or coffee?
Which way shall we turn? [*i.e.* to the right or to the left?]
What did he say?
What woman would dare to say that?
Whose child is he?

These pronouns are distinguished in a different way from the same forms when used relatively (**19.**7) : *which* asks for one (or more) out of a restricted number, while *who* and *what* ask indefinitely. While *what* as a primary is always neuter, it may (like *which*) be put as an adjunct to all kinds of words. The question " What is he? " refers to character, office, place in society, or the like, while " Who is he? " asks about his identity.

Prepositions are idiomatically placed at the end :

What are you looking at?
Who(m) is that letter from?

Examples of interrogative adverbs :

When did he say it?
Where did he say it?
Why did he say it?
How did he say it?
How often did he say it?

In the last sentence *how* does not ask about manner, but about degree ; thus also in *how much?* and *how many?* The change in meaning is parallel to that of *so* (**16.**3₄).

28.5₃. Interrogative words are often strengthened colloquially by some supplement, chiefly to indicate impatience or similar feelings :

What on earth (Whatever) are you hinting at?
Who the dickens (Whoever) told you that nonsense?

28.6₁. Questions are shown to be such by intonation, by word-order, by a special interrogative word, or, finally, by two or three of these means in the same sentence.

The rising tone characteristic of questions is, of course, most pronounced in questions which are not marked as such by any other means, e.g. *Tom ? Alone ? At night ?*

In questions containing an interrogative word the high or rising tone is generally concentrated on this pronominal word.

In simple nexus-questions the tone rises towards the end of the sentence, as this intonation implies incompleteness : the speaker asks the hearer to complete his thought. But if a second alternative is added, as in disjunctive questions, the sentence ends on a falling tone : In " Did John drink sherry or port ? " *sherry* has a high, and *port* a low tone. If, on the other hand, we pronounce the sentence in such a way that *sherry* has a middle and *port* a high tone, we have not a disjunctive, but a simple question, in which *sherry or port* forms one idea, as when we express surprise at John's drinking such strong wines.

The tone varies naturally with the degree of feeling expressed.

28.6₂. The word-order characteristic of questions consists in placing the verb before the subject. This is opposed to the general tendency of the language, which is to have the subject before the verb. But the two tendencies are reconciled when the verb placed first is a comparatively insignificant auxiliary, while the really important verb comes after the subject ; thus, using the same symbols as in **10.4** :

$$v—S—V—O$$

Can he take photos ?
Will he take photos ?
Would he take photos ?
Has he taken photos ?
Is he taking photos ?

During the last few centuries the use of *do* (*does, did*) has become the rule in such interrogative sentences as contain no other auxiliary ; instead of the old " Swims he ? " etc., we now say :

Does he swim ?
Did he swim ?
Did you have the picture framed ?

(Cf. the use of *do* in emphatic and negative sentences, **28.1₂**, **28.2₃**.)

But *do* is not required in those sentences in which the subject naturally precedes the verb, *i.e.* when it is an interrogative pronoun or an equivalent :

Who swims?
What happened?
How many people signed the petition?

28.7₁. We have curious double-barrelled questions in " Who is who? " = ' Who is one, and who is the other? ' (found as early as Chaucer). Thus also " He does not know which is which " or " what is what."

28.7₂. Questions are often elliptical :

What about lunch?
What if we should fail to find them?

Note also " I'll tell you what," in which *what* is virtually an indefinite pronoun = ' something.'

28.7₃. A related use of *what* is to introduce alternative words, chiefly to indicate the (combined) reason for something :

What with eating above stairs, and drinking below, with receiving your friends within, and amusing them without, you lead a good pleasant bustling life of it (Goldsmith).

This is often used very loosely.

28.7₄. The interrogative words *what* and *how* are frequently used in exclamations, but the word-order generally shows that the sentences are not to be taken as questions :

What beautiful hair that girl has!
What a fool he was to reject our offer!
How we shall laugh when he comes back!
How great was my surprise when they were engaged!

Note here the difference between *what* before mass-words and *what a* before thing-words in the singular. Very often the exclamation contains only a predicative :

What fun!   What a funny sight!
How curious!

28.8. What from a formal point of view is a question is often not really meant as such. " How do you do? " is generally a greeting that does not require an answer (**1.**2). Rhetorical questions implying the opposite meaning of the corresponding direct statement have been mentioned in **28.**4₄. A surprise may be expressed in the form of a question, *e.g.* " What! are you here? " which certainly is not said in order to be informed whether the other person is here.

28.9. On dependent interrogative clauses, see **33.**2. The conjunction *whether* (which originally meant ' which of two ') was at first used in disjunctive questions only (*whether . . . or no* or *whether . . . or not*), but is now often used when no second alternative is expressed.

DEPENDENT NEXUS

29.1₁. While an independent nexus forms a complete piece
of communication (a sentence), a dependent nexus forms only
a part of a sentence, and thus may be either a primary in a sentence (subject or object), a secondary (an adjunct) to a primary
in a sentence, or a tertiary in a sentence.

A dependent nexus may take the form of either :

(1) a simple collocation of a primary and a secondary
(XXIX) ;
(2) a nexus-substantive, which shares the ordinary qualities
of a substantive (XXX) ;
(3) a gerund, which is a special kind of nexus-substantive
(XXXI) ;
(4) an infinitive (XXXII) ; or
(5) a clause (XXXIII-XXXV).

In a clause we find the same constructions as in a sentence
(subject, verb, object, etc.). The relations of what in an ordinary
sentence would be the subject and object are not so simple in
other forms of dependent nexus.

Simple Nexus as Object

29.1₂. The object of a verb is often a nexus expressed by
a simple collocation of a primary and its adnex. As a first
example we may take " I found the cage empty," which is easily
distinguished from " I found the empty cage," in which *empty*
is an adjunct. In the former sentence the whole combination
the cage empty is naturally the object (cf. " I found that the cage
was empty" and "I found the cage to be empty"). This is

particularly clear in sentences like " I found her gone " (thus did not find her !)

Further examples :

> I saw my face reflected in the mirror.
> I heard it spoken of in the club.
> We think this a great shame.
> They held the Government responsible for all the outrages.
> They called (baptized) him James.
> Will you keep me informed about the affair?

The adnex may be any word or combination of words which can stand as a predicative (**13.**6), *e.g.* a prepositional group.

> Could she have believed herself in the way ?
> Her friends held her of little account.

This remark applies to the following paragraphs as well.

After *wish* and *want* we have an approach to an object of result :

> Don't tell Mrs M. anything you wish forgotten.
> I want my room ready by seven in the morning.
> She only wished the dinner at an end.

29.1₃. A nexus as an unmistakable object of result is found in the first place after such verbs as denote in themselves the production of a result :

> Much learning doeth make thee mad (AV.).
> Her stubbornness made him angry.
> They elected Jones President of the Society.
> What makes you in such a hurry ?
> The respect that makes calamity of so long life (Sh.).

Next, after some verbs the original physical meaning of which is more or less effaced :

> This will drive him mad.
> Set the prisoners free.
> You will lay yourself open to censure if you go on.
> The great thing was to get the book talked about.
> It would be a relief to get the meeting over.

29.1₄. A special case is *have*, which is used not only of what is unintentional on the part of the subject, as in

> King Charles the First had his head cut off ;
> The General had two horses shot under him—

but also (with an object of result) serves to express causality
on the part of the subject :

> I had my hair cut.
> I went to a dentist's to have a tooth out.
> They had their fortunes told them.
> He was some years older than when he had had his picture
> painted.

The distinction which is made between this construction and
the perfect and pluperfect, *e.g.* between " he had the books
bound " and " he had bound the books " would seem to disappear in a relative clause : " the books which he had bound " ;
but in natural spoken language *had* would in one case have
a full vowel [hæd], and in the other be run together with
he [hi·d].

29.1₅. Finally we have the extensive use of nexus after other
verbs to express the result of the action or state expressed by
the verb itself. If it is transitive it can thus take an object
that is quite different from its usual object, as in

> He drinkes you with facillitie your Dane dead drunke (Sh.).
> He had drunk all the officers under the table.

Intransitive verbs, which can otherwise have no object, also
admit this construction :

> He slept himself sober.
> A lovers eyes will gaze en eagle blinde (Sh.).

Other examples (with transitive and intransitive verbs) :

> She flung the window open.
> I stripped myself stark naked.
> It will bore you stiff.
> He bowed her into an armchair.
> Eating his father out of house and home.
> You cannot explain the contradiction away.
> We must live this down.
> The novel with which he had read himself to sleep.

29.1₆. In all the examples given so far we have the natural
word-order corresponding to the usual order in an ordinary
sentence (subject before the verb). To bring about this order

the use of preparatory *it* (**16.1₆**) is often required.   The opposite
word-order is exceptional, but permissible if the adnex is very
short, especially in fixed combinations like the following :

> He *cut short* all interruptions.
> By now they must have *made good* (=effected) their retreat.
> This amounts to *letting loose* a tiger on a crowd.
> He has *seen fit* to escape.

29.1₇. When sentences like those dealt with in this chapter
are turned into the passive, *e.g.*

> The cage was found empty ;
> He was made angry by her stubbornness;
> The window was flung open—

we may call the words *empty, angry, open* simply predicatives.
But if we analyse the sentences in the same way as we did in
11.2, we see that the (notional) subject is the whole nexus,
the cage . . . empty, he . . , angry, the window . . . open
(which was the object in the active sentence) : this is what
was found, made, flung.   Cf. **32.**5 : split subject containing an
infinitive.

29.1₈. A simple nexus may be the object not only of a verb,
but also of a preposition.   In ordinary language this is chiefly
found after *with*, which is quite natural, as *with* often means
virtually the same thing as *having*, though its meaning is in many
cases very vague indeed :

> Will Fortune never come with both hands full? (Sh.).
> Don't speak with your mouth full.
> I can't write with you standing there.
> Morning?   It seems to me a night with the sun added (Browning).
> I can't live on my wages with prices what they are.
> It was pitch-black outside, with the moon not yet up.
> With Sister Glegg in this humour, there was a cheerful prospect
>   for the day.
> She came the whole length of the immense room, with every one
>   looking at her.
> She sat looking in his face, with the colour quite gone from her
>   own face.
> What a lonely world it will be with her away.

29.1₉. A nexus is sometimes found as the object of the preposition *without* :

> Without permission given or asked for, he brought to me a large parcel.
> They had passed without a single word spoken.
> Like a rose, full-blown, but without one petal yet fallen.

After other prepositions such a nexus is rare ; Milton's " after Eve seduc'd " and Dryden's " the royal feast for Persia won " are no doubt due to conscious imitation of Latin syntax.

Simple Nexus as Tertiary

29.2₁. A simple collocation of a primary and an adnex may serve as a tertiary in a sentence. This construction belongs to literary style rather than to colloquial speech. The case of the primary is not often shown, but when it is, it is the nominative, as it is felt to be the subject :

> He being rich and I poor, everybody took his side against me.

29.2₂. These grammatical constructions occur most often in set phrases. They serve, in the first place, to indicate reason or condition, very often with the participle *being* :

> Weather permitting (God willing) we shall start on Monday.
> All things considered, the offer seems reasonable.
> The season being over, I was my own master.
> There being no taxis, we had to walk.
> Their conversation being in Chinese, I did not understand one word.
> That being so, he wasted no words on the matter.
> Other things being equal, the simplest explanation is the best.

In this case *it* is occasionally dropped before *being* :

> Being Sunday, the shops were all closed.

29.2₃. Next, a time-relation may be indicated :

> This done, he bade us good-night.
> These preliminaries over, we began to talk business.
> (There were only fifty prisoners, all told.)
> The Captain having first set the example, we all began to dance.

> This duty being performed, my son and I went to pursue our usual industry (Goldsmith; now rather . . . having been performed, or with *when*).

The temporal meaning may be strengthened by *once* :

> Once the door closed, they all began to talk together.
> The cup once sipped, would he consent to put it down ?

We must specially mention *ago*, as in

> He came back a few minutes ago,

which is a participle of an obsolete verb *ago* =' go ' ; the old form was *agone*.

29.2₄. In the third place, the nexus contains descriptive details and indications of attendant circumstances, generally added after the main part of the sentence, and sometimes very loosely connected with it :

> She stood silent, her head slightly on one side.
> The two still knelt, tears running down their cheeks.
> I waited, every nerve upon the stretch.
> She said her prayers at home, her heart full of love and tenderness.
> Helen ran back to the dining-room, her brother following.
> He spoke with a strong foreign accent, the result being that he was arrested as a German spy (=and the result consequently was . . .).

29.2₅. In descriptions we often have condensed expressions, in which qualifications that are necessary in other combinations are omitted :

> He stood there, hat in hand and pipe in mouth (with his hat in his hand and a pipe in his mouth).
> He tumbled down head foremost.
> We turned the tortoise upside down.
> Head over heels (said to be a corruption of " heels over head ").
> We met face to face at last.

29.2₆. A few participles are generally placed before the primary in this construction :

> Given these persons in this situation, such and such events will follow.
> Granted health, he may still live to pay off his debts.
> By diplomatic pressure, if possible, or, failing that, by force.

It is from such combinations that *during* and *pending* have become prepositions :

> During the war = while the war dures or dured.
> Pending his return, Kate and her mother were shown into a dining-room.

29.2₇. We may finally mention constructions in which the adnex is an infinitive with *to,* expressing what is destined or enjoined (as in *he is to go,* **32.**2₉) ; the expression " he himself being to . . . " is avoided :

> He proposed a picnic, he himself to pay the railway tickets, and John to provide the food.

CHAPTER XXX

NEXUS-SUBSTANTIVES

Formed from predicatives or from verbs.—Subject or object.—
Genitive or *of*.—Active or passive import.—Both subject and
object.—Concrete meaning of nexus-substantive.

30.1. A dependent nexus is very often expressed by means
of a substantive. We have two kinds of nexus-substantives.
In the first kind an adjective or a substantive is at the basis
as a predicative : *cleverness* = ' being clever,' *wisdom* = ' being
wise,' and similarly *pride, ease, constancy, friendship, chaplaincy,
heroism,* etc.

In the second kind a verb is at the basis : *arrival* = ' the act
of arriving,' *belief, existence, sleep, fight, examination, collision,
judgment,* etc.

These latter are often called ' action-nouns,' but some of
our examples have already shown that this name is not quite
appropriate, as many verbal ideas do not indicate any action.

30.2. Nexus-substantives serve to express complicated ideas
in a short and handy way. If we compare the sentence :

> The doctor's extremely quick arrival and uncommonly careful
> examination of the patient brought about her very speedy
> recovery ;

with

> The Doctor arrived extremely quickly and examined the patient
> uncommonly carefully ; the result was that she recovered
> very speedily—

we see that the three ideas are brought together as one organic
whole instead of being presented as pearls on a string. Note
the grammatical changes necessitated by this rearrangement,
as also in :

> We noticed the doctor's astonishing cleverness ;

as compared with

> We noticed that the doctor was astonishingly clever, or
> We noticed how astonishingly clever the doctor was.

The use of nexus-words is accompanied by a change of the rank of many words. Two consecutive adverbs are avoided by means of *with* and a nexus-word : " he spoke with absolute freedom " instead of " absolutely freely " ; similarly, *with perfect ease, with approximate accuracy*, etc.

30.3. The most interesting thing from a grammatical point of view about nexus-substantives is to see how the element that in an independent sentence would have been a primary (subject or object) is combined with these substantives. It is evident that very often no such indication is needed ; then we understand the whole as predicated either (1) of the ' generic person ' (**15.6**) or (2) of the subject of the main sentence :

(1) Pride goes before a fall.
(2) He found happiness in work and temperance.

30.4. But just as often the primary has to be indicated. In the case of a predicative nexus-word, and one formed from an intransitive verb, this presents no difficulty : either the genitive (or possessive pronoun) or the preposition *of* is used :

The doctor's cleverness (his cleverness), the cleverness of the doctor.
The doctor's arrival (his arrival), the arrival of the doctor.

The same is true of substantives formed from such transitive verbs as cannot on account of their meaning take a person as object :

The doctor's (his) suggestion, decision, supposition ; the suggestion (etc.) of the doctor.

30.5. In such cases there can be no doubt that in an independent sentence the word in question would be the subject. But in other cases it might as well be the object : *the love of God* may just as well be the love felt by God as the love we feel for God. Note also the following combinations :

A manual for the use of teachers.
What is the use of teachers ?
Your praise encouraged him.
She is full of your praises.
His assistance was required.
We must come to his assistance.

In other words the nexus-substantive has sometimes an active, and sometimes a passive import; the latter is always the case after such a verb as *need* or *want* :

He needs support, he asks for approbation, etc.

In the following cases the substantive will naturally be taken in the active sense :

John's (his) discovery, admiration, love, respect, approbation, etc.

But in all those cases in which more interest is taken in the person who is the object of an action than in the person who is the agent, the substantive will be taken in the passive sense :

A man's (his) defeat, overthrow, arrest, deliverance, education, etc.
The Prime Minister's reception in London was unique.
The criminal escaped recognition.

Now it is possible to have one and the same substantive accompanied by two words, one to express the subject and another the object; the former expressed by a genitive (or possessive pronoun) and the latter by an *of*-combination :

His instinctive avoidance of my brother.
He won praise by his release of his prisoners.
Lady Miller's reception of her guests.
He had overcome her dislike of him.

30.6. It will thus be seen that both the genitive and the possessive and the *of*-combination have really a double function with nexus-substantives. To remedy the awkwardness and want of clearness resulting from this we have two means. One is to use the preposition *by* for the subject (just as with a passive verb, **12.**7)—a use which has been increasingly common since the middle of the nineteenth century. This is generally combined with *of* before what would be the object :

The accidental discovery by Miss Knag of some correspondence (Dickens).
Every government of one nationality by another is of the nature of slavery (Lecky).
Mrs Wright's account of her courtship by Joseph Wright (=Joseph Wright's courtship of her).

But a possessive may also be used :

His expulsion from power by the Tories.

30.7. The second is to use prepositions for the object other than the ambiguous *of* :

Your love for my daughter.
The love of Browning for Italy.
There would have been no hatred of Protestant to (for) Catholic.
The control of mind over matter (=of matter by mind).
Their organized attack on the Government.

30.8. It should be noted that many substantives are used, not only of the action, but also of the thing produced by the action : *a construction, invention, institution, collection*, etc.

In a similar way substantives derived from adjectives may be used to denote that which has the quality : *beauty* (" Isn't our puss a beauty ? "), *a truth, the realities of life*, etc. In slightly different ways : " he was the pride of his parents " (what they were proud of), " His Royal Highness."

CHAPTER XXXI

THE GERUND

Hybrid between substantive and verb.—Treated as substantive.
—Similarities with verbs.—Active and passive meaning.—Object.
—Subject.—Genitive or possessive.—Difficulties.—Common case.
—Personal pronouns.—Gerund or participle ?—*Of* and *by*.—The
gerundial nexus itself subject.—*It* and *there*.

31.1₁. The gerund is a nexus-substantive like those dealt with
in the previous chapter, but differs from them in several important
respects. In the first place it has the advantage that it can
be formed—and formed in the same way, through the addition
of *-ing*—from any verb (with the exception of *may, shall* and a
few other auxiliaries of the same type). And then it has taken
over certain syntactic characteristics of the verb which are not
found in other nexus-substantives : it may therefore be termed
a hybrid between these two word-classes, and as such has become
an extremely supple means of combining and subordinating
ideas. One of the reasons why the gerund is thus treated like
a verb is evidently the formal identity with the first participle
(cf. **31.**4).

31.1₂. Let us first consider those points in which a gerund
resembles and is treated like a substantive.

It can be used as a subject, predicative or object—also, and
this is very important, as the object of a preposition. Examples
of gerunds as objects of adjectives are found in **11.**9.

It can form a plural : *his comings and goings, sayings and
doings* ; this is especially frequent when a gerund has acquired
a completely concrete signification and thus is more or less
detached from the verb from which it is formed : *buildings,
drawings, savings, leavings, blessings.*

It can form a genitive, though, on account of the restrictions
in the use of the genitive (**14.**8), chiefly before *sake* : reading
for reading's sake.

It can take various adjuncts in the same way as other substantives : *the beginning*; *a good beginning*; *any beginning*; *public speaking*.

It can enter into compounds in various ways : *a wedding-ring*; *a dwelling-place*; *blotting-paper*; *the getting-up bell*; *sight-seeing* (in combinations like : he is fond of sight-seeing) ; *holiday-making*; *house-keeping*; *cock-fighting, prize-fighting*. In *laughing-stock* and *growing-pains* we have gerunds in compounds, in *a laughing child* and *a growing pain* participles as adjuncts.

31.1₃. In the following respects a gerund differs from other nexus-substantives. It has a perfect and a passive, also a perfect passive. It can be freely combined with adverbs and other tertiaries. It can take an object (without *of*) and a predicative. It can sometimes have a subject without having to put it in the genitive or possessive. The following sentences will illustrate all these points :

> (Active) : I have some suspicion of the police having never properly searched the room.
> (Passive) : I have some suspicion of the room having never been properly searched by the police.

31.1₄. We shall now consider the constructions of the gerund more in detail.

Tertiaries are freely combined with gerunds, both when they form a necessary part of the verbal idea and when they are more loosely connected with it :

> He is tired of looking out for jobs.
> The possibility of their ever knowing the truth.
> He was nervous from having never before spoken in public.

A gerund may be combined with a predicative :

> She was proud of being a woman as well as of the prospect of becoming a mother.

On the tenses of the gerund enough has already been said **(23.9₄)**. Besides the active perfect gerund we have also a passive perfect :

> He expressed a doubt of their having ever been married.
> He prided himself on having never been beaten at chess.

31.1₅. What was said above **(30.5)** about nexus-words being sometimes taken in an active and sometimes in a passive meaning applies to gerunds as well.   A passive meaning is found, *e.g.* in

> The tale did not lose anything in the telling.
> The garden wants weeding. (Cf. He wants to weed the garden.)
> That needs explaining.
> The annihilation of his own life's work did not bear thinking about.
> It is difficult to obtain a hearing in these circles.
> People who are dissatisfied with their own bringing up.
> He is past praying for.
> What is worth doing at all is worth doing well.

Both the passive and the active meaning are found together in

> She deserved punishing for punishing me.

This passive meaning was formerly more frequent than now, see, for instance :

> Shall we . . . excuse his throwing into the water? (Sh.).

The ambiguity of this form has led to the development of a new passive with *being* ; we should now say :

> Shall we excuse his being (or having been) thrown into the water?

The passive form is seen, for instance, in

> He was three times very near being murdered.
> Each of them for the first time knew the double pride of loving and being loved.
> The soldier's trade is not slaying, but being slain (Ruskin).

31.2₁. What in an ordinary sentence would be the object, is very rarely put in the possessive before a gerund :

> They were eager after his undoing (Thackeray),

where we may take *undoing* in the passive sense and *his* as the subject-part of the nexus.

Of is chiefly found when the substantival character of the gerund is shown by the use of the definite article or some other adjunct :

> On account of his deliberate buying up of stocks. (Cf. On account of deliberately buying up stocks.)
> To take him in the purging of his soule (Sh.).
> He imitated the putting of a noose about a man's throat.
> This will certainly be the making of you.

31.2₂. The most usual construction, however, is for the gerund to take an object without *of*; after the definite article this was frequent in former times, but is now generally avoided :

> Nothing in his life Became him like the leaving it (Sh.).
> What else can joy be but the spreading joy ? (Byron).

Examples without the definite article abound ; a few may suffice here :

> He entered the room without greeting anybody.
> Different ways of making money.
> I always take great pleasure in hearing him play.
> I thanke thee, Jew, for teaching me that word (Sh., thus even with two objects).

31.2₃. An object is found also in the idiom " there is no -ing " (= ' it is not possible to . . .'), though one might expect that the adjunct *no* would require *of* :

> There was no avoiding him.
> There is no denying the fact that most Germans are diligent.

31.3₁. We now come to the treatment of what in an independent sentence would be the subject of the verb. No indication is needed in the numerous cases in which the subject is either the ' generic person ' or identical with something mentioned in the main sentence, generally the subject :

> (1) Complimenting is lying.
> (1) Now, I call that talking.
> (2) We lost no time in making inquiries.
> (2) On returning from the war he took to writing for the papers.
> (2) He felt indignant with his father for cutting him off with a shilling.
> (2) The pain in my throat made speaking difficult.

31.3₂. The genitive and a possessive pronoun are used here just as with other nexus-substantives :

> We were naturally surprised by John's (his) asking us to dinner.
> He repaired there in person, on Kate's agreeing to undertake the management.
> She strongly resented Mr Watson's drawing so close to her.

Examples of possessives are found in great number in other paragraphs of this chapter.

The possessive *our, your, their* may be qualified by *all* or *both* :

I insist on your all meeting me there.
Assurance of their both being alive.
He liked to hear of our being all near together.

31.3₃. With regard to the occurrence of genitives before a gerund it may be remarked that it is sometimes doubtful whether we have a genitive or a common case.

In the ordinary plural the common case and the genitive are identical in sound, and the distinction now made in writing between *kings* and *kings'* is comparatively recent. Hence, when we find in Sh. :

Breake the story off, Of our two cousins comming into London—

we cannot tell which case is intended. Jane Austen writes :

Mrs Bennet, who had calculated on her daughters remaining at Netherfield—

without any apostrophe, but might just as well have written *daughters'*.

31.3₄. The genitive is to some extent falling into disuse before a gerund, at any rate in the spoken language. This tendency is strengthened by the fact that, even apart from the combinations occupying us in this chapter, the formation or use of a genitive presents some serious difficulties.

Some words have no genitive (or possessive) at all ; if they have to be used as subjects before a gerund it is therefore necessary to take the common-case form ; the same holds good of some word-groups, which cannot easily be put in the genitive :

He would not hear of that being possible.
In spite of those three telling the same story, I could not believe it.
I am not surprised at young or old falling in love with her.
You wonder at one so poor and friendless having an attachment.
He would not hear of Mrs Mackenzie and her daughter quitting the house.
Upon my application for her address being refused, I had resigned my own post.
The ludicrous idea of a gentleman of his fashion scrambling for coppers.

31.3₅. The difficulty is even greater if one of the words joined in this way is a personal pronoun ; hence such constructions as these :

> Laughing at Sir John Walter and me falling out.
> Some remark about my patient and me being well qualified to keep each other company.
> Without either of us knowing that the other had taken up the subject.
> There was no need of both of them making a journey.
> A dream of my father and myself driving out together in a beautiful car.

31.3₆. As there is a general disinclination to use the genitive of words which do not designate a person, constructions like the following are rare :

> His mother kicked a little at first against the money's having gone to him.
> There seemed to be some slight appearance of the gale's abating.

Such words are therefore frequently put in the common case before gerunds :

> In the event of a breeze springing up.
> There is a chance of some record being left.
> We were surprised at her beauty being made so much of.

31.3₇. Even in the case of words denoting living beings, a genitive of which is easily formed, the common case is frequent in this combination. The following sentences are all of them taken from writers of repute (nineteenth and twentieth centuries) :

> Surprised at his ward appearing in public.
> I have no objection to the author being known.
> The chances of the disconsolate widower bestowing his hand on her daughter.
> It ended in the doctor being sent for.
> There is nothing ridiculous in an English gentleman entertaining feelings of loyalty.
> In consequence of the Shah having marched an army into Herat.

You can talk to me of other women being charming, and of Patti singing divinely.

It would lead to some noble gentleman marrying her.

What is the good of a man being honest in his worship of dishonesty ?

She would never get stout, as there was every danger of Clara doing.

The use of the common case makes constructions like the following possible, where the genitive would be awkward :

They objected to Tom getting nothing and John everything.

We speak of good people going to heaven, and wicked people to the Devil (Defoe).

The tendency to use this common-case construction is stronger when the whole idea is vague than when it is definite or concrete ; thus after such words as *possibility, chance,* etc., and when the subject is indefinite (*a man, people, anybody*). *No one* could hardly be made into *no one's* in :

He insists on no one knowing about the experiment.

31.3₈. With regard to pronouns we must first mention that *its* is probably used more frequently than *it* in this position :

Only think of its being three months since I went away.

In honour of its being Christmas day.

He had no doubt of it being highly agreeable to Fanny.

The use of the objective case of a personal pronoun instead of the possessive is looked upon by many (not all) theorists as incorrect ; still it is found in good writers :

I'm so afraid of you being angry (Emily Brontë).

To think of me kissing Mr Heldar after all he's done to me! (Kipling).

You say nothing about us calling (Bennett).

I'm afraid of *you* misunderstanding me (Galsworthy).

31.3₉. *Prevent* admits of three constructions : (1) *prevent his falling,* (2) *prevent him falling,* (3) *prevent him from falling.* In (3) *him* alone is the object, in (1) and (2) the gerundial nexus is the object, with the objective and the possessive, respectively, as the subject-part.

31.4. In some cases one may hesitate about the analysis of a combination, which may be taken to contain either a participial adjunct or a gerund, thus in

> I remember my grandfather giving me a sovereign (I remember him as he was when he gave; or I remember the act itself).
> I laughed at the thought of me going to that hideous chapel.
> We hear of Harriet continuing her Latin studies.
> He was aware of an odd, light footstep drawing near.

But in most combinations there can be no doubt that we have not a participial adjunct, but a nexus. When Thackeray writes : " I have not the least objection to a rogue being hung," it is not the rogue (who is being hung) that he approves, but his execution —or, grammatically speaking, the object of *to* is not the substantive *rogue*, but the whole combination.

Similarly this analysis is evident in

> There was no doubt as to the crime being a political one.
> I hate people being unhappy (different from ' I hate unhappy people ').

31.5. As with other nexus-substantives (**30.4**) the subject may be represented by an *of*-combination :

> On the breaking out of the war.
> The time had come for the sailing of the emigrant ship.
> They were surprised by the sudden coming in of a stranger.

This is possible with intransitive verbs only, as *of* is used for the object with transitive verbs ; with the latter the subject may rarely be preceded by the preposition *by* (cf. **30.6**) :

> How well I understand now the shooting of officers by their men.

31.6. In all the cases so far considered the gerundial nexus is the object either of a verb or of a preposition. But it may be itself the subject of a sentence. Here the genitive or a possessive may be used :

> Sophia's having seen them did not greatly surprise us.
> Her thus turning her back on me was fortunately not a snub.

Frequently, however, a substantive is put in the common case, as it is felt to be the subject of the main verb (though more correctly it is only part of the subject) :

> Parliament breaking up immediately after gave the officials a good excuse for doing nothing more.
> Is the lady bothering you any reason for you to come bothering me ?

31.7$_1$. The gerundial construction may be represented by preparatory *it* (**16.**1$_6$) :

> It has been just splendid meeting you here.
> It was the merest chance my taking these pills.
> It is no use your trying to deceive me.

Here " you trying " is often said, but it is generally considered less correct.

> You must find it rather dull living here all by yourself.
> I call it abominable, his leaving us in the lurch like that.

31.7$_2$. A gerund may be preceded by preparatory *there* (cf. **4.**9$_4$, **10.**8) :

> No one would have dreamed of there being such a place.
> He denied there being anything uncongenial in their character.

THE INFINITIVE

32.1₁. Comparative grammar has shown that the infinitive in prehistoric time was a fully inflected verbal substantive. In course of time its distinctive endings have worn off, so that now it has become identical in form with the base of the verb. In a combination like " I can sing," *can* originally meant ' know,' and *sing* meant ' singing,' which was the object of the verb. Gradually the infinitive adopted more and more of the syntactic peculiarities of verbs, and lost those of substantives, going in that respect even further than the gerund.

The infinitive is now a purely verbal form. This is shown negatively by the fact that it cannot be preceded by the definite or indefinite article, an adjective, or a genitive, and positively by the fact that it can take an object and an adverb (or other tertiary), and that it possesses a perfect (**23.**8) and a passive. On the other hand, it has so far retained its substantival character as it can stand as a subject or object, etc. ; a reminiscence of its origin is also the mixed active-passive character of the infinitive in some cases (**32.**2₂, 2₄, 2₇). On account of all these things a classification of the manifold uses of the infinitive offers considerable difficulty.

32.1₂. The sphere of utility of the ' bare infinitive ' has been gradually restricted so that now it is used chiefly after the so-called auxiliary verbs and in a few other cases in which the connexion between the infinitive and what precedes it is very close ; these cases will be specified below. In all other cases the infinitive is preceded by *to*. This was at first the ordinary preposition indicating direction or purpose, as it still does in some combinations, *e.g.* " he goes to fetch his hat " and " he was led to believe it." While a trace of this meaning may be said to exist in " ready to go, I wish to go," it is totally obliterated in " I refuse to go " and " To see her is to love her," etc. The weakening of the meaning of the preposition is similar to that mentioned above (**11.**7₄) ; the meaning of direction is also lost in the combinations *today* and *tomorrow*. Before an infinitive *to* may now be considered a grammatical implement with no meaning of its own.

It would be legitimate to speak everywhere of such forms as *go, see*, etc., as infinitives and of combinations like *to go, to see*, etc., as infinitives with *to* or infinitive phrases ; but for shortness sake I shall in this chapter use the term infinitive so as to include both the ' bare infinitive ' and the ' *to*-infinitive,' it being understood that the latter is used everywhere except where the use of the former is expressly stated.

Infinitives as Primaries

32.1₃. The infinitive may stand as the subject :

> To see you is always a great pleasure.
> To err is human, to forgive, divine (Pope).

The subject is often placed in extraposition, represented before the verb by the preparatory *it* :

> It is a great pleasure to see you.
> It always pays to tell the truth.

The infinitive here is always used with *to* : in such colloquial expressions as

> Better wait and not say a word about it at present.
> As well be hanged for a sheep as for a lamb !—

we can hardly call the infinitive the subject ; no *to* is used because the whole is felt as short for " We had better wait . . ."

(cf. **32.1₅**) or " One may as well be hanged . . ." ; *to* would always be required in " It is better to wait."

32.1₄. An infinitive may be a predicative :

My chief purpose has been to point out the difficulties of the matter.

When we have infinitives both as subject and predicative, as in

To see her is to love her—

the sentence does not really denote complete identity of the two acts, for it is not possible to reverse the terms ; what is meant is that seeing immediately leads to loving. Another example is

Where but to think is to be full of sorrow (Keats).

These combinations are thus different from corresponding ones with the gerund, *e.g.* :

Complimenting is lying,

which means that complimenting is one form of lying, one of the ways in which you may lie.

Other combinations in which *to*-infinitives are used as predicatives will be mentioned under infinitives as secondaries (**32.2₇**).

32.1₅. The infinitive may be the object of a verb. Without *to* this is only found after the auxiliaries *can, may, must, will, shall, do,* and a limited number of verbal phrases, namely, *had better, had sooner, had as soon,* and the obsolete *had liefer, had as lief.* In these the shortened forms *I'd, he'd,* etc., are often understood as containing *would* instead of *had.*

With *dare* and *need* there is some vacillation. The general practice, which, however, is not strictly observed, is either to treat these verbs like the above-mentioned auxiliaries, *i.e.* to use them without -*s* in the third person, without *do,* and then without *to* before the infinitive,—or else to treat them as ordinary full verbs, with -*s, do* and *to* :

He dare not (daren't) object. He does not dare to object.
Dare you contradict me ? Do you dare to contradict me ?

Need he ever know? This is all he needs to know.
He needn't know more than that. He does not need to know
more.

32.1₆. The verbs which can take an infinitive with *to* as object
are very numerous, e.g. *wish, want, refuse, like, prefer, hope,
begin, continue, cease, forget, try, attempt, intend, mean, promise,
purpose, pretend.*

In a few cases we may have an indirect object alongside of
the infinitive which is the direct object :

> ⌐ They gave us to understand that no pardon would be given.
> They promised us to refrain from hostilities.
> Our parents taught us to speak the truth and to fear nothing.
> He never allowed any one to shoot on his ground.

This construction cannot be separated from that to be considered in
32.4₃.

32.1₇. Among verbs taking infinitive objects we must specially
mention *have.* When we say " he has a difficult task to perform," *task* is the object, and *to perform* is an adjunct to *task*,
and has the passive import mentioned in **32.2₄**. But in sentences
like Shakespeare's :

> Of my instruction hast thou nothing bated
> In what thou had'st to say—

it is possible to take *to say* as the object of *hadst*, and *what* as
the object of *say*. In a relative clause the distinction is thus
effaced between two constructions which are contrasted in
Trollope's saying that " the writer, when he sits down to com-
mence his novel, should do so, not because he has to tell a story,
but because he has a story to tell."

I have to with infinitive means ' am obliged to,' and has in
the last few centuries been very extensively used as a substitute
for *must*, chiefly because it allows of tense and other distinctions
not found in *must* : *I had, had had, shall have, should have to go,
having to go*. Combinations with *have got to* are also frequent
colloquially in the same sense. Negative *have to* is not
equivalent to negative *must* : *I have not (got) to do that* means
' I am not obliged to do that,' while *I must not do that* means
' I am not allowed to do that.'

32.1₈. Some verbs which cannot take an ordinary object, but require a prepositional group, nevertheless take an infinitive as object :

> I long to see her again (I long for the sight of her).
> I don't care to be famous (I don't care for fame).
> We agreed to set out the following day (We agreed on a plan).

In a similar way some substantives and adjectives which cannot otherwise take an object can have an infinitive as object :

> A desire, a wish, a hope to see her again.
> Anxious, eager, desirous, afraid, able to see her again.

32.1₉. The infinitive may be used as the object of a preposition. The only preposition that is nowadays used regularly before a *to*-infinitive is *about*, and that only in the signification ' on the point of, going to ' :

> He was about to retire (in this sense also sometimes *about retiring*).

Otherwise a gerund is required after a preposition, thus also after *about* as in

> He spoke about retiring (= of retiring).

If the bare infinitive is often used after *but, except, save*, it is because these words are conjunctions just as well as prepositions. Here we often have the plain infinitive :

> He cannot but admire her.
> He could not choose but laugh.
> I have done nothing except send for the constable.

After *than* we have *to*, for instance, in

> He knew better than to interfere in our affairs.

But after *rather than, sooner than* the bare infinitive is usual, not only when necessitated by a preceding word like *would*, but also in other cases :

> He would die rather than yield.
> He cannot bear spiders, but puts them out of doors sooner than kill them.
> A dying man who had crawled up to a dead comrade rather than die alone.

Infinitives as Secondaries

32.2₁. An infinitive may be used as an adjunct placed before a substantive, but only if it is preceded by an adverb :

> This never-to-be-forgotten day.
> His not to be alienated inheritance (Dickens).

32.2₂. Infinitives with *to* are very often used as adjuncts placed after a substantive : *to come* denotes simple futurity (*in days to come*, etc.) ; other infinitives denote ' what might, would or should, or (in other connexions) what can or may . . .' :

> She is not the kind of girl to encourage lovers.
> Clive was not a man to do anything by halves.
> The Duchess was to be the one to bell the cat.
> There are always plenty of people to believe this nonsense.
> We may find something to interest us in the town.
> A maid whom there were none to praise, And very few to love (Wordsworth).
> There isn't a girl in London to beat her.
> This is not a good place to rest in.

A mere fact is indicated in

> He was always the first to come and the last to leave the office.

32.2₃. *To do* used in this way means ' connected with ' :

> Would that be anything to do with the war?
> He dislikes anything to do with politics, but is interested in everything to do with the stage.

This use probably arose from phrases like " It's nothing to do with his health," in which *s* originally stood for *has*, but was interpreted as *is*, and this then led to the extension : " I hope it has been nothing to do with his health."

32.2₄. While the infinitives we have so far been dealing with have active import, we find others seemingly parallel to them with passive import ; this is a survival of the original substantival character of infinitives and should be compared with the similar phenomenon in the case of nexus-substantives and gerunds (**30.**5, **31.**1₅). Examples :

> A house to let.
> A black tie was the proper thing to wear.

He is not a man to know (='worth knowing ').
We could think of nothing to say.
The brisk manner of a woman who has had her own way to make
in the world (cf. **32.1₇**).

A preposition naturally comes last :

A young lady eats nothing to speak of.
Is he quite the sort of man to confide in ?

The passive and the active senses are combined in

She wants somebody to love and somebody to love her.
Nothing can be done with a corporation, because it has neither
a soul to save nor a body to kick—

here we might say that the understood subject of the first
infinitive is the corporation and that of the second is somebody
else.

32.2₅. Not only the meaning, but also the form may be passive
in adjuncts placed after the primaries :

The next thing to be considered was food.
This leaves nothing to be desired.

The reference to futurity is clear in

A difficulty felt by others in times past, and to be felt again in
times to come.
A higher legal authority presently to be defined.

The distinction between active and passive infinitive has sometimes hardly any importance :

There is only one thing to do | to be done.
There is nothing to fear | to be feared.
There is a lot to do yet | to be done yet.
There was no time to lose | to be lost.

But the following example shows a clear distinction :

There were always four little boys to pick up the balls and at
least three dozen balls to be picked up.

Note the distinction between the active and passive infinitive
in :

Pictures are not the only things to see at Florence (=worth
seeing).

In the street, umbrellas were the only things to be seen (=that could be seen).

32.2₆. Combinations with *about* and *to*-infinitive can be used in this way as adjuncts :

No one could have had the slightest foreboding of anything about to happen.
With drooping head like a prisoner about to receive his sentence.

(Cp. also " a deed not likely to be forgotten.")

32.2₇. A related use of the infinitive, which we are therefore entitled to call a secondary, is found in the predicative after the verb *be*. In some stock phrases the infinitive, though active in form, has a passive sense :

The house is to let.
He is to blame.
What's to pay ?
The causes were not far to seek.
She did what there was to do.

The passive infinitive may, however, be used :

This house is not to be let (always : The house is to be sold or let).
He is to be blamed for this.

32.2₈. Apart from such stock phrases, the passive infinitive is always used. In the first few examples the meaning is the same as in a paraphrase with *can*, in the rest as *should* :

He was nowhere to be found.
Beer like that is not to be had outside of Germany.
His long figure was often to be seen in the streets.
The great and wealthy are not always to be envied.
He is to be congratulated on his brilliant discovery.
I rather tell thee what is to be fear'd Then what I feare (Sh.).
It is to be hoped that he will be present.
His failure is not to be ascribed to want of diligence.
The letters to the lawyers were still to be written.

A preposition which belongs closely to the verb is placed last :

This is not to be thought of.

32.2₉. The corresponding use of the active *to*-infinitive after *be* generally serves to express what is determined, planned or destined, thus dependent on some foreign will :

> I am to meet them at five.
> Am I to stand here for ever? What am I to do?
> When an old bachelor marries a young wife, what is he to expect?
>   (Sheridan).
> We know that something dreadful is to happen, but do not know
>   what.

Note the expression of a necessary condition (cf. **32.3₅**) :

> You must speak out, if we are to remain friends.

A mere future result is indicated in

> The weary ages that have been and are yet to come.
> I had no children in my marriage—that was not to be.

In this way we arrive at the " after-past " (**26.9₆**), as in

> This I was only to find out later.

Infinitives as Tertiaries

32.3₁. An infinitive with *to* is very often used as a tertiary. The original meaning of the preposition *to* is still easily discernible after a verb of motion :

> He came to see it in a different light.
> How can I get to know her?
> He was led to believe everything she said (cf. was forced to obey,
>   **32.5₂**).
> Loud-speakers tend to become a nuisance.

32.3₂. In the infinitive of purpose the original meaning of the preposition *to* is also evident :

> He came here to speak to me, not to you.
> He has been to see the doctor (cf. He has been to Paris; thus only
>   with the perfect and pluperfect).
> He opened his lips to make some remarks.
> The car was waiting at the door to take them out.
> He works hard in order to keep his family in comfort.
> He nodded his head as much as to say, " I consent."
> Don't trouble to dress.

Note especially the infinitive of purpose after *make*, which should not be confused with the use mentioned in **32.4₄, 5₂** :

> She made her own clothes, and made them to last.
> Women are made to be loved, not to be understood (Wilde).

32.3₃. An interesting subdivision under the infinitive of purpose is seen in sentences like the following, in which the purpose does not belong to anything mentioned in the sentence, but to the speaker (a kind of mental parenthesis) :

> The controversy was carried on with acrimony, not to say venom.
> To give him his due, he's a clever fellow in his way.
> To tell the truth, it does not always pay to tell the truth.
> To change the subject : have you heard nothing of Graham ?
> (He left his property—that is to say his landed property—to Tom.)

32.3₄. Related to the infinitive of purpose is the infinitive of result :

> She woke suddenly to find someone standing in the doorway with a candle.
> He needed only a few words to be convinced.
> I hope you will see your way to pay me yet.
> What have I done to offend you ?
> He raised our expectations only to disappoint them.
> I am afraid that prohibition has come to stay.
> He will live to be ninety, he is so strong.
> In 1899 he left England never to return (This might be called the infinitive of providential purpose).

32.3₅. From the infinitive of purpose we are led to the following constructions, in which the main verb expresses a necessary condition to obtain a result :

> To be effective, a poem must be beautiful (also : In order to).
> The evidence, to be of value, must be independent of hear-say.
> I could not write a sonnet to save my life.

32.3₆. Further illustrations of the use of infinitives as tertiaries :

> Cousin, I am too young to be your father. Though you are old enough to be my heire (Sh.).
> What a lucky fellow I am to have such a wife.
> Woe is me, T'have seene what I have seene, see what I see (Sh.).

Who am I to quarrel with Providence ?
The money is his to do what he pleases with.
To look at him you could hardly help laughing.
A man would be blind not to see that.
I know her to bow to.
He was shocked to hear her vulgar expressions (This to some extent resembles the use in **32.1₈**).

Primaries in an Infinitive-Nexus.

32.4₁. We must now deal with the question, how those words which in a complete sentence would be primaries (subject and object) are treated in connexion with an infinitive.   With regard to the object, this presents no difficulty (it did to some extent with gerunds, **31.2**), the verbal character of the infinitive shows itself by its capacity of having objects :

I want to give you a piece of advice : don't make Jack your intimate friend.

32.4₂. With regard to the subject of an infinitive the question is more involved.   Here, as in **31.3₁**, there are innumerable cases in which no indication is necessary, because the subject would be either the generic person or identical with the subject of the main verb, or at any rate evident from the context :

(1) It always pays to tell the truth.
(2) Napoleon wanted to conquer the whole world.
(2) He is old enough to know better.
(2) It is your obvious duty to protect your old mother.
(2) It was stupid of us to consent.

The subject is also left unexpressed in some few expressions after another verb (among those mentioned in **32.4₃** ff.) :

Live and let live.
The children made believe that they were Indians.
I have heard say that your country is very beautiful.
They all helped lay the table for tea.

32.4₃. But very often the subject has to be expressly indicated. We shall first mention an important construction, in which the nexus consisting of a primary and an infinitive is the object of a verb ; the primary is put in the common case if it is a sub-

stantive, and in the objective if it is a pronoun. This construc-
tio.1, which is merely a subdivision of the simple nexus as object
considered in Chap. XXIX, is generally termed ' the accusative
with infinitive ' ; we need no other term than infinitival nexus
(as object).

In the following sentences examples are given of the chief
types of verbs admitting this construction :

> I saw (heard, watched) him run.
> He felt his hands tremble.
> I found my attention wander.
> His family had never known him beg for a shilling.
> Did I understand you to say that you refuse ?
> I judged (took) him to be about sixty years of age.
> They firmly believed him to be innocent.
> I do like a man to be smart.
> I should hate you to miss the train.
> I can't bear you to be unhappy.
> He suffered himself to be interviewed.
> (He never allowed any one to shoot on his ground, 32.1$_6$.)
> We will let the matter rest there.
> (Leave him be—modelled on *let him be*.)
> I have forbidden my children to smoke.
> I defy (dare) you to repeat that phrase.
> Will you come and help me (to) develop some photos ?
> This is not, as some authorities would have us believe, a fraud.
> I did not mean you to hear what I said.
> We must tell them to wait.
> He whispered Juan not to be afraid (Byron ; more usual : *to J.*).
> They wanted Dora to sing.
> They asked (prayed, enjoined, invited, ordered, charged) him to
> follow them.
> I'll thank (trouble) you to pass the mustard.

32.4$_4$. Cases like those just exemplified form the transition to
others in which the infinitive-nexus is undoubtedly an object of
result, as in the following sentences :

> Nothing will make him work, the mere idea of work makes him
> shudder.
> Their brilliant conversation made the hours fly.
> He caused the prisoners to be put to death.
> He forced (compelled) them to obey.
> They could not bring themselves to believe it (cf. **32.3$_1$**).

32.4₅. It will be noticed in these examples (**32.4₃** and 4₄) that the bare infinitive occurs chiefly after those verbs that belong to the most familiar sphere of language; many of the *to*-constructions (*e.g.* after *think, believe, know*) are literary rather than colloquial. No hard-and-fast line can, however, be drawn between the two strata, and in former times people were less strict than now with regard to the use or non-use of *to* (*e.g.* the half-obsolete *bid* without *to*).

With regard to word-order we have here the same rule as above (**29.1₆**): the primary is generally placed before the infinitive. Exceptions occur chiefly with *let*, when it forms one sense unit with the following infinitive :

Let goe the hand of that arch-heretique (Sh.).
Having let slip the golden moment.
He let fall some of the most unpleasant remarks I've ever heard.

Instead of " I saw (heard) him come " we may say " I saw (heard) him coming " ; the latter generally implies the same modification of the meaning as the expanded tense, and is therefore more descriptive : ' he was coming when I saw (heard) him,' while the former means ' he came, and I saw (heard) it.'

32.4₆. Such an infinitive-nexus consisting of a primary plus an infinitive may be the object not only of a verb, but also of a preposition, or rather, of a phrase consisting of a verb and a preposition. The infinitive generally has *to*, but in some cases, where the phrase means the same thing as a verb which does not require *to*, the bare infinitive may be found (*look at* = ' see,' *listen to* = ' hear '). Examples :

I hoped I could count on you not to interfere.
She can hardly prevail upon him to eat.
I rely upon you to be discreet.
Look at Lord Clodworthy come into a room with his wife (Thackeray).
Listening to the rain patter on the shrubs.
I'm not ashamed of myself to talk so.
Pen longed for the three years to be over.
He did not wait for her to speak.
We are quite prepared for things to go wrong.

> Jenny had arranged for Irene to pick her up in the course of the evening.
> He had fixed for the marriage to take place at eleven.
> I couldn't bear for us not to be friends.

As is seen in the last few sentences, the construction with *for* is extended to some verbs which do not otherwise take *for*.

32.4₇. The same construction with *for* is found after adjectives, not only such as are also otherwise constructed with *for* (as in the first two examples), but also others :

> He was anxious for his sister and Esther to get acquainted.
> I should be sorry for you to think that.
> His mother was frightfully keen for Michael to stay with them.
> He was quite willing for every one else to come.

The same remark holds good with regard to substantives as well :

> He gave immediate orders for all his family to be summoned round him.
> The decree for our army to demobilize was issued yesterday.
> I'm in no hurry for him to do anything in the matter.

Infinitives with a preceding *for* are very frequent after *too* and *enough*. From such obvious constructions as " This stone is too heavy for you to lift," in which *for you* is immediately connected with *too heavy*, and *to lift* may be considered an appended explanation (' in respect of lifting '), we get freer combinations, in which the word or words standing after *for* are intimately connected with the infinitive as what in a complete sentence or clause would be the subject :

> One word is too often profaned For me to profane it (Shelley).
> Am I too wicked for you and me to live together ?
> A tiny boy—now too big for it to be desirable that I should mention his name.
> Mr Darcy had been standing near enough for her to overhear a conversation between him and Mr Bingley.

32.4₈. An infinitive preceded in this way by *for* may express a purpose, design or determination :

> I thought you had kindly left the book here, on purpose for me to read.

He stood aside for her to enter.

In order for a poet to be taken seriously by the public, it must first be clear that he takes himself seriously.

Something ought to be left for ingenious readers to find out.

That is for you to decide.

This isn't a world for an innocent girl to wander about in.

32.5₁. We now come to constructions in which the subject plus an infinitive is in itself the subject of the main verb. We saw already in **11.**2 that in a sentence like " he happened to fall " *he* is not the subject in the ordinary way : what happened was " he . . . to fall " : in reality the (notional) subject is the infinitive with its subject (*he*), which is separated from it. Other examples of such ' split subjects,' as we may term them, are :

He seems *to be all right.*
They would be certain *to miss him.*
She is not likely *to be up so early.*
I fail *to see* any justification for his behaviour.

32.5₂. The same grammatical analysis applies to the passives of the constructions dealt with in **32.**4₃, 4₄, *e.g.*

He has been seen to enter the house at night.
He was heard to mutter some words under his breath.
His pupils were never known to tell a lie.
He is supposed to be honest.
He is said to be quiet.
We were never allowed to smoke, when we were small.
His beard was shaven on his chin, but was let to grow on his cheeks.
I am forbid To tell the secrets of my prison-house (Sh.).
He is told to be quiet.
He must be made to work.
They were forced to obey.

In all these cases, except occasionally after *let*, the infinitive requires *to*. Note the difference in meaning between *said* and *told* ; the former verb is not used in this way in the active.

Cf. the passive constructions in **29.**1₇.

32.5₃. In the cases dealt with in **32.**5₁ and 5₂ there is naturally no preposition before the subject. But in other cases the preposition *for* is used with the subject-part of an infinitival nexus which is in itself the subject of a sentence. This arises from constructions like

It is good for a man not to touch a woman (AV.).

Here we have the preparatory *it* representing the infinitive " not to touch a woman " : this negative attitude is what is good for a man. But the point of view is shifted : " It is good for a man | not to touch a woman " is felt as containing the two components " It is good | for a man not to touch a woman." In other words the *for*-group is felt as belonging closely to the infinitive as its subject-part. Thus through sentences like

It was no uncommon thing for him to be away days and nights on end ;

It was the custom for the players to receive their weekly stipend on the Saturday ;

When will it suit your convenience for me to call ?—

we arrive at sentences in which the word-order or other things show clearly that the *for*-group cannot be anything else but the subject of the infinitive :

What I like best, is for a nobleman to marry a miller's daughter. And what I like next best, is, for a poor fellow to run away with a rich girl (Thackeray).

The custom of most Indian villages is for a few boys to take the cattle out to graze in the early morning.

For a man to tell how human life began Is hard (Milton).

For anything to happen in spite of her was an offensive irregularity.

For you to stop here is an outrage against common-sense.

What can be more ridiculous than for gentlemen to quarrel about hats ? (Swift).

Nothing so easy as for a young lady to raise her expectations too high (Jane Austen).

The only way for a woman to provide for herself decently is for her to be good to some man that can afford to be good to her (Shaw).

'Tis quite enough for me to offer advice, for him to scorn it.

32.5₄. An infinitive may be preceded by *there* in the same way as we saw in the case of gerunds (**31.7₂**) :

Let there be light.

Would you like there to be a revolution in this country ?

It was too late for there to be any taxis.

Final Remarks on Infinitives

32.6₁. As already remarked, the verbal character of the infinitive is shown, among other things, by the freedom with which it can be combined with adverbs. These may be placed after the infinitive, especially if they are descriptive (she will dress carefully | she wants to dress elegantly), or before *to* (we want never to see him | in order not to trouble them). This latter place is often perfectly natural, in some cases even inevitable. But there is a third place, namely, between *to* and the infinitive : this order is found as early as the thirteenth century and is favoured by many distinguished writers, especially of late, but nevertheless it is often condemned by grammarians, who have invented the name " split infinitive " for the phenomenon. The name is misleading, for the preposition *to* no more belongs to the infinitive as a necessary part of it, than the definite article belongs to the substantive, and no one would think of calling " the good man " a split substantive. The word-order with the adverb after *to* seems in some cases to be unobjectionable ; it has probably been brought about through the influence of similar word-orders : " with the object of further illustrating the matter," " he further illustrates," " that he may further illustrate " lead naturally to the construction " in order to further illustrate." Note also instances like the following, to which no one would object, and in which *to* stands nevertheless separated from the infinitive :

The power to understand and fully sympathize with him.
All they have to do is to sit down and faithfully copy it.
You ought to describe and accurately define these phenomena.
She tried to, and did not, feel brave (cf. **32.6₃**).

32.6₂. The position after *to* makes the meaning perfectly clear in some cases, which would otherwise be open to misunderstanding :

No one claims to completely understand it.
For the first time she seemed to really know and feel the sort of lives they led (Galsworthy).
He prepared to silently accompany her.
He liked to half close his eyes.

Any details which would help the reader to exactly identify the cottage.

He made up his mind to once more become a suitor to her hand.

He was palpably too ill to really carry out his duty.

Clearness is also achieved by the position in

A vicious back-hander, which I failed to entirely avoid—

which indicates imperfect success, while " I failed entirely to avoid " might mean complete failure.

" We will split infinitives sooner than be ambiguous or artificial " (H. W. Fowler, *Dictionary of Modern English Usage*).

32.6₃. The phenomenon here described may be taken as evidence of the fact that *to* is often felt as belonging more closely to the preceding verb than to the infinitive. This is shown even more conclusively by the possibility of using *to* by itself instead of a clumsy repetition of the whole *to*-infinitive. Just as we may say :

Will they play ? Yes, they will (=will play).

Did they play ? Yes, I made them (=made them play)—

we may say :

Yes, I asked them to (=asked them to play), but they didn't want to.

Not obey ? I'm afraid you'll have to.

His book will sell well, it's bound to.

They will call your father a rogue, and will have a right to.

" Congratulate me."   " I should be happy to, if I could."

This use of *to* does not seem to have become frequent till the nineteenth century ; formerly without *to*, e.g.

If a write, I will say whatever you wish me (Jane Austen).

32.7₁. As the spheres of utility of the infinitive and the gerund are about the same, it is not to be wondered at that there is a good deal of overlapping, though in many cases idiomatic usage allows only one construction : only the gerund is permitted after *avoid, resist, have done, give up, postpone*, only the infinitive after *wish, hope*, etc. But both constructions are found, *e.g.* after *begin, continue, omit, prefer.*   Sometimes there is a difference, *e.g.*

> I remember seeing him (past happening).
> You must remember to call on him (future act).
> I hate lying (the vice in general).
> I hate to lie (myself, in this particular case).
> I don't like smoking.
> I should like to smoke now.
> In his distress he tried praying, but that did not ease his mind (made an attempt with praying).
> In his distress he tried to pray, but could not concentrate on it (made an attempt at praying).

32.7₂. In some constructions, in which *to* has more or less the meaning of direction towards an aim, either the infinitive or the gerund may be used :

> He is accustomed to use (using) his left hand.
> With a view to facilitate (facilitating) research.
> I have no objection to mention (mentioning) names.

Sometimes both an infinitive and a prepositional group with the gerund may be used concurrently :

> Was there no chance to get away (no chance of getting away)?
> His power to decide (of deciding).
> I have the honour to address you (of addressing you).

In some of these the infinitive is slightly more formal than the gerund.

Similarly after an adjective :

> Unworthy to take his place (unworthy of taking his place).

32.8. An infinitive sometimes by itself serves to form an independent sentence (related to amorphous sentences, **10.**9). Thus in a question :

> What to do?   Where to go?
> How to get rid of that bore?

In these, the meaning is related to that found in **32.2₉** : What is one to do? etc.   But no *to* is found in

> Why not go at once? (=Why should you not, or Why do you not, go?)
> Men of England, wherefore plough For the lords who lay ye low? (Shelley).

Further, an infinitive stands by itself as a wish :

Oh, to be in England Now that April's there! (Browning).

Finally, in sentences of deprecation in which an idea is, as it were, brushed aside as unthinkable :

For shame, Tony.   You a man, and behave so! (Goldsmith).
To think of that man having the impudence to call!
You fresh from Rugby, and not know your Thucydides better than that? (Thackeray).
I say anything disrespectful of Dr Kenn?   Heaven forbid! (G. Eliot).

CHAPTER XXXIII

CLAUSES AS PRIMARIES

33.1_1. A whole clause may, under certain conditions, be a
primary (subject, object either of a verb or of a preposition).

Content-clauses

A content-clause is a clause containing a statement which is
not a sentence by itself, but is made part of a sentence. Such
content-clauses are very often introduced by means of the
conjunction *that*. They can be used as primaries in various
functions.

The content-clause is the subject :

That he is dead seems tolerably certain.

It is the predicative :

The worst thing is that he never answers our letters.

It is the object of a verb :

I believe that he is dead.

After a verb expressing fear, *lest* may be used instead of
that :

I trembled lest they should see us.

33.1_2. Very often the content-clause is placed in extraposition at the end and is represented in the body of the sentence
by *it* (**16.1_6**) :

It seems tolerably certain that he is dead.
Is it certain that he is dead ?
We think it highly probable that he is dead.

Some verbs require the same representative *it* immediately before the clause :

> The men to whom we *owe it* that we have a House of Commons.
> I *take it* that he gives his consent.

Compare also the insertion of the words *the fact* :

> This could not hide the fact that he was growing old.

33.1₃. A content-clause may be the object of a preposition :

> I know nothing *except* that he was found dead.
> Men differ from brutes *in* that they can think and speak.

This, however, is nowadays rather exceptional, for in most cases it is necessary to prop up the clause with some introductory word :

> You may rely *on it* that I shall give you a full account.
> See *to it* that no harm comes to her.
> Everything points *to the fact* that he had been very seriously ill.

Content-clauses without *that*

33.1₄. We may say either " I think he is dead " or " I think that he is dead " ; but it would be wrong to imagine that in the former expression the conjunction *that* is omitted. The historical explanation is the following. In both expressions we had originally two independent sentences : " I think : he is dead " and " I think that (demonstrative pronoun pointing to what follows, namely) : he is dead." But in course of time *that* was accentually weakened (**4.**9, note now the obscure vowel [ə] different from the full vowel [æ] which we pronounce in the demonstrative pronoun), and this weak *that* was eventually felt to belong to the clause instead of to what precedes, and by that very fact became what we now call a " conjunction."

The distinction between the two constructions, therefore, is now that in one the subordination of the clause is left to be inferred from the context, while in the other it is expressly indicated. Consequently *that* is often desirable, in some cases even necessary, to make the connexion between the two ideas perfectly clear. But where no doubt is possible the construction without the conjunction is generally preferred, at any rate in colloquial speech, as being more direct and straightforward.

33.1₅. The conjunction will generally be felt to be indispensable

(1) when the clause is placed first :

That time is money has never been realized in the East;

(2) after a substantive like *belief, conviction,* etc. :

My suggestion that he was mad was not accepted by everybody;

(3) when the preparatory *it* is placed first :

It is to be regretted that he should have come just now. (But in very short sentences *that* is not always necessary : it is true he did not say that | It was good he came.)—

(4) in the second of two coordinate clauses, especially if the first is long :

He only wished he dared look at Maggie, and that she would look at him.

Interrogative Clauses as Primaries

33.2₁. When a question is made into a dependent member of a sentence, we have what is called an interrogative clause.

Questions undergo certain grammatical changes by being made into clauses : persons and tenses are shifted as in other kinds of indirect speech ; the word-order is changed, and the auxiliary *do* is not required.

Compare the two columns :

Is she glad ?	He wanted to know if she was glad.
Who is she ?	He wanted to know who she was.
What am I to do ?	He wanted to know what he was to do.
What do you say ?	He wanted to know what you said.
Why do you say that ?	He wanted to know why you said that.

33.2₂. An interrogative clause may be the subject of a sentence :

How he got hold of the veronal was the problem.
Whether Shakespeare wrote *Titus Andronicus* or not will always remain a secret.

Note the use of preparatory *it* :

> It does not interest me in the least who will be Prime Minister in
> fifty years.

The clause may be a predicative :

> It is not who rules us that is important, but how he rules us.

33.2₃. Examples of interrogative clauses as the object of a
verb have already been given.   While literary language prefers
a construction with *if* or *whether*, the inverted order of a direct
question without any conjunction is often retained in colloquial
style, though person and tense may be shifted :

> She whispered something, and asked was that enough (Dickens).
> Ned put his flat and final question, would she marry him, then
> and there (Hardy).

33.2₄. An interrogative clause may be the object of a preposition ; some theorists, however, object to this construction :

> To be truly happy is a question *of* how we begin and not *of* how
> we end, *of* what we want and not *of* what we have (Stevenson).
> I thought of the fifty guineas, and *of* how very useful they would
> be to me.
> I shall not fuss *about* how the trick has been done (Shaw).
> It depends *on* how far he had gone.
> There is some doubt as *to* whether the document is genuine.
> (*If* is never used after a preposition.)

In such a sentence as " I have no idea of what he is going to
do " the object of the preposition is the whole clause, and not
the introductory pronoun ; this is obvious when we notice that
the pronoun may be governed by another preposition (at the
end of the clause) :

> I never had the least idea *of* what you charge me *with* (Sheridan).
> I tremble to think *of* what poor Emilia is destined *to* (Shelley).

33.2₅. Infinitive constructions of the kind described in **32**.8
are often made into clauses :

> How to begin is more difficult than where to stop.
> He never knows when to go.
> She hasn't even learnt how to make tea.
> I am at a loss what to answer.

No Preposition before a Clause

33.3. The general feeling is that clauses governed by pre-positions are clumsy constructions ; therefore clauses are often added without a preposition to words which otherwise require one.   Thus Goldsmith writes : " And are you *sure of* all this, are you *sure* that nothing ill has befallen my boy "—where *of* is necessary before *this*, but would be impossible before *that*. Examples of the two classes of clauses we have here dealt with :

I *insisted* he should come up with us.
I shall make it my business to *see* you are no loser [=see to it that . . .].
In future I am going to be *careful* what I do.
I don't *care* what people say.
It all *depends* how you handle it.

Relative Clauses as Primaries

33.4₁. Though relative clauses are most often used as adjuncts (see Chap. XXXIV) they may also in some cases be primaries. Let us first give some examples before offering any comment.
The relative clause is the subject :

Who steales my purse, steales trash (Sh.).
Whoever says so is a liar.
What you say is quite true.
What puzzles me is that he got hold of the key.
What money I have is at your disposal.
Whatever I get is at your disposal.

33.4₂. The relative clause is the object of a verb :

You may marry whom you like.
He wants to shoot whoever comes near him.
He will take what you offer him.
She will give you what money she has.
He will eat whatever he sets his heart on.

33.4₃. The relative clause is the object of a preposition :

You may dance with whom you like.
He will shoot at whoever comes near him.
He only laughed at what we said.
He will be thankful for what help you can offer him.
He will pay attention to whatever you may say.

33.4₄. In all these sentences it is the relative clause itself in its entirety that is the subject or object. It would not do to say that in the first sentence (in **33.4₁**) *who* stands for *he who*, and that *he* is the subject of (the verb in) the main clause, and *who* that of the relative clause, for the supposition of an ellipsis of *he* is quite gratuitous—and in many of the sentences quoted it would be impossible to insert any pronoun that would give sense and that might be said to have been omitted.

The correctness of this analysis, which makes the whole clause the subject, etc., is brought out clearly when we consider those cases in which a clause which is itself the object of a preposition contains a preposition having for its object the relative pronoun :

To take a note of what I stand in need of (Sh.).
I had been writing of what I knew nothing about (Ruskin); cp. the similar phenomenon with interrogative clauses, **33.2₄**.

In fact, the relative pronoun may fulfil any function in the clause, totally independent of the role the clause itself plays : the reader may go through the examples given above and find out the role of each pronoun. Therefore we have the correct use of *whom* as the object of *love*, while the whole clause is the subject of *die*, in Byron's " Whom the gods love die young " ; the nominative *who* is correct in Kingsley's " Be good, sweet maid, and let who can be clever," and similarly *whoever* in " he was angry with whoever crossed his path." But writers who have been taught to avoid the form *who* in the objective are often led by a false grammatical analysis to use *whom* instead of *who* in clauses like the following :

To bring ruin on whomsoever hath shown kindness to me (Scott).
For the benefit of whomsoever should call (Hardy).

33.4₅. While *what* is used very extensively in clause primaries, the same is not true of *who*. Sentences like " Who steals my purse steals trash " are not heard in colloquial speech, and have for centuries been literary or archaic only. There is, however, one condition on which similar clauses may be used in natural speech, namely, that the meaning is distinctly generic and that the indifference of choice is expressly indicated. This may be done in one of two ways, either by means of the added adverb *ever* (*whoever* with the archaic variants *whoso, whosoever*) or else by such a verb as *choose, please, like* in the clause itself. It is possible to say " you may marry whom you like " or " he abuses whoever crosses his path," but not " he abuses whom he knows " or " he abuses who crosses his path."

Whoever, whatever, and *whichever* are in common use, but the forms with *-so* and *-soever* are now obsolete. In former times *soever* might be separated from *what* :

> What reason soever he might give (S. Johnson).

It is worth noting that in these clause primaries the same distinction between these pronouns is made as between them when used interrogatively ; it is thus different from that made in the case of the ordinary relative pronouns. *Whichever* refers to a choice between a definite number without regard to gender, and may therefore refer to persons (though the relative pronoun *which* cannot be thus used) :

> It was agreed that whichever first received news should communicate with the other.

33.4₆. A relative clause may be placed in extraposition and then resumed later by a personal or demonstrative pronoun :

> Whosoever shall smite thee on thy right cheeke, turne *him* the other also. And whosoever shall compell thee to goe a mile, go with *him* twaine (AV.).
>
> What thou wouldst highly, *that* wouldst thou holily (Sh.).

33.5. We must here mention a peculiar class of relative clauses though they are not properly primaries in a main sentence : in a kind of mental parenthesis the speaker (writer) interrupts the flow of the sentence to give his own comments on some idea or expression ; such clauses are introduced by *what* or *which.* Examples :

> He can say it all; and what is more strange, will not.
>
> Her notions were what is called advanced.
>
> Kropotkin was not a communist, but an anarchist, which is quite a different matter.
>
> I regard marriage as sacred, and when, which God forbid, it proves unsacred, it is horrible.
>
> He is one of the moderns, whatever that may mean.

Relative or Interrogative

33.6. Though the relative and interrogative pronouns and adverbs beginning with *wh* are identical in form, it is possible in most cases to tell whether a clause is relative or interrogative. *What* is relative in " I insist on paying what it has cost," but interrogative in " I insist on knowing what it has cost." We have an interrogative clause in " As I have not yet read all his novels, I cannot tell you which I like best " ; note that it would be possible here to say " which one " or " which ones," but this addition is not possible in the case of the relative pronoun ; besides, *which* has here the specializing meaning peculiar to the interrogative pronoun, and we may use it of persons : " As I do not know all the new boys, I cannot tell you which (of them) I like best." Note the double use of *when* : if your friend is out and you ask : " When will he be in? " the servant may say either : " He didn't tell me when he would be back " (interr.) or " He didn't tell me when he went out " (rel.)—or she may combine the two : "When he went out, he didn't tell me when he would be back."

Sometimes a relative construction is used where strict logic would require an interrogative clause :

> What is freedom?—ye can tell That which slavery is, too well (Shelley).
> I had no idea of the kind of person Roddy was (=what kind).

CHAPTER XXXIV

CLAUSES AS SECONDARIES

Relative clauses.—Restrictive and non-restrictive.—Double restriction.—*It is.*—Form of relative clauses.—Clauses with *wh*-pronouns. — *Which* as adjunct. — Two co-ordinated clauses. — Contact-clauses.—Clauses with *that.*—*Wh*-pronouns preferred in speaking of persons.—*That* however used.—Other cases.—*That* a conjunction. — *As.* — *But.* — Final remarks. — Place of preposition.—Irregular continuation.—Concatenation of clauses.—Adverbs *whereof*, etc.

34.1$_1$. The only clauses that can stand as secondaries (adjuncts) are the so-called relative clauses. (Other relative clauses are primaries, see **33.4.**)

Like other adjuncts (**9.2$_2$**) relative clauses may be either restrictive or non-restrictive. In the former, as in " Tom has found the key that you lost yesterday," the clause gives a necessary determination to the words *the key*, which by that means are made more precise. A non-restrictive (or loose) clause, on the other hand, may be left out without injury to the precise meaning of the word it is joined to, as in " The Prince of Wales, who happened to be there, felt sorry for the prisoners."

A subdivision under loose relative clauses is formed by continuative clauses, *e.g.*

> He had seen my aunt give this person money in the moonlight, who then slunk away and was seen no more (Dickens): *who* =and he.

> He drank the profits, and left the embankment to his deputies, who left it to their assistants, who left it to itself.

34.1$_2$. The following are examples of (A) restrictive and (B) non-restrictive clauses ; the reader may try for himself whether it would be possible to substitute other relative words for those here given :

(A) All the soldiers that were brave pushed on.
(B) The soldiers, who were all of them brave, pushed on.

(A) I met the boatman that had taken me across the ferry.
(B) I met the boatman, who then took me across the ferry.

(A) He had four sons that became lawyers.
(B) He had four sons, who became lawyers.

In (A) we may expect some continuation like " and two that became clergymen " ; in (B) we may insert " all of them."

(A) There were very few passengers that escaped without serious injury.
(B) There were very few passengers, who escaped without serious injury.

Examples of both classes used side by side :

I have spoke With one that saw him die, who did report, That very frankly hee confess'd his treasons (Sh.).

Scott, who when a boy did little that would attract notice.

They divide women into two classes : those they want to kiss, and those they want to kick, who are all those they don't want to kiss.

34.1₃. Double restriction is found when there are two relative clauses of which the second restricts the primary as already defined by the first :

Can you mention any one that we know who is as talented as he?

Is there anything you want that you have not?

They murdered all they met whom they supposed to be gentlemen.

How seldom do we find a man that has stirred up some vast commotion, who does not himself perish, swept away in it (Carlyle).

The only artists I have ever known who are personally delightful are bad artists (Wilde).

34.1₄. Sentences that are introduced by *it is* are logically interesting. When we say " It is the wife that decides " or " It was the Colonel I was looking for," what we mean is really " the wife is the deciding person " and " the Colonel was the man I was looking for " : the relative clause thus does not restrict " the wife " or " the Colonel," but belongs really to *it*. " It is champagne I like best " means " champagne is what I like best." This explains why it is possible in such sentences to have a *that*-clause or a contact-clause after a word which is in itself so definite that it cannot be further restricted :

It is you that must suffer for it.

It was the battle of Waterloo that decided the fate of Europe.

We now see the logical connexion in some proverbial sentences, which, analysed differently, will give no sense :

> It is an ill bird that fouls its own nest.
> It is a wise child that knows its own father.
> It is a poor heart that never rejoices (*i.e.* the heart that never rejoices is poor).

34.1$_5$. With regard to form we must distinguish three classes of relative clauses :

(1) Clauses with one of the two *wh*-pronouns, *who* and *which* ;

(2) clauses without any connecting word : contact-clauses, and

(3) clauses with one of the connecting words, *that*, *as*, *but*.

Clauses with *wh*-Pronouns

34.2$_1$. The *wh*-pronouns were originally interrogative, but in Middle English *which*, *whom*, and *who* came into use as relative pronouns (in the order indicated) and have since then been gaining ground at the expense of *that*, chiefly in the last few centuries and in the more pretentious kinds of literature. One of the reasons for this preference was probably that these pronouns reminded classical scholars of the corresponding Latin pronouns. When Addison in the *Spectator* complains of the injury done recently to the two pronouns *who* and *which* by the " Jacksprat " *that*, he turns all historical truth topsy-turvy, for *that* was really the favourite relative word in literature from the Middle Ages on ; but in deference to his erroneous view of the historical development he corrected many a natural *that* into a less natural *who* and *which*, when he edited the *Spectator* in book-form.

On the distinction between *who* and *which* see **19.**7, on the genitive *whose* **19.**8, on the case-form *whom* **14.**1, **14.**2, **14.**4$_3$.

These pronouns may be used in non-restrictive as well as in restrictive clauses.   Some examples have already been given.

In speaking, a pause, and in writing, a comma, often comes before a *wh*-clause, especially if it is continuative.

34.2₂. The relative *which* may be used as an adjunct both with words denoting things and persons, though as a primary it is always neuter :

> Between six and seven o'clock, at which latter hour they would dress for dinner.
>
> A young woman with a wedding-ring and a baby, which baby she carried about with her when serving at the table.

34.2₃. If we have two co-ordinated relative clauses, the second nearly always has a *wh*-pronoun :

> She possessed gifts that were not only higher than a ready tongue, but which paid better in the long run.
>
> Not even a glimpse of those I love, and of whom I must ere long take leave for ever.
>
> The penal laws we have passed and which, for the time, have been severe and numerous.

Contact-Clauses

34.3₁. Relative clauses without any connecting word are here called *contact-clauses*, because what characterizes them is the close contact in sound and sense between the clause and what precedes it : in sentences like " this is the boy we spoke of " and " he falls in love with all the girls he sees," the words " the boy " and " all the girls " are felt to be just as intimately connected with what follows as with what precedes them. No pause is possible before a contact-clause. Contact-clauses are very old in the language and have for centuries been extremely frequent in speech as well as in all kinds of literature, except in translations which tend to reproduce foreign idioms. The construction is hardly found at all in the Bible, while examples abound in Shakespeare and most good writers, although Dr Johnson and some of his followers avoided it as " a colloquial barbarism."

Contact-clauses are always restrictive.

34.3₂. Contact-clauses are most frequent in those cases in which the pronoun, if present, would have been the object :

> The seed ye sow, another reaps; The wealth ye find, another keeps (Shelley).

It was all he could do to keep from screaming.
How much was it he stole?
One of the women he had made unhappy.

Very frequently also the relative pronoun, if expressed, would
have been the object of a preposition (which is placed after the
verb) :

You are not the first I have said no to.
What is it he is staring at?
The family he lived with simply adored him.

34.3₃. The relative pronoun would have been the predicative :

I am not the man I was when you knew me first.
She speaks like the eccentric woman she is.
(I am not the madman you thought me.)

34.3₄. The pronoun would have been the subject ; this is not
common nowadays except in some well-defined instances, chiefly
after *it is*, *there is* (*are*), *here is* (*are*) :

It isn't every boy gets an open chance like that.
It wasn't I let him in.
I wonder who it was defined man as a rational animal (Wilde).
There is a man below wants to speak to you.

34.3₅. Contact-clauses beginning with *there is* are pretty
frequent :

She taught me the difference there is between what is right and
     what is wrong.
As if I could write a better book than any there has been in this
     country for generations.

34.3₆. We finally come to cases in which the relative pronoun,
had it been expressed, would have been a tertiary :

The moment he entered the room, I felt myself prejudiced against
     him.
By the time I had told my mother they had all left.
Dolly was looking up at Archie in the way they do, you know.

Clauses with *that*, *as*, or *but*

34.4₁. It is customary to call the relative (connecting) word
that a pronoun, but it would be more correct to term it a relative

conjunction or particle. It differs from the pronoun *that* in having no separate plural form and through tolerating no preposition before it; besides, it is now pronounced with the indistinct vowel [ə], while the demonstrative pronoun has the full vowel [æ] (**4.9₁**). It is therefore best to recognize the two *thats* as distinct words:

Demonstrative pronoun, singular *that* [ðæt], plural *those*.
Conjunction (uninflected connective particle) *that* [ðət].

Note the similarity between the two kinds of clauses, both possible with or without the introductory *that*, as in

I know the man (that) you mentioned, and
I know (that) you mentioned the man.

(Cf. also **34.4₆** at the end.)

34.4₂. The relative *that* was formerly used in all kinds of clauses, but is now found in restrictive ones only. Here it is freely used in clauses referring to things, but there is a certain reluctance to use it after names of persons; note thus the difference after *all* (plural and singular):

The dog frightens all who come near the house.
We have now exhausted all that his room can teach us.
It was all that the two jailors could do to keep him on his legs.

Similarly (though less strictly) after *the same* and *those*:

The same man who was afterwards assassinated.
Give girls the same advantages that you give their brothers.
Those who admire Shelley are not identical with those who read Keats.
Chains like those that hang to a lady's watch.

(On *as* after *the same*, see **34.4₇**.)

34.4₃. There are, however, instances in which *that* is freely applied to persons, thus after *it is* (**34.1₄**) and in the following instances:

(1) After superlatives and similar words:

You're the best friend that he has, and the only one that has access to him at all times.
Of all the women she is the last that would triumph in this way.
(Tennyson is the poet that he likes best—with the superlative inside the clause.)

(2) When a relative clause restricts an interrogative pronoun, *that* is generally preferred, not only after *who* (where two *who's* would be awkward), but in other cases as well :

> Who that has such a home to return to, would travel about the country like a vagabond?
> Which of us that is thirty years old has not had his Pompeii? (Thackeray).
> Who ever lov'd that lov'd not at first sight? (Sh.).

(3) After *anybody, everybody,* etc., *that* and *who* are perhaps equally frequent :

> Was there anybody there that (who) applauded him?

(4) *Who* cannot be used in the predicative (because predicatives are felt as neuters) ; hence we have *that* in cases like these :

> Remembering the sweet little girl that she used to be.
> I let him escape, fool that I was.
> The carrier was in high spirits, good fellow that he was.

(5) *That* is customary in phrases like the following, which serve to indicate a time-relation :

> Do you mean Lady Jenny Forbes that was?
> Mrs Dombey that is to be, will be very sensible of your attention.
> People began to talk of her as Lady Cheyne that was to be.
> Mrs Harrison, Miss Brown that was.

34.4₄. After these examples of *that* applied to persons it will not be necessary to give many examples of *that* in similar clauses referring to things :

> You'll just ask me anything that I don't make clear.
> Nothing should be done in a hurry that can be done slowly (Stevenson).
> The most important thing that happened in the Victorian era was that nothing happened (Chesterton).
> The letter that arrived this morning was from my nephew.

After *much, little, few, that* is generally, but not always, used :

> His writings contain little that is new or startling, but much that is old and even trite.
> All the trains—the few that there were—stopped at all the stations.

34.4₅. *That* is always used in *that I know* and similar phrases after a negative = ' so far as I know ' :

> He took a book sometimes, but never read it that I saw.
> I never was hand and glove with him, that I remember.

34.4₆. *That* is often used (as a tertiary) in a way that would be impossible with the *wh*-pronouns (where a preposition would be necessary), thus to indicate time :

> This is the time that the unjust man doth thrive (Sh.).
> By the time that you are dressed, breakfast will be ready.
> The moment that he entered, everybody stopped their chatter.
> (Now that the war is ended, we shall all bury the hatchet for good.)

The corresponding use of *that* after words indicating manner, etc., is " now considered slipshod " (N.E.D.) :

> Who riseth from a feast with that keene appetite that he sits downe? (Sh.).
> He spoke with the same good-humoured ease that he had ever done (Jane Austen).
> We parted in the same cordial fashion that we met.

A similar use is found after adverbs of place :

> They are taken up mountains, anywhere that a mule can find a road (Kipling).

The phenomena just considered cannot be separated from the use of *that* in cases like the following :

> It was there (or, in Italy, in my early youth, then, in this way, etc.) that I first made his acquaintance.
> It is because he is so cruel to animals that I dislike him.
> It is with the younger firm that I am transacting business (cp. It is the younger firm that I am transacting business with).

This use shows that we are right in calling the relative *that* a conjunction rather than a pronoun and in ranging it with the *that* dealt with in Chaps. XXXIII and XXXV.

34.4₇. *As* is used as a connective (relative) particle after *the same, such, so* and *as* :

> He would after to-night never be the same man as he was before.
> If he attaches the same meaning to a certain symbol as the sayer does.

We rode the same way as we had come out the evening before.

Let me have men about me, that are fat, Sleeke-headed men, and such as sleepe a-nights (Sh.).

He was such a listener as most musicians would be glad to welcome.

There are as good fish in the sea as ever came out of it.

No one of them has as much brains in his whole body as Bentley has in his little finger.

A girl, poorly dressed, but as neat as could be.

He is a brave man, as are all of his house (cp. **16.3₆**).

In vulgar speech *as* is used extensively as a relative :

Though I say it as shouldn't.

34.4₈. *But* is used after a negative expression as a relative connective :

There is no vice so simple, but assumes Some marke of vertue on his outward parts (Sh.).

No gentleman but wishes to avoid a scene.

Few of these men but at some time of their lives had worn the clog.

Final remarks on Relative Clauses

34.5₁. The invariable place of relative *that, as* and *but* is at the beginning of the clause.   This is also the natural place of the *wh*-pronouns, but with these there are some exceptions to the rule, as we shall see.

A preposition is very frequently placed at the end of a relative clause : this is imperative in contact-clauses (**34.3₂**) and in those which begin with *that, as* or *but,* as these conjunctions cannot be preceded by a preposition ; it is in a great many cases also the only natural place in clauses beginning with a *wh*-pronoun. Very often the verb and the preposition form together a set phrase which cannot well be separated.   Thus we have, *e.g.*

All the things he is fond of.

All the things that he is fond of.

All such things as he is fond of.

These things, which he is fond of.

Similarly with phrases like *longs for, takes care of, makes use of, is afraid of, wonders at, laughs at, delights in, comes across, cannot do without,* etc.

In the same way, " a girl whom he makes love to " or " is in love with."

34.5₂. Some examples of end-position with *that* and *as* :

The thousand naturall shockes That fleshe is heyre to (Sh.).
Rather beare those illes we have, Then flye to others that we know not of (Sh.).
You will never say anything that's worth listening to.
It is not you that I am angry with.
Bookcases filled with books that no gentleman's library should be without.
We are such stuffe as dreams are made on (=of, Sh.).
He was not half such a coward as we took him for.

34.5₃. But there are cases in which it is preferable, or even necessary, to place the preposition first, and then a *wh*-pronoun must be used. The preposition may sometimes be preceded by some word or words. Thus with partitive *of* :

These names of which he remembered some (or some of which . . .).
He had two daughters, both of whom were married.
He had two daughters, one of whom married a judge (If we say " of whom one married a judge," we expect some continuation about the other daughter).

It is possible to say " the knife that (or which) he cuts with," but we must say " observe the dignity with which he rises," because *with* belongs closely to *dignity*, so that the two together form one adverbial idea.

Among prepositions which are always placed before relative pronouns, we may mention *beyond, besides, round, opposite.* Cp. also *than whom* (**14.**2), *than which.*

34.5₄. A few literary examples may be given of both positions with *wh*-pronouns :

(1) I would have told you of good wrastling, which you have lost the sight of (Sh.).
That which I was afraid of, is come unto me (AV.).
The two waiting-maids . . .; whom also her Majesty could not travel without (Carlyle).

A magnitude of blessing which her husband would not part with for all the earth itself (Ruskin).

A reflection exceedingly just in itself but which I failed to profit by (Stevenson).

(2) But thou, to whom my jewels trifles are (Sh.).

Given to them for whom it is prepared (AV.).

That bitter Valley of Humiliation, into which only the wisest and bravest of men can descend (Ruskin).

Like a repeating clock of which the spring has been touched (Shaw).

Solacing himself with a draught of ale, a huge flacon of which stood upon the table (Scott).

The Balkan provinces, from a tour in which he had just returned (Galsworthy).

One who is not fortunate in life, and the many reasons for not insulting whom you are old enough to understand (Dickens).

Delicious entertainments, to be admitted to one of which was a privilege (Thackeray).

The Hispaniola herself, a few yards in whose wake I was still being whirled along, seemed to stagger (Stevenson).

Constructions like the last-mentioned ones should not be used too often.

34.5₅. Sometimes a relative clause is continued irregularly, a personal pronoun taking the place of the relative, whose force is exhausted :

A fellow whom you must make drunk before you get a word of truth out of him (Boswell).

A man of whose whereabouts and condition—nay of his very existence—she was unaware (Trollope).

A person whose intellectuals were overturned, and his brains shaken (Swift).

Mrs Strachey and Mrs Montague, with both of whom and their households I became acquainted (Carlyle).

34.5₆. A relative clause may be concatenated with another clause :

A man whom she soon found it would be impossible she should ever marry.

A little house which he had found was to be let.

Ferdinand, whom they suppose is droun'd (Sh.), cf. **14.**4₄.

To anyone, whom he knew had direct communication with me (Shelley).

The details and the whole, which an artist cannot be great unless he reconciles (Ruskin).

Thackeray had the kindness which I, for one, have never met a journalist who lacked (A. Lang).

34.5₇. Compound relative adverbs, *whereof, whereby*, etc., instead of combinations of preposition + *which*, were formerly frequent, but are now generally considered stiff or pedantic :

All the movables Whereof the king, my brother, was possest (Sh.).

A continent, on the south-side whereof was a small neck of land (Swift).

The lungs wherewith they breathe (Raleigh).

CHAPTER XXXV

CLAUSES AS TERTIARIES

Place.— Time.— Contrast. — Manner. — Comparison. — Cause. — Purpose. — Result. — Condition. — Restriction. — Concession. — Indifference.—Parallelism.—Amorphous clauses.

35.1₁. Clauses are very frequently used as tertiaries, introduced most often by particles (conjunctions), but also sometimes in other ways. We shall now give a selection of examples, arranged roughly according to the meaning of the clauses. It will be noticed that while clauses of place are uniformly introduced by *where* (and archaic *whither*), those of time and also some of the others present a great variety of construction; further that some conjunctions (*as, while, since*) are used with different meanings, and that *that*, which we met with in primary and secondary clauses, is used also in some of the classes here enumerated. There is thus a good deal of overlapping in such a classification.

35.1₂. Place

Dick lay *where* the grass was thickest.
Whither thou goest, I will goe; and *where* thou lodgest, I will lodge (AV.).

35.1₃. Time

When he comes, tell him to wait.
After he had lost his wife, he settled in France.
It seemed scarcely a week *since* he had been there last.
As soon as she saw him, she shouted "Alfred!"
By the time you get back, the document will be ready.
He got up *before* the sun had risen.
Don't open the door *till* the train stops.
He stayed in Paris *as long as* he had money.
Repairs done *while* you wait.
Just *as* he was passing, she looked out of the window.
Every time he appears her face brightens up.
Now I come to think of it, I suppose you are right.
You are safe enough, *once* you are outside the gate.

35.1₄. Contrast

Whereas Mr Brown had been delighted at the news, his wife saw
that it might mean trouble.

While everything was scrupulously clean in the sitting-room, the
kitchen was abominably dirty.

These conjunctions do not originally indicate a contrast, but
place (*whereas* another form for *where*) and time.

35.1₅. Manner

He has a right to spend his money *how* he pleases.

You may come just *as* you are ; don't dress.

35.1₆. Comparison

Everything is left just *as* it was when the murder was discovered.

The others felt exactly *as* he did.

He spoke well, *like* he always does (considered vulgar).

The water was much deeper *than* we had expected.

He spoke loud *as if* we were deaf.

Maggie's heart thudded *as though* she had been running hard.

A derived use of *as* is found in attestations like :

As I live, I shall repay you.

35.2₁. Cause

He was angry, *because* no one spoke to him.

As the train does not come till 5.30, we have plenty of time.

Since you have nothing else to do, why not remain with me ?

His impressions of Russia cannot be valuable, *inasmuch as* he
does not speak the language.

She could hardly keep still, *so* delighted was she to be home
again (or . . . she was so delighted to . . .).

Who am I *that* I should presume to offer advice to you ? (giving
the reason why the question is asked).

35.2₂. Purpose

Place yourself there, *that* I may see your face clearly.

He raised his hand *in order that* the bus might stop.

She turned her head away *lest* he should see her tears.

He wrote down the number, *for fear* he should forget it.

35.2₃. **Result**

He spoke so well *that* he convinced everybody of his innocence.
The burglar wore gloves, *so that* there were no finger-prints
    visible.
It's so hot I can't sleep.

35.3₁. **Condition**

If he comes back, what are we to do ?
Suppose (*supposing*) he comes back, what are we to do ?
Don't come *unless* I call.
I don't care, *so long as* (*provided*) the weather keeps settled.
It matters not who finds the truth, *so only* the truth is found.
In so far as the weather remains settled, we shall start to-morrow.
I shall take the thermos, *in case* anybody wants some coffee.

Condition, combined with unreality or improbability, has been dealt
with in the chapter on tense (**24.**2), where are given also examples of
condition implied in relative clauses.

Sometimes *if* does not really imply a condition : " if the offer
was rejected, it was because people distrusted him" is a rhetorical
device to express the reason why the offer was rejected.   Compare also the familiar saying :

She is fifty if she's a day.

A peculiar way of indicating condition is by word-order without any conjunction (**10.**4₃) ; this is historically developed from
questions and was formerly used more extensively than now,
when it is found in imaginative clauses only and chiefly with
had, were (**24.**2₅) and *should* :

Had he been faithful, everything would have been all right.
Woe to the man, were he the Emperor himself, who dares lay
    a finger on her ! (Shaw).
I would go even to Africa for her sake, should it be necessary.

35.3₂. **Restriction**

As far as (*so far as*) I can see, he cannot be more than thirty.
That is all right, so far as I am concerned.
He has never been here, *that* I know.

35.3₃. Concession

Though (*although*) the hall was crowded, they managed to find seats.

Deep *though* (*as*) her sympathy was, she still had no words to offer.

Even if it isn't fine, we must start.

Even had she been alive, we should not have seen her (**10.**4₃).

However annoying his behaviour may be, we cannot get rid of him.

35.3₄. Indifference

Whether he answers or no, I shall go on distrusting him.

No matter what the others may say, I stick to my opinion.

Thus also with other subordinate clauses (no matter *how* he behaves, *when* he comes back, *where* he stays, etc.) :

Whatever he may say, don't you believe it.

Whoever you may be, I'm deeply grateful to you.

These clauses should be contrasted with the similar ones mentioned in **33.**4, in which the clause acts as a primary (subject or object) in the main sentence.

A special class is introduced by the base of a verb, which may be considered governed by a following auxiliary :

Go where he will, he is sure to find people who speak English.

Get up as early as he may, he will find the room ready.

Try as he would, John could not remember a word of the sermon.

35.3₅. Parallelism

The sooner we get there, the more likely are we to get seats.

You may pay me little by little, *according as* your salary falls due.

A man will not always succeed *in proportion as* he exerts himself.

35.4. A type of clause often met with contains only an introductory word and a predicative referring to the subject of the main sentence :

When asked his opinion he remained silent.

If in need, don't hesitate to ask me for money.

Don't speak until spoken to.

To be left till called for.
Though cold, it was a fine morning.
He looked round, as if in search of something.
Any government, however constituted, must respect the people's
wishes (Macaulay).

There are other types of more or less amorphous clauses, *e.g.*

He greeted us very cordially, if rather shyly.
His figure would have been noticed anywhere, if only for its
physical health and shining cleanliness.
We wondered what answer, if any, he would give us.

35.5. It is possible to have clauses within clauses, *e.g.*

He has now nothing to live on, because whenever he had a
good job, the more he earned the more he spent, so that
he never saved anything.

Cf. concatenated relative clauses, **34.**1$_3$, **34.**5$_6$.

CHAPTER XXXVI

RETROSPECT

Synopsis of grammatical means.—The unchanged word.—Stress
and tone.—Other modifications.—Endings.—Separate roots.—
Grammatical words.—Word-order.—Grammatical synonyms.

36.1. Our task is ended. We have tried to give an idea of
the grammatical structure of the English language as it is spoken
and written in the beginning of the twentieth century, with
occasional glimpses of earlier stages. But it will be well here
to retrace our steps and to give a short synopsis of the various
means used in English for grammatical purposes.

In the first place we have the use of the **unchanged word.** In
a great many cases the same form may serve in various word-
classes, the context alone showing which is meant in each case.
If it is a substantive, it is taken to be in the singular, if a verb
(the base of a verb), it may be either the infinitive, the present
indicative or subjunctive, or the imperative.

36.2. Next, we have **stress and tone.** Stress serves to show
which words in a sentence are more important than others; the
place of the stress often serves to distinguish a substantive from
a verb : *a record* : *I record*. Tone serves more emotional purposes
and is of special importance in amorphous sentences and in
questions.

In connexion with weak stress we often find a reduction of
vowels, which are made indistinct or even dropped altogether.
This is seen in many compounds, but has particular grammatical
importance in the weak forms of prepositions and auxiliary
verbs; note especially the distinction between *that* as a pronoun
of pointing and as a conjunction, and the similar distinction
between full and weak *there*. The weak form of *not, n't*, is fused
together with auxiliaries. In connexion with phonetic weakening we have often loss of the original full meaning, as when *have*
is used to form the perfect and *will* (*'ll*) to indicate future time
without any regard to volition.

36.3. **Modifications** of words other than those caused by stress :
a distinction between voiceless and voiced consonant serves to
differentiate substantives from verbs : *a belief* : *I believe* | *the
use* : *to use.* The same distinction in connexion with the *s*-ending
serves to differentiate the plural from the singular in words like :
thief : *thieves* ; *path* : *paths* ; *house* : *houses.* Vowel-changes are
used to form plurals of some substantives : *man* : *men* ; *woman* :
women ; *foot* : *feet,* etc., and to form preterits and participles
in many verbs : *drink* : *drank* : *drunk* ; *run* : *ran* ; *shine* :
shone, etc.—often in connexion with other changes : *bring* :
brought ; *fly, flew, flown,* etc.

36.4. **Endings** are used very extensively for grammatical purposes. The most important ending is *s* (with three phonetic
varieties), which in substantives serves to form the plural and
the genitive : *princes, kings, dukes, prince's, dukes',* etc., and in
verbs the third person singular present : *he wishes, sings, looks,*
etc. Further *-ed* (also with three pronunciations) to form
preterits and second participles of verbs : *added, begged, kicked.*
The ending *-er* forms comparatives : *thicker,* and agent-nouns :
baker ; *-est* forms superlatives : *thickest,* and the obsolete second
person in verbs : *thou thinkest.* The ending *-ing* forms
first participles and gerunds ; *-ly* forms adjectives : *daily,* and
adverbs : *happily.* An added *-en* in one case forms a plural :
oxen ; it often serves to form participles : *broken, given,* and
verbs from adjectives and substantives : *soften, strengthen.*
This enumeration is not complete : a selection of other endings
to form words of various word-classes has been given in
Chap. VII.

36.5. In a few cases **separate roots** are used in flexional forms,
thus in verbs : *be, am, is, was* ; *go, went* ; in pronouns : *I, me,
we, us, our* ; *he, she, him, her, they* ; in adjectives and adverbs :
good, well, better, etc.

36.6. Further, we must mention the extremely important use
of **grammatical (" empty ") words.** These are in some cases
verbs (auxiliaries) : *have, had* in the perfect and pluperfect, *be*

in the passive, *will, shall, is going to, may, is to* in expressions for the future time, *would, should* in conditioned sentences, *do* in questions and negative expressions. In other cases we have pronouns, such as the two articles *the* and *an (a)*, the prop-word *one*, and preparatory *it*, or else prepositions : *of* in *the roof of the house, all of us*, etc.; *to* in *give a penny to the boy*; *he means to go*, etc. ; *by* in *he was punished by his teacher*. The adverbs *more* and *most* are used in the comparative and superlative : *more natural, most natural*.

36.7. Last, but not least, we have **word-order**. This serves to show which of two collocated substantives is secondary and which primary : *garden flower* : *flower garden*. The subject is normally placed before and the object after the verb : *Jack loves Jill*. But in questions and wishes the verb comes before the subject : *Is he ill? Long live the King !* Word-order shows the difference between a question and an exclamation : *How old is he? How old he is !* The indirect is placed before the direct object : *We offered the butler a reward*. Hence also in the passive : *The butler was offered a reward*.

Prepositions are generally placed immediately before their objects ; but in certain well-defined cases they stand by themselves at the end : *She must be taken care of* | *What is the letter about?* | *The boys he played with* | *He had no one to play with*, etc.

36.8. The interplay of the two last-mentioned factors is of the utmost importance and makes a great many things easy and supple which otherwise would be cumbrous and inconvenient. A genitive is placed before the governing word, and the indirect before the direct object ; but unwieldy combinations are avoided by means of the prepositions *of* and *to*, e.g. in " The views of those of our friends who have never been to France " and " Do not tell this to those of our friends who have never been to France." The use of preparatory *it* makes it possible to place long infinitive-groups and clauses in extraposition, while it would be inconvenient to have them in the places required by the usual rules, *e.g.* in " He finds it difficult to believe in her innocence," "He thought it highly probable that she was guilty." The extensive use of auxiliary verbs enables one to place a verb before the subject to indicate that the sentence is meant as a question or wish, etc., and yet to have the subject before the really important verb, *e.g.* "Does he smoke?" "May he live long!" "Let us sing!" "Are you coming?" "Will he die soon?" In a similar way auxiliaries make it possible in a negative sentence to have *not* before the verb that is really negatived, and yet affixed to a verb : "I shan't sleep," "He doesn't smoke."

In such instances, and in the frequency of constructions like "He had a wash," "He took a walk," etc. (**7.**8$_2$), we see the result of what is one of the distinctive features of Modern English grammatical structure—the tendency, that is, to have in the beginning of the sentence a small verb indicating person, number and tense as well as showing whether the meaning is positive, negative or a question, and to let this be followed by an invariable word denoting the main idea.

36.9. There is one fundamental principle which should be apparent from the whole of this book—namely, that two expressions may have exactly or approximately the same meaning and yet, grammatically speaking, belong to totally different categories, so that they should not be named by the same term. See, for instance :

Shakespeare's plays.
The plays of Shakespeare.

What's the time?
Please tell me the exact time.

I beg your pardon.
What did you say ?

Silence !
Don't say a word !
You mustn't say a word !

I gave John an apple and Jane a pear.
I gave an apple to John and a pear to Jane.
John got an apple and Jane a pear from me.

He may be rich.
It is possible that he is rich.

He happened to fall.
He fell accidentally.

On entering the room he greeted everybody most kindly.
Entering the room he greeted everybody most kindly.
When he entered the room he greeted everybody most kindly.

I leave tomorrow.
I shall leave tomorrow.

This hat doesn't belong to me.
This hat isn't mine.
This is not my hat.

He came to the tryst because he admired her.
He came to the tryst because of his admiration for her.
His admiration for her was the reason why he came to the tryst.

INDEX

References are to chapters and sections. Very often the matter concerned is dealt with not only in the section referred to in the index, but in one or more subsequent sections.

[æ] is placed between ad and af ; [ð] between d and e ; [ε, ə] between e and f ; [ŋ] between n and o ; [ɔ] between o and p ; [ʃ] between s and t ; [þ] between t and u ; [ʌ] between u and v ; [ʒ] after z.

A

[aˑ] 2.1$_3$, 2.4, 3.9, 4.2$_2$.

a, an 4.9, 5.4, 5.7, 17.2, numeral 17.2, means 'same' 17.2, place 17.5 ; repeated 17.5$_4$,—a from on 5.4.

(Ablaut 3.1$_2$)

About to, infinitive 32.1$_9$, 32.2$_6$

(Absolute construction 29.2)

Abstract substantives as predicatives 13.7

(Accusative with infinitive 32.4$_3$)

acquaintance 21.4$_5$

(Action-nouns 30.1)

Adjectives 7.2, 7.7$_3$, $_4$, $_7$, from substantives 7.9$_2$, as primaries 8.3, as tertiaries 8.7$_3$, with proper names 16.5$_3$, 16.8$_4$, place 17.5 ; XXII

Adjunct 9.1, restrictive 9.2$_2$, various kinds 9.3, with compounds 9.4, 9.5, infinitive as 32.2

Adnex 9.1, 9.7, 29.1$_2$, 29.2

Adverbs 7.5, from adjectives 7.7$_7$, 7.9$_4$, as primaries 8.3$_4$, as secondaries 8.6$_2$, as predicatives 13.8, comparison of 22.4, place with infinitive 32.6

[æ] 2.1$_3$, 2.4, 3.9, 4.2$_2$

[aˑə] 2.8

Affirmation 28.1

after, tense with 23.4$_4$, 23.6$_9$, 23.7, 23.9$_4$

After-future 23.1$_3$

After-past 23.1$_2$, 26.9$_6$

ago 29.2$_3$

[ai] 2.8, 3.5

albeit 27.3

all 18.1, primary 8.3$_7$, tertiary 8.7$_4$; *not all* 28.3$_4$, *all that, all who* 34.4$_2$

Alternations 3.2, 3.4$_2$, 3.8, 3.9, 4.5$_1$, 4.7$_2$, 4.9, 5.6

am 4.9$_2$

American 3.4$_2$, 3.5$_2$, 4.1$_2$, *will* 25.4$_4$, *would* 26.3$_2$

Amorphous sentences 10.9, with infinitives 32.8, clauses 35.4

an, *a* 5.4, 17.2, numeral 17.2, means 'same' 17.2, place 17.5 ; *an* or *a* before *h* 5.7

Analogy 3.4$_2$

and 4.9$_3$, before isolated predicative 13.4$_4$

Animals, sex XIX

Animated XVI

any 17.9, (*anybody, any one, anything*) 8.3$_6$, as tertiary 8.7$_4$

Apophony 3.1$_2$

Apposition 9.6, 14.7$_3$, 18.1$_4$

Appositional *of* 14.9$_3$

Appreciative grammar 1.3

are 4.9$_2$

Article 7.4$_2$, 7.4$_4$, in predicative 13.6$_2$, definite 16.4, no article 16.5, indefinite 17.2, generic 21.5, definite with gerund 31.2

as 5.6$_2$, 10.4$_9$, case after 14.2$_2$, with indefinite article 17.5, relative 34.4$_7$

Assertion 28.1

Assibilation 5.8

at 4.9$_3$

at that 16.2$_4$

Attraction, relative 14.3$_2$, negative 28.2$_1$, 28.2$_7$

[au] 2.8, 3.5

aught 17.9$_5$

Auxiliary verb, full and weak forms 4.9$_2$; with object 11.4$_3$, place 10.4, in perfect and pluperfect 23.5, in passive 24.1, in negative sentences 28.2$_2$; no *s* in third person 23.1$_4$; cf. *be, have, may, shall, will*

B

[b] 2.1$_2$, 2.6

Back-shifting, see Indirect

Back vowels 2.4

Bare infinitive XXXII *passim*

100, 106